W8-BVK-366

D0122522

THE GOLDEN DREAM

THE
GOLDEN DREAM

Suburbia in the Seventies

Stephen Birmingham

HARPER & ROW, PUBLISHERS

NEW YORK   HAGERSTOWN   SAN FRANCISCO   LONDON

Portions of this work originally appeared in the *Ladies' Home Journal* and *Los Angeles Magazine*.

FIRST EDITION

Designed by C. Linda Dingler

Library of Congress Cataloging in Publication Data

Birmingham, Stephen.
  The golden dream.

  Includes index.
    i. Suburbs—United States.   2. United States—
Social conditions—1960–   I. Title.
HT351.B55   301.36'2'0973   76-57891
ISBN 0-06-010334-5

78 79 80 81 82 10 9 8 7 6 5 4 3 2 1

Contents

The Suburban Dream   vii

SOUTHWEST—AND A MOUNTAIN STATE

1. Blood and Money   3
2. The Casual Life   11
3. Wide Streets   19

MIDWEST

4. Connecticut on Lake Erie   33
5. Company Town   39
6. Small Town   47
7. Pointes and Points   57

SOUTH

8. The Country Club Set   67
9. Rules and Regulations   78

EAST

10. The Rockefellers on the Turnpike   85
11. Troubled Darien   99
12. The Lively Art of Commuting   106
13. Three Ryes   115

14. The Grandeur That Was   122
15. Nil Admirari   131
16. Summer Camps   141

WEST

17. "A Feeling of Separation"   153

CITY VS. SUBURB

18. The Price of Status   171
19. Swinging   179
20. The Vanishing Living Room and Other Phenomena   186
21. Back to the City?   192

Index   205

The Suburban Dream

*T*hey came to the suburbs in pursuit of a dream—the way, in the 1920s, people flocked in droves to Florida looking for a land of sun and space. They came in search of green grass and trees, away from the hassle, a place where children and pets could run and play unattended, where there was room for a garden, a terrace, a backyard swing, a swimming pool, a tennis court, or a gazebo. They came to escape the city's dirt and noise and crime and traffic, and to escape the tyranny of rents and landlords. They came for the promise of better schools, lower taxes, less indifferent police, more convenient shopping, to find an amorphous quantity called "greater freedom," and to leave behind the alleged anonymity of city living. Many came for racial reasons, to escape what seemed an "invasion" of blacks, or Puerto Ricans, or Jews, or Mexican-Americans. More than anything else, they came because the suburbs symbolized the Good Life, and one of the most important factors of the Good Life—in America, at least—has been to own a home of one's own, or at least to own a part of it, and to be invited to join the country club. The suburbs symbolized "making it." They came by the millions.

The flight to the suburbs began before the turn of the century, encouraged at first by the coach and ferry, then spurred by the development of the railroad and the automobile. By 1925, suburbanization had become as national trend. But it was not until the economically booming days of the 1960s that the trend became a roaring phenomenon. In the decade between 1960 and 1970, the twenty-five largest cities in the United States had, all together, gained about 710,000 in population. Their suburban areas, meanwhile, gained 8.9 million people—or twelve times more. The suburbs of New York, for example, now have more residents than the city itself—nearly nine million—making the New York suburbs themselves the largest "city" in the country.

The escapees to the suburbs have found many of the things they were looking for: the grass, the trees, the cleaner air, and so on. But they have also found other things which they did not bargain for. They have found spiraling taxes, soaring real estate prices, schools that often seem less than satisfactory. They have found drugs, and crime, and dirt and noise from the freeways. They have found zoning battles, bond-issue fights, dirty politics, corruption in government, water shortages, crab grass, red spider, and the Dutch elm disease. They have watched the encroachment of industry, of high-rises, of tract developers, and of shopping centers set amid acres of asphalt. They have watched the racial minorities they hoped to avoid follow them, and they have cursed at suburban rush-hour traffic jams. They have discovered the value of the spite fence, and they have discovered boredom. Most of all, they have also discovered that curious anomie, that sense of disorientation, that indefinable "feeling of separation," which living in suburbia so often seems to convey.

SOUTHWEST—AND A MOUNTAIN STATE

1

Blood and Money

When the Keith Jacksons of Houston, Texas, became, like so many young Texans, suddenly petroleum rich, the first thing they felt they needed was "a good address!" In Houston, the only good address worth mentioning is River Oaks—a suburb that, because of its proximity to the city, is convenient for businessmen and that, because of the sheer opulence of its residences, is probably unmatched among American show-off communities.

Jackson, who was too busy to house-shop himself, dispatched his wife to drive around River Oaks and select a house she liked. In River Oaks, a zoning ordinance prevents owners from putting "For Sale" signs on properties, but that didn't particularly worry the Jacksons, who figured that whether or not a house was actually for sale didn't much matter, since the Jacksons were prepared to offer the owner of whatever house Mrs. Jackson fancied a price the owner couldn't refuse. For several days, Mrs. Jackson prowled the shady, Spanish-moss-hung streets of River Oaks, peering through majestic gateways and down long drives, examining façades. Finally, she announced that she had found the house of her dreams. "It's nice and big," she explained, "and has beautiful grounds. There's a pool, there are tennis courts, and there's even a golf course." When the Jacksons prepared to make their offer, however, they discovered that the place Mrs. Jackson had in mind was the River Oaks Country Club. The Jacksons weren't able to buy the country club, but they did end up with quite a nice place—a two-million-dollar house which contains, among other things, a Steuben Glass staircase. At the time, a friend commented, "I didn't know Steuben Glass made staircases." "Neither did Steuben Glass," replied the Jacksons, "until we ordered it."

River Oaks relishes its tales of residential extravagance, and takes great civic pride in each new splurge. When, for example, the Kenneth Schnitzers—who are big in supermarkets—bought their house, Joan Schnitzer wanted a tennis court. But there was no room for one. So the Schnitzers simply bought the place next door, took an acre for their tennis court, and sold what was left. Mrs. Collier Hurley travels around town in a chauffeur-driven Cadillac that has a bar. When she travels to New York, for shopping, as she frequently does, she flies with her four poodles and a small freezer full of fresh, extra-thick lamb chops, which, she insists, are the only meat her dogs will eat. Mrs. Anthony Villa, who is famous locally for the size and number of the diamonds she wears, has a thing about pineapples, and so, when the Villas bought their River Oaks house, Mrs. Villa ordered an array of enormous ornamental pineapples placed on the rooftop. The place has become a landmark, and a neighbor giving directions to his house may say, "I live three doors down from the pineapple house." When Earl Dow—who runs an expensive fast-food chain—bought his River Oaks house, he had it painted to match the colors of Neiman-Marcus shopping bags— chocolate brown and beige. And so it goes. Costly idiosyncrasies are applauded in River Oaks.

River Oaks likes nothing better than to entertain visiting royalty. Mr. and Mrs. Robert Herring have achieved something of a record in this category, since they have been host to four heads of state in the last two years, with a perhaps understandable emphasis on Arab leaders, and the Herrings spare no expense. At a party for King Hussein of Jordan, for example, Joanne Herring and her decorator turned one large room into a "shah's discotheque"—an indoor Arabian Nights tent with lush pillows scattered about the zebra-patterned floor. Joanne Herring had assigned various Houston beauties to lounge, harem fashion, on the cushions when the king made his entrance, but somehow a cue was missed and when Hussein entered the tent, all the women were standing. "I thought you were all going to be lying around on the floor!" cried Mrs. Herring. "Quick! Get on the cushions." The ladies complied, and a Mexican mariachi band—a Texas touch—struck up a tune. On her cushion, a young Houston woman named Annie Owen found herself seated

4

next to the king. She reached for a cigarette, and the king reached for his lighter. When Miss Owen admired the lighter—gold, embossed with the royal insignia—Hussein proved that he could be as extravagant as any Texan, and asked her to keep it. At first Miss Owen demurred, but he insisted. "If I don't take the lighter, will you be insulted?" she asked. "I will," replied the king. So Miss Owen kept the lighter. Though King Hussein's visit at the Herrings' lasted only thirty minutes—he had to dash on to a meeting with former U.N. ambassador George Bush—it was all considered worth it.

River Oaks loves its reputation for outrageousness. "Everything they say about us here is true," is a comment the visitor hears frequently at local dinner parties, between discussions of the merits of Cavalier jets and the relative reliability of various Beechcraft agencies in the area. (In River Oaks, airplanes are compared with as much enthusiasm as automobiles are in Grosse Pointe, Detroit's suburb.) River Oaks likes to boast that some of its leading society ladies are former call girls, and it is definitely chic here to have a past that is shady or worse. When someone makes it big in River Oaks, it is a cause for general rejoicing, another reminder that people get richer quicker in Texas, and spend their money more ebulliently, than anywhere else on earth. When a River Oaks girl named Sandra Hovas married Baron Enrico di Portanova, everyone applauded, and they applauded even more when she changed her name from Sandra to Alessandra. ("Remember, I'm the Baroness Alessandra di Portanova," the baroness reminded society reporter Shelby Hodge at the King Hussein party.) Houston itself supports a wealthy and socially active gay community. At the Old Plantation—an expensive nightclub hard by River Oaks—men dance with men and women dance with women, and nobody thinks a thing about it. But within the confines of River Oaks, a firm line is drawn. Everyone wishing to buy a house in River Oaks must pass a screening committee, and one of the firmest rules is that no house can be purchased jointly by two gentlemen or two ladies. For years, no Jews were permitted to buy in River Oaks, though an exception was made in the case of the department store Sakowitzes. And there are still no blacks here, though there was a fuss stirred up a while back when it was rumored that Muhammad Ali was shopping for River Oaks property (he wasn't, as it turned out).

River Oaks people also have a zesty, pioneer fondness for good old-fashioned bloodshed, and nothing is more welcomed than a spicy murder scandal. When socialite Joan Robinson Hill, the daughter of oilman Ash Robinson, was allegedly poisoned by her plastic surgeon husband, who was then, in turn, dispatched by a killer allegedly hired by her father, River Oaks couldn't have liked the ensuing trial more. The killings later became the subject of a book called *Blood and Money* by Thomas Thompson, and River Oaks got excited all over again. Visitors were routinely driven past the house where Dr. Hill was murdered. *"There*—right in that doorway—is where the killer shot down John Hill." Hill had never been convicted of killing his wife, but in the mind of River Oaks there was no question that he did it. "The minute I heard she was dead, I said to myself, 'John did it,'" says one woman.

There was spirited talk, too, about the civil-court trial of millionaire Ash Robinson for, allegedly, having hired a gun to kill his son-in-law.

"There isn't a juror in this town who would find against Ash Robinson," said one woman. "Too many people in this town love old Ash. Too many people loved Joan and hated that creep husband of hers, and *admire* old Ash."

In the event, Ash Robinson was cleared by the civil-court jury. But the case was a popular topic of dinner-table conversation in River Oaks, where they say, "Don't we have the best old murders here? Don't we have the best old time? Aren't we *somethin'*?"

In addition to the splendid quality of local murders, River Oaks likes to boast of the splendid shopping. There is the sparkling new Galleria shopping center, for example, which contains, among other things, "the most beautiful branch of Neiman-Marcus." Then there is Jamail's, which can only be described as a supermarket for the super-rich. Jamail's abounds in all sorts of costly delights, such as fresh fruits out of season and vegetables imported from all over the world, displayed and arranged as though for a Tiffany window. The live Maine lobsters may cost twelve dollars a pound, but Jamail's will have them. "You can buy *anything* at Jamail's," they say, and an account at Jamail's is as important to River Oaks as a Neiman's charge plate. Jamail's will prepare exotic hors d'oeuvres and deliver them to your party. Jamail's will also prepare whole meals and cater parties from a menu of a hostess's choosing. A number of River Oaks families, too busy to be bothered with cooking and tired of coping with the kitchen-staff problem, simply give Jamail's carte blanche and have all their meals delivered to their homes on a daily basis.

Extravagances like having Jamail's do your cooking are brushed aside in River Oaks as mere practicalities—a simple way of solving life's little problems. In the same spirit, Mrs. Harvey Steinburger built a new house of "only" fourteen-thousand square feet because, she explained, "All the children are off and gone, and I needed a place for some of my pretty things." Some of her pretty things included all the chandeliers from New York's old Astor Hotel, one of which hangs ninety-two feet from her living room ceiling. And in the same spirit, elderly residents of River Oaks keep suites of rooms at Methodist Hospital on a permanent basis, "Just in case we should ever need them." It's merely practical.

Though, as in Phoenix, there is no downtown living in Houston, there have been attempts to spruce up older, run-down areas of the city outside River Oaks, and to make these once-fashionable neighborhoods fashionable again. Such efforts have met with a certain limited success. In the old Heights area of town, for example, there are many fine old Victorian mansions—with high-ceilinged rooms, bay windows, turrets and towers—built for an earlier generation of Houston rich. In recent years they had fallen into disrepair. Though no part of Houston is very "high," the Heights houses had views of sorts, and several years ago, bright-eyed young designers and architects discovered that mansions in the Heights could be bought for a fraction of their original cost and, with a little money and imagination, stripped down and renovated to something approaching their original glory. Greenhouses and swimming pools were added and, all at once, the Heights became fashionable again. Or somewhat fashionable. The trouble was that as restoring old houses in the Heights became chic, the owners of old houses in the area became greedy. Real estate prices shot up to the point where decaying mansions are no longer much of a bargain. And so restoration projects in the Heights have come to a standstill, and the Heights remains partly a good address and partly not.

Older Houston families like to point out that though Houston's oil fortunes are spectacular, there was wealth in Houston long before the petroleum industry. Lumber was once big business here, and second to that came cotton. Old Houston pre-oil families included the Garrows, the Clevelands, the Neuhauses, Carters, Dicksons, Myerses, and Autrys (cowboy actor Gene Autry is kin of the Houston Autrys). Nearly all these families' in-town mansions are gone now. The sites of the old H. B. Rice house on Crawford Street and the James A. Baker house on Main Street are now parking lots, and the

7

Italianate palace the James Butes built on Milam Street has given way to the Tenneco Building tower. But at least one in-town street has managed to retain much of what was its original suburban charm, and that is Courtlandt Place.

Courtlandt Place was planned as a walled, gated, limited-access street for the wealthy, who, by the turn of the century, were moving away from downtown's Main Street and wanted something that at the time seemed very much like "country." According to the rules drawn up by the founding fathers of the Courtlandt Improvement Company in 1906, the purpose of Courtlandt Place was to "create a district restricted to the erection of residences of good class and to surround such and the locality generally with conditions assuring as far as possible freedom from noise, dust, constant traffic and other annoyances incident to a populous city." The founders of this idyllic enclave also decreed that "No business house or houses, sanitarium, hospital, saloon, place of public entertainment, livery stable, resort or dance hall or other place of business shall ever be erected on said lot, or any part thereof." And they meant *ever*.

What were erected, instead, were large homes of brick and granite. Architects from the East were imported, as was then the fashion—including the firm of Warren and Wetmore, who designed New York's Ritz-Carlton and Biltmore hotels, as well as 17 Courtlandt Place. Courtlandt Place houses were built with detailed interior paneling, dumbwaiters, wine and preserve cellars, vast kitchens with servants' callboards, hand-cut crystal doorknobs. And since the Eastern architects didn't know about the problem of Houston "gumbo"—the muddy ooze that runs off silty soil when it rains—most Courtlandt Place mansions were built with commodious, if occasionally damp, basements.

But as the suburbs grew, fashionable Houston began moving out to Memorial Drive and River Oaks. One by one, the old families moved away and by now most of the big houses have changed hands several times. An exception was the so-called Carter Complex, and three of four houses built for members of the Carter family are still family-owned. (Victor Carter III, a grandson of the original Courtlandt Place owner, Victor Carter II, recently renovated and moved into his grandfather's old home.) At the same time, Courtlandt Place managed to find favor with new arrivals from out of town (one Louisiana couple thought Courtlandt Place reminiscent of New Orleans's Vieux Carré), and so the stately flavor of the street was preserved.

In the early 1920s, residents of the newly developed subdivision of Montrose demanded easy access to downtown Houston, and the easiest access seemed to be straight through Courtlandt Place. Down came the brick wall that barred the way, and through came the traffic, carrying with it the cul-de-sac's air of privacy. Better transportation to and from the city was called for, and along came the Montrose trolley, which ran down Hawthorne, turned left on Taft, and clanged to a stop at the east gates of Courtlandt Place. Peace and quiet vanished. But still Courtlandt Place held on, refusing to succumb to the growing city around it. Nearby streets filled with businesses and business traffic, and yet Courtlandt Place—now a suburb within a city—remained undaunted. In the late 1950s and early 1960s, the neighboring streets filled with "hippies" and undesirables, but Courtlandt Place stood firm.

In the 1960s, the neighborhood was dealt its most severe blow. The Brazos ramp of the Southwest Freeway appeared on the drawing boards of those in charge of the Interstate Highway System, slashing through the old east gates of Courtlandt Place, where the crescent-shaped parklike entrance to the street had been. At the time, Courtlandt Place became sharply and bitterly divided between those who felt the neighborhood was doomed and wanted to sell, and those who preferred to stay on and fight regardless. Though the fight against the ramp was intense, the freeway, as all freeways do, inexorably came. And yet the little street, though aesthetically marred by the ramp at one end, almost miraculously remained unchanged otherwise.

Today Courtlandt Place is a proud and handsome strip of green lawns and old cottonwood trees in the middle of a bustling city. The Courtlandt Place residents are united again and, through their Courtlandt Association—to which every home owner belongs—determined that Courtlandt Place will remain as it is forever, a pocket of large, expensive private homes. "We are an example to other cities of what can be done to preserve fine old neighborhoods," says one association member. Plans are afoot to have Courtlandt Place declared a historic preservation district, like Audubon Place in New Orleans and King William Street in San Antonio. And, as a gesture of neighborhood solidarity, Courtlandt Place tosses an annual Christmas party for all present and former residents.

Of course, out in the perfumed reaches of River Oaks, no one would think of living "down there." Some River Oaks people have never heard of Courtlandt Place, and many are not sure exactly how to get there. River Oaks isn't much concerned with the preservation of old places, being more concerned with preserving its private police force and its private garbage-collection service and its meals catered by Jamail's, with seeing to it that no apartment buildings invade the "right" side of San Felipe Boulevard, and with its favorite preoccupations—money and blood. There was all sorts of talk in River Oaks, for example, when a prominent society woman was knocked down by the bouncers at the Old Plantation, and then beaten up in the parking lot, allegedly for trying to bring her small dog into the bar. As they say in River Oaks, "Don't we have the most *wonderful* scandals here?"

2

The Casual Life

*E*very new house in the gilded suburb of Scottsdale, Arizona, is built with a "family room." Family rooms are almost as popular in Scottsdale as high school basketball—and flagpoles. Scottsdale, which bills itself as "The West's Most Western Town" (the slogan is emblazoned on the town's official stationery), may have more flagpoles per home than any suburb in the country. Scottsdale is proud of its flagpoles, and of the flag, because Scottsdale considers itself a particularly patriotic city. Its motto might well be "America's Most American Town." This is, after all, Barry Goldwater country, where America comes first.

Patriotism, here, is serious business. No wonder everyone was shocked when, at a recent American Legion meeting, veterans of World War II were asked to stand up, and a German-born member of the Scottsdale City Council rose proudly to his feet. He had fought in World War II, all right—but on the other side. No wonder there was further shock when he couldn't seem to understand why everyone was shocked.

One of Scottsdale's current heroines is Miss Lori Cox, now a freshman studying pre-law at nearby Arizona State University. Miss Cox, posed in front of an American flag, has been labeled in Scottsdale "The *real* Miss America." It all started when Lori Cox was a little girl growing up in this Phoenix suburb in the early sixties, and saw, on a local telecast, a group of student demonstrators set fire to an American flag. "Mommy, Mommy," she reportedly cried

11

out. "Please make them stop it!" Then, in 1971, the Scottsdale school board banned the recital of the pledge of allegiance in the classrooms of Scottsdale's public schools. Lori was even more upset. She went to her principal, Robert Hendricks, and protested. "But he refused, saying it would create a disciplinary problem."

In 1974, Senator Barry Goldwater came to speak to the pupils of Coronado High School, where Lori was a sophomore, and the students were instructed, on this occasion, to stand and recite the pledge. The students did, but there was a lot of grumbling about it, and, says Lori, "The hypocrisy of the situation bothered me." So she carried her crusade a step further. She went to the Scottsdale school board, confronted the Superintendent of Secondary Education, and requested that the pledge be reinstated. He replied that "The pledge of allegiance on a daily basis would prove to be a traumatic experience for some students," a judgment no one quite understood.

But Lori Cox was not to be deterred by officialdom. The following week she and a group of friends stationed themselves outside various Scottsdale supermarkets and collected some three thousand signatures in favor of restoring the pledge to Scottsdale schoolrooms. In November, 1974, she carried her petition to the school board, which voted four to one (with one member abstaining) in favor of bringing the pledge back. But her victory was short-lived. For the next five months there were all sorts of disruptive incidents. Flags were ripped down from front-yard flagpoles, and flagpole ropes were cut. One day at school, during the singing of the national anthem, a student marched down the hall carrying a Communist flag. Although only a minority of the students were actually involved in the protests, a majority voted that the pledge to the flag was "meaningless." "Many of the kids said they were too tired to stand in the morning," Lori says. "It seemed as though nobody really wanted the pledge back." She received unpleasant phone calls and threatening letters. "My name was on all the bathroom walls," she says. "I missed all the parties and lost friends. But the thing that hurt me most was their disrespect for the flag."

As a result of all the dissension, five months after it had voted to reinstate the pledge the school board reversed itself and voted to ban the pledge again and to substitute, instead, a "once-a-week patriotic observance."

Lori was crushed but not defeated. "This is the only country in the world where a fifteen-year-old girl could approach the legislature," she says, which is precisely what she did. After another futile round with the Board of Education, she took her case to the Senate Education Committee of the Arizona State Legislature in Phoenix, asking the committee to pass a bill that would give students the daily opportunity to recite the pledge of allegiance to the flag in all Arizona public schools. There was, she says, much opposition, but in the end the bill was passed and signed into law by Governor Raul Castro on June 13, 1975. "The bill doesn't force anyone to make the pledge," Lori says, "but it does permit someone to make it if he wants to."

Still, Lori says, it has not been easy. She has been subjected to jeers and sneers and catcalls at high school, and was even the object of derision—from faculty as well as students—during her freshman year at Arizona State. She bore it all bravely, and now, at last, things are beginning to quiet down. Lori boasts proudly of the congratulatory letters that have poured in from patriotic people like herself all over the United States, Canada, and even the U.S. Virgin Islands. "I would do it again," she says, pointing out that she was taught "the advantages of American education and freedom of speech" by her parents. "I feel very close to God and think He is guiding me. Otherwise I wouldn't have had the strength to go on."

Recently, Lori Cox embarked upon another patriotic project, which she calls Operation Mailbag. In February, 1977, with the backing of the Disabled American Veterans, their auxiliaries, and various other flag-proud organizations, some four million letters were sent out to United States congressmen and to President Carter, urging that an annual National Patriotism Week be established. The letters were all mailed on February 21, the eve of George Washington's birthday. If the drive accomplishes its purpose, as Lori prays it will, we will have a National Patriotism Week by 1978.

Lori Cox may have been ridiculed by some of her young contemporaries in Scottsdale and by the "self-styled intellectuals" in Tempe (where the Arizona State University campus is located), but young people and intellectuals are not what Scottsdale is all about. It is about wealthy, frontier-spirited, Republican families who boast that they never read anything more mentally taxing than *Vogue* and *Playboy*. It is about sprawling houses with family rooms, cactus gardens, and—the new rage—private tennis courts, and that famous casual life style in which, as they say, "everybody has a pool." As for Phoenix itself—well, all *real* living is suburban. No one goes to the city unless he happens to work in one of the banks, mortgage companies, or state office buildings. There is only one first-class downtown restaurant, the Eagle's Nest, on the top of the Valley National Bank building, and that is primarily a men's lunching place. Everything else is in the suburbs, including the big department stores—Saks Fifth Avenue, Bullocks, and I. Magnin. The supermarkets in the suburbs sell everything—liquor, baked goods, even clothing. You can find a barbershop or beauty salon, even visit your dentist, without leaving the supermarket.

Scottsdale is almost aggressively casual. Cut-off jeans and tank tops are standard wear for cocktail parties, and men who wear neckties are regarded either as sissies or dumb Easterners who don't know better. "If you wear a tie, someone will ask you who died," says one man. Instead, men wear Western "bolo" string ties with turquoise beads, or gold chains. (Scottsdale women wear very little jewelry, but men wear lots of it—massive silver-and-turquoise rings, wide, mean-looking leather belts with huge silver buckles, silver-embossed cowboy boots.) The necktie is held in such contempt in Scottsdale that if a man enters the popular Pinnacle Peak restaurant wearing a tie, he will promptly have it cut off by a headwaiter with a pair of scissors. This is considered a great joke, and the victim of the vandalized necktie is supposed to laugh it off. To have one's necktie severed at the knot at Pinnacle Peak has even become a local status symbol. The management takes the cut-off ties and nails them to the ceiling, and the hundreds of dangling bits of haberdashery have become part of the restaurant's décor. To each tie, furthermore, is stapled the calling card of the gentleman who wore it.

For the last decade, Americans have been moving to Arizona towns like Scottsdale lured by the climate and the casual life. It has been advertised that casual means inexpensive, and it is claimed that an individual can live in Arizona on 25 percent less gross pay than he can in chillier regions of the country. Developers have been having a heyday here, and there is a booming business in the selling and reselling of building mortgages and in commercial paper, all of which has become so lucrative that the Mafia is said to be taking an interest in Scottsdale and nearby Paradise Valley. Families buy Scottsdale houses and lots sight unseen, and often a new development will be completely sold before there are any houses, streets, sewers, or utility lines on it. Everyone in Arizona, it sometimes seems, is involved in land speculation in one form or another, and the favorite topics of conversation at Scottsdale dinner parties are the costs of lots and houses and how values have appreciated in how many years' time. So bullish is the building industry here that banks are offering mortgages to home owners for no money down. Enticed by this situation, families in the Northeast and Middle West are pulling up stakes, emptying their savings accounts, and heading for a new life. But it turns out that jobs are not all that easy to find in Arizona. Furthermore, many are hoodwinked by unethical developers and end up having to sell their new houses, at distress-sale prices.

Scottsdale, however, prides itself on the fact that "there are no poor people here." Scottsdale streets are immaculate and well tended, outdoor advertising is restricted to small, tasteful signs, no neon is permitted, and yards and gardens are fenced for security and privacy. Even the Scottsdale Telephone Company building is cleverly disguised to look like a private house and not a commercial structure. Yet some newcomers from the East have found life in Scottsdale vaguely disappointing. "The accent here is all on sports and outdoor life," says one transplanted New Yorker. "There's no intellectual life, and not much cultural life." It is true that a young man imported to be resident director of a small theater company arrived in Scottsdale and saw his season fold after its first production of *The Glass Menagerie.* On opening night, only about thirty people were in the audience. Of the Arizona Ballet, the local company, one woman says, "It's really pretty bad; they drop people, and people fall down." The Phoenix Symphony is really the Phoenix Pops. Arizona State University is not particularly good. There is no one on the faculty who is a member of the National Academy of Sciences. Even its football team is rated one of the ten worst in the country. When Leonard Goodstein was recruited to be head of the Psychology Department at the university, he was offered a lower salary than he had been making in the East. When he protested this, the recruiter "launched into an elegy about the raptures of the climate and the clear night skies and the magnificent views." Finally Professor Goodstein said, "Are you offering me the head of Psychology or Physical Education?" Still, Goodstein confesses, "The casual life can be terribly seductive. Here, you drink your Coors beer straight out of the can—that sort of thing. But sometimes I miss the elegance of the East. Here, there is almost a *demeaning* of elegance."

The casual life means that high school basketball and football and college baseball scores are front-page items in the politically conservative *Arizona Republic,* which also gives space to letters to the

15

editor that want to know: "Why are we picking on the Postal Service? Let's pick on the Commies!" From Paradise Valley—where Barry Goldwater lives—front-page attention was recently given to the efforts of a citizens' group to recall the mayor, the vice-mayor, and two members of the town council who had the temerity to vote for the widening of Lincoln Drive from two lanes to four between Tatum Boulevard and Scottsdale Road. Neither in Scottsdale nor in Paradise Valley do people want wider roads. Wider roads encourage heavier traffic. In fact, the most fashionable Scottsdale streets are not paved at all, in order to discourage incursions from sightseers, rubber-neckers, and other unwanted visitors, who might be Communists or similarly dangerous types.

The casual life in Scottsdale means that Scottsdale goes to bed rather early. Scottsdale parties usually are called for six or six-thirty, and by ten o'clock, everyone is shaking hands and saying good night. A lot of this has to do with the desert climate. Scottsdale's days can be very hot, and its nights are chilly. Often, the national high and low record temperatures are set in Scottsdale within a single twenty-four-hour period. This means that if one is going to get one's tennis game in, one must rise early and play before the heat of the day begins. Also, Scottsdale's bankers and stockbrokers and corporation executives have to time their business day according to Eastern time, and this, too, means rising early. Arizona and Hawaii are the only two states that completely refuse to go on Daylight Time (the feeling is that there is something a little un-American about Daylight Time), and so in the summer months businessmen are often at their desks at six-thirty in the morning, and come home at half-past two. Construction work, to take advantage of the cool mornings, starts as early as five-thirty, so in booming, building, expanding Scottsdale it is often impossible to sleep much after that hour.

In the opinion of some, Scottsdale and its casual life have attracted just too many people. After all, the population of the place is climbing toward 100,000, and in winter there are hordes of vacationing tourists and conventioneers. Scottsdale, as they say, just isn't what it used to be, and so, several years ago, a clever developer had the idea of building an even more exclusive suburb of exclusive Scottsdale. In the rugged mountains twenty-two miles north of Scottsdale, Carefree and The Boulders were created. Carefree's altitude is about 1400 feet above Scottsdale's, which means that Carefree's days are somewhat cooler; further, some of the world's most expensive houses have been built in Carefree for the very, very rich who no longer have to worry about when the business day begins. In The Boulders, houses have been placed upon, within, and around the great rounded granite rocks that scatter across the mountainside like huge marbles tossed from the sky. The scenery is as spectacular as the houses, which feature indoor-outdoor pools fed by artificial waterfalls. Nearby, the Carefree Inn offers its golf course and tennis courts, and the Carefree Shopping Center sells nothing that is not expensive.

Carefree was designed as a refuge for wealthy retirees, and they have come to Carefree from all over the United States. Some have built houses that, in architectural style, are rather like the houses that were left behind in, say, Minneapolis, but most have adopted the prevailing adobe or Arizona Territorial style. Hugh Downs has a house in Carefree, and so does Dick Van Dyke. Though Carefree does not like to think of itself as a retirement community exactly, most of its residents, as television writer Kathleen Hite puts it, are "not in their first bloom of youth." Lazy pastimes are favored in Carefree—golf rather than tennis, a bit of hiking, rock collecting, and a great deal of contract bridge. Again, Carefree goes to bed not long after one of its predictably exuberant desert sunsets.

Carefree was the extravagant brainchild of two promotion-minded developers named Thomas Darlington and K. T. Palmer, who, at the time, described it as "the most expensive development in the world," and "like a limited edition of a fine piece of art," and "only for a few very special people." A private airport was provided for the special people's private planes. All utility lines were run underground, and all lots zoned to a minimum of two acres (a few condominiums have since crept in). Messrs. Darlington and Palmer (their enterprise has been taken over by the Sundial Realty Company, which carefully screens prospective buyers of property) were responsible for the enclave's quaint street names, which some people find a trifle cloying. The developers were determined that Carefree streets should sound very Western—more Western, perhaps, than "The West's Most Western Town"—and so the winding lanes between the big gray rocks and the big houses were designated Six Gun Road, Long Rifle Road, Staghorn Lane, Stage Coach Pass, Mule Train Road, and Eagle Claw Drive, among other such flights of fancy. More than anything, however, the developers wanted Carefree street names to sound—well—carefree. There is a Serene Street, a Nevermind Trail, a Whileaway Road, a Rocking Chair

Road, a Sleepy Hollow Road, and a thoroughfare called Languid Lane. For bridge players, tennis players, and golfers, there is Foursome Way. There is a Ho Road, and a Hum Road, and yes, there is an Easy Street. (Ho, Hum, and Easy Street intersect.)

There is only one aspect of the casual life which the promoters, developers, and current residents of Carefree have not been able to harness completely, and that is the area's large indigenous population of rattlesnakes. Carefree people have learned that it is unhealthy, while gardening, to poke around with one's hands under shrubbery and in flower beds. When walking out of doors (though rattlesnakes have been known to enter houses), it is wise to keep one's eyes on the ground. But the developers have taken care of an even greater nuisance, and have made sure that there will be no pledge-of-allegiance crisis in Carefree such as the one that rocked Scottsdale. Carefree is not particularly fond of children, and is less fond of teen-agers. And so, while Carefree provides every amenity a rich person might desire, from hydrotherapy pools to a private jetport, there are no schools.

"A school," says one Carefree woman in her typically carefree way, "gives a community nothing but trouble."

3

Wide Streets

*I*n the summer of 1847, when Brigham Young led his weary little party of pioneers—143 men, three women, and two children—into the valley of the Great Salt Lake, he was suffering from exhaustion and fever. But upon reaching the valley's rim, Young lifted himself from the pallet of the covered wagon that bore him, gazed into the expanse beyond, and uttered the prophetic words: *"This is the place."* At the time, no one could imagine what he saw that was so appealing. The valley floor was dry and desolate, bereft of vegetation except for a single scrubby pine and miles of tumbleweed and cocklebur. It hardly seemed an auspicious location for the promised new Zion, the earthly abode of God, that Young and his fellow Mormons had set out to seek when persecution had driven them out of Nauvoo, Illinois, some three and a half months earlier.

But Brigham Young must have seen something, because today, just 130 years later, Salt Lake City, which Young founded, is a gleaming place of steel-and-glass skyscrapers where hundreds of thousands of members of the Church of Jesus Christ of Latter-day Saints have prospered and some have become enormously wealthy. A local joke tells of the departed Mormon who arrived at Saint Peter's gate, gave his name, and was asked to state his religion. When the man replied that he was a Mormon, Saint Peter consulted his great book, but could not find the new arrival's name on his list. Finally, after much searching, Saint Peter announced, "Ah, I see what the trouble is. I have you down under 'Real Estate.'" Visitors to Salt Lake City are often told that the huge statue of Brigham Young at the center of Temple Square, in the heart of town, depicts Young with his left hand proudly pointing at the new Zion's First National Bank building across the street.

Young designed the irrigation system—based on reservoirs and the river he renamed the River Jordan—which turned the valley green and fruitful, and he laid out the plan for the city's streets, using a unique system of his own devising which was designed to show the traveler exactly where he was at any given moment. The 500 block of South Fifth Street West, for example, would be five blocks west of State Street and five blocks south of Temple Square. As the city has grown, however, Young's numbering system has evolved into one of mind-boggling complexity confusing even to the natives, who would have trouble directing you to an address such as 1185 South 1300th Street East, or 4567 West 5055th Street South. Young insisted that his city have wide streets—wide enough to turn a Conestoga wagon around in—and these streets are a source of great civic pride today. "Have you noticed our beautiful wide streets?" the visitor is always asked. When, not long ago, in order to lure shoppers away from the proliferating suburban malls and back into the downtown shopping area, the city widened the sidewalks on both State and Main streets, and studded them with trees, fountains, benches, and gazebo-like shelters, the result was narrower streets. "We've *always* had wide streets," complains Mrs. Joseph Mendenhall, whose grandfather came out to Salt Lake with Brigham Young. "We love our wide streets. Why would we need wide sidewalks, for heaven's sake? If you ask me, what they've done with those sidewalks is a *mess*!" (It has also been noted that the wider sidewalks have not appreciably increased pedestrian shopper traffic along State or Main.) Once the city even went so far as to propose moving Brigham Young's statue to another part of town in order to relieve traffic at the intersection of Main and Temple. But this was too much. The citizenry made it quite clear that it would never stand for that.

For all that the city has prospered, expanded, and changed, there is a pervading reluctance to see things change much more. This is a proud and conservative place. And though it was once a desert in the middle of nowhere, it is now a city in the middle of nowhere, and Salt Lake City likes its splendid isolation from other places almost as much as it likes its wide streets. The nearest city of any size is San Francisco to the west. The closest city to the east is Denver, and to the south there is only Phoenix. "We're not a part of any megalopolis," says Dr. Duncan McDonald, a prominent ophthalmologist, "and our isolation and distance from other big cities keeps us free from other cities' influences. That's kept us about ten years behind the times. And there are advantages to being ten years behind the times: the problems of other cities haven't caught up with Salt Lake." But Dr. McDonald also calls Salt Lake City "an island of mediocrity." He says, "Salt Lake has no pronounced intellectual or social elite, and no pronounced lower class, either. Everyone is on a mediocre level somewhere at the middle." Salt Lake is also a city that lives entirely in its suburbs, like both Phoenix and Houston, and, as Dr. McDonald puts it, "The Democrats live on the west side of town, and the Republicans live on the east."

The east side of Salt Lake is by far the most fashionable. There, in the low foothills of the Wasatch Range, sprawling ranch-style houses face the often spectacular sunsets against the Oquirrh Mountains to the west. But there is no real "best address" in Salt Lake City. Federal Heights is an older suburb, near the campus of the University of Utah and not far from the Salt Lake Country Club (the area just below Federal Heights, so another local joke goes, is "Federal Depths"). As the city has grown, it has tended to sprawl eastward and southward, and expensive houses have been built in such newer developments as Olympus Cove and in the mouth of Cottonwood Canyon. Originally, Salt Lake suburbanites took to the hills to escape from the coal dust that hung over the town from the valley's mining operations. Now that the air is cleaner, the attraction of the hills has been the views and the sunsets, and building and development have climbed higher and higher. But when Salt Lake found itself faced with the prospect of having its ruggedly beautiful Wasatch Mountains completely covered with suburban houses and swimming pools, a zoning ordinance was passed requiring that all new houses built at an altitude of 5200 feet or over be placed on lots of at least sixteen acres. Since mountainside acreage is measured on the horizontal, the few people who have ventured higher than 5200 feet have pieces of property that, if laid out flat, would stretch for miles. At least one property owner confesses that he has never really visited the upper reaches of his land.

The Mormon influence in Salt Lake City—and indeed in all of Utah—has created all sorts of interesting anomalies. There is no clear-cut "Mormon area" of Salt Lake, and Mormons, non-Mormon Christians, and Jews live next door to one another (though wealthy Jewish families, such as the Bambergers, Auerbachs, and Rosenblatts, who made money in everything from railroads to the clothing business, tend to favor Federal Heights). At the same time, there is relatively little social intermingling among the religious groups. In Mormon terminology, any non-Mormon is classified as a Gentile. But to many Mormons the word "Gentile" has a stronger meaning: anti-Mormon. Correspondingly, in the Gentile community, any Gentile who affiliated himself with a predominantly Mormon business or organization was for years branded a "Jack Mormon"—a traitor who collaborated with the Mormon enemy. For years, the Mormon and Gentile communities did not mingle except in some sort of conflict or confrontation. There was a Mormon economy and a Gentile economy. There was a Mormon (Peoples) political party and a Gentile (Liberal) party. There were Gentile holidays, and Mormon holidays, such as the twenty-fourth of July, marking the anniversary of Brigham Young's entry into the valley. Thus the "irrepressible conflict" and the "Utah problem" divided Salt Lake City into two irreconcilable worlds. Though individual Mormons and Gentiles could, and did, strike up occasional personal friendships, Mormons and Gentiles could not afford the social stigma of publicly being in any way nice to one another.

Those days, they like to say, are gone—but not entirely. The Mormon dietary restrictions present a problem, for one thing. A good Mormon is not supposed to drink coffee, tea, or any other "heated liquid," including, presumably, hot soup. He cannot smoke, drink alcohol, or partake of any other stimulant, including Coca-Cola. And yet, not long ago, when a prominent Mormon businessman was reported to have installed a Coca-Cola machine in his office building, the scoop was that the Mormon Church had invested in some Coca-Cola stock and, therefore, the machine was working for the Church. Though Mormons are not supposed to touch alcohol, the story goes that it was a Mormon group that started the area's first brewery in the foothills at the entrance to the valley—in order to attract newcomers (and potential converts) to the growing city.

There are no ashtrays in Mormon homes or offices, and visitors who ask if they may smoke are requested not to. "Some of my Mormon clients might smell the smoke in the office," says another Mormon businessman. And yet, away from the office, he smokes and, on the sly, drinks coffee and Scotch whisky, and keeps a well-stocked bar in his house. Old Melbourne Romney, a prominent Mormon, was even seen smoking his cigar right on Main Street. Mormons, when they are invited to Gentile dinner parties, traditionally arrive one hour late, in order to avoid the cocktail hour. But at the same time, it is the worst-kept secret in the town that many of these late arrivals both drink and offer liquor in their own homes. Because of situations like these, Gentile Salt Lake citizens have the impression that most Mormons are not as serious about their religion as they pretend to be—an attitude that only widens the social abyss between Mormons and Gentiles.

The Mormon taboo against alcohol has accounted for Utah's quaint liquor laws. Utah has many state-run stores (where liquor is heavily taxed), but liquor cannot be sold at bars. It must be "brown-bagged" in, and this has led to a thriving business—in bottle-bag manufacturing. Salt Lake stores offer all sorts of canvas and leather bottle carriers in a variety of designs and sizes. At the larger hotels, the state liquor store is usually right next door to the bar, for the convenience of drinkers. The person desiring a drink buys his bottle at the store, then carries it into the bar, where the bartender will sell setups but, if he is a Mormon, will not mix the drink. As a result, it is futile to order a Margarita or a frozen Daiquiri in Utah. Perhaps, as another result, Utah has one of the highest alcohol-consumption rates—and one of the highest alcoholism rates—of any state in the country. "I'm sure it's because when you have the bottle right there on the table, you tend to pour stronger drinks, and pour them oftener, than when you're ordering an ounce-and-a-half drink from a waiter," says one man. "At least, I know I drink more under this silly system."

The fact that many Mormons drink is shrugged off by other Mormons, who do not see it as apostasy or hypocrisy—necessarily. As one Mormon bishop puts it with a wink, "You got to sin to know what sinnin' is." Mormons also belong to the various private drinking clubs that have proliferated all over Salt Lake City, such as D. B. Cooper's, named after the successful skyjacker who bailed out of his hijacked plane and disappeared. At clubs like Cooper's, members either keep their own bottles at the bar or buy one outright from the bartender. To offset Utah's high tax on liquor, Salt Lake City has Wyoming—with cheap liquor as well as cigarettes—just across the border.

Salt Lake's Mormons are equally ambivalent on the controversial subject of polygamy. It is estimated that in Salt Lake City and surrounding Davis County as many as twenty-thousand families may be practicing polygamy, or "multiple marriage," as the Saints prefer to call it, and of course, all of them are doing so illegally. The Mormon Church officially abolished polygamy in 1896—it was a condition of Utah's admission into the Union. Today, polygamy is grounds for excommunication and, in addition, legal arrest. But both the Church and Utah law-enforcement officials have tended to take a soft line on the issue, and to look the other way. The polygamists, meanwhile, consider themselves part of a reform, or fundamentalist, brand of Mormonism, and, as such, candidates for the first circle of Glory when they are gathered to their ancestors— of whom most Mormons keep elaborate track. (Mrs. Mendenhall, for example, can trace her ancestry to the thirteenth century, and has a thick sheaf of documents to back her up.)

If the Mormons of Salt Lake City have one common enemy, it is that amorphous body in Washington known as "the Government," or in the twangy Western vernacular, "the Gummint." Whenever the subject of the Gummint comes up, there are angry snorts of general disapproval, because the Gummint is forever threatening to "come in here" and change things around. "The Gummint isn't going to tell *us* what to do," is a phrase frequently heard in Salt Lake City. The fact that the Gummint opposes polygamy is probably why Salt Lake City Mormons continue to tolerate it, and if the Gummint were not behind the welfare program, the Mormons would be more willing to accept it. It is the Mormons' contention that "We take care of our own," and they often boast that there are no members of the faith on welfare. Meanwhile, a number of Mormon families in Salt Lake *are* on welfare—particularly the polygamous ones. Some polygamous families are rich, having made money in mining, banking, and real estate, and at least one family lives in an enormous ranch-style house near Cottonwood Canyon. But many of the multiple-marriage families, with numerous wives and even more numerous children, are poor, and the wives and children are said to put an enormous strain on the welfare rolls and, in turn, on the non-Mormon taxpayer. This is another cause of friction between Mormon and Gentile. Several years ago, a number of Mormon merchants banded together to build an elegant downtown shopping complex called the ZCMI Center, the initials standing for Zion Cooperative Mercantile Institution. Non-Mormons jeeringly say that the letters actually stand for "Zion's Children Must Increase."

Still another sore point between Gentiles and Mormons involves public education. The public schools of Salt Lake City offer an hour of religious education—in the Mormon faith—every day, which strikes many people as a violation of the church and state separation provisions of the American Constitution. To be sure, the Mormon children arrive an hour early for their religious instruction, which is not part of the regular curriculum for non-Mormons. But—in some outlying areas, at least—youngsters receive full scholastic credit for the religious courses, which prompts at least one Gentile cynic to say, "There is *no* separation of church and state in Utah."

As a group, the Mormons are proud, thrifty, hard-working, and clannish. The late Howard Hughes chose Mormons for his closest business associates because of their acumen and probity. "A man who never drinks never forgets," he once said. And the manner in which members of the Mormon faith elect to raise their children is perhaps the greatest force dividing the Mormon and the Gentile worlds, and keeps the two in "irrepressible conflict." Though Mormon and Gentile children may go to school together, their lives outside the classroom are totally different. On the theory that the devil finds work for idle hands, Mormon families keep their children so busy with planned activities that there is no time for them to get into mischief. Immediately after school, youngsters report to various Mutual Improvement Societies, church-sponsored groups designed, as the name implies, to improve the members. The Mutual Improvement Societies offer activities ranging from religious and language study to arts, crafts, sports, and calisthenics. In a proper Mormon household, dinner is on the table promptly at six o'clock. Afterward, there is an evening regimen of study groups, seminars, lectures, and cultural events. On weekends there are church-organized sports and, in the evenings, young people's dances. Dancing is one of the few frivolities of which the Mormon Church approves, and dances—particularly square dances—are an important part of Mormon social life. By the time a Mormon teenager collapses into bed at night he is, so the theory goes, too exhausted to masturbate.

If you see a youth with hair hanging below his collar, or with a beard, or a girl wearing tight pants or a skirt with a hemline above the knee, you will be certain that he or she is not a Mormon. At nearby Brigham Young University, a strict dress and grooming code is enforced—despite occasional protests. Women's Liberation has made few inroads in Salt Lake City, because a Mormon's world is a man's world. The president of the Church has always been a male,

25

and always will be, and so are the apostles, who correspond roughly to bishops. High officials of the Church are chosen in visions, which occur with computer-like regularity on Monday afternoons in the Temple—though it has been noted that whenever a new president is chosen, the deciding vision manages to elect that senior member of the Council of Twelve Apostles who is next in line.

At the age of nineteen, or after he has completed one year of college, every young Mormon male begins his required two years of missionary work. After two months of intensive training—often in a foreign language—he departs for one of the Church's many far-flung missions around the world (avoiding Catholic countries, where Mormonism is anathema). He is expected to survive on a stringent allowance of $160 a month, which the Church will pay only if he cannot. When he returns, his standing in the community will depend on how many converts to the faith he has been able to collect. Mormon youth, in other words, is programmed to such an extent that there is almost no time for intermingling with Gentiles, other than in missionary work. And, it has been noted, when young Mormons return from their long months in the field, that a distressing number of them require psychiatric help. There is also a high rate of youthful suicide and, ironically, a disturbing number of drug-related deaths. A Mormon's life, after all, is not intended to be easy.

Though many Mormon families have become very rich, their way of life is generally Spartan. Mr. Obert J. Tanner, for example, one of the town's richest men—his fortune was made in the jewelry business, with college rings and fraternity pins—lives comfortably but without frills in a modest suburban house on the southeast slopes, and drives his own car. Mormon frugality has managed to rub off on the Gentile community, and most forms of conspicuous spending are frowned upon in Salt Lake City. There are only eight Rolls-Royces in the entire Salt Lake Valley, and the most popular family car is the four-wheel-drive Jeep. Mr. George Eccles (non-Mormon) is something of an exception. He is president of the First Security Bank and keeps the only Mercedes limousine in town. Mr. Obert Tanner's one extravagance is his fondness for giving fountains to the city; among others, he has donated the fountains in front of the Federal Building and his own headquarters.

As part of their religious regimen, Mormons are required to keep a two-year supply of food and staples in their homes as a form of insurance against what they believe will be an inevitable holocaust; at any time, without notice, a family may be ordered by Church elders to live for a specified period on its stored goods alone. Gentile families deplore this sort of hoarding, but at least one Salt Lake housewife—non-Mormon—says that Mormon marketing habits affect her own. "When I see a Mormon woman with her supermarket basket filled with hundreds of rolls of toilet paper, I think I'd better load up on toilet paper too—in case there's going to be some sort of shortage."

Among the great Mormon families of Salt Lake are the Kimballs (Spencer W. Kimball is the current president of the Church as well as a prominent banker), the Tanners, Larkins, Youngs (descendants of Brigham), Smiths (descendants of Joseph Smith, the founder of the church), the Romneys, Vancotts, Cannons, Whitneys, and Marriotts (of the hotel/restaurant chain). The leading Gentile families would include the McCormicks, Cullens, Hanauers, and Walkers (who came to the valley as Mormon converts, but later left the Church). Over the years, the town's leaders on both sides of the religious fence have mingled to a limited extent within the confines of the Alta Club, a men's social club modeled on San Francisco's Union Club. Originally, the Alta Club was strictly a Gentile club. But as it evolved into a social arm of the Salt Lake City Chamber of Commerce, it became impossible to exclude Mormons from membership since they represented the most powerful commercial force in the city. Still, during lunch hour at the club, Mormons and Gentiles tend to eat at separate tables.

It strikes many outsiders as curious that, as the Salt Lake suburbs have expanded for miles in a southeasterly direction from the center of town, the citizenry have ignored the natural phenomenon of the Great Salt Lake itself, which lies to the northwest. It is the largest body of water west of the Mississippi and the largest saline lake in North America, measuring fifty by seventy-five miles and surrounded by a wild and ruggedly beautiful shoreline. It is also an ecological curiosity in that the southern arm of the lake has a water level almost two and a half feet higher than the northern arm, a result of the higher degree of salinity in the northern half. Still, aside from the chemical companies that mine the lake for Salt Lake shrimp (used in pet foods), table salt, and other minerals, no one in Salt Lake City has ever quite known what to do with it. A few suburban areas, such as the northeast ridge called "Pill Hill" (many doctors live there), have views of the lake shimmering in the distance, but most Salt Lake citizens visit their lake—and then reluctantly—only when out-of-town visitors insist on being taken to see it. The lake is disparaged. At certain seasons, to be sure, the lake has a strong briny odor, quite different from the smell of the sea. "It smells as though someone should flush it," says one Salt Lake City man. And there is the problem of the brine flies, which bite. But from the rocky hills and promontories along the shore there are breathtaking stretches of blue water and white "sand" beaches—not really sand, but the pulverized shells of prehistoric sea creatures which once inhabited the original Lake Bonneville.

In the early 1900s, the lake was used for recreation. On summer afternoons, Salt Lake City families used to board the little trains—one open, for those who preferred the sun, one closed for those who liked shade—that chugged slowly out to Saltair, a huge Victorian pleasure dome on the lakeshore that offered swimming, boating, and other outdoor delights. But the trouble was—and is—that the shoreline of the lake keeps changing due to the rising and falling water level. In years of heavy rainfall, an increase of just a few inches in the water level can extend the area of the lake by miles, and in years of drought the lake shrinks just as drastically. The Saltair resort found itself either standing on its pilings in the middle of the water or standing high and dry with the water miles away. By the late 1920s, Saltair had fallen to rot and decay.

Various proposals have been put forth for controlling and stabilizing the water level of the Great Salt Lake through dredging, dams, pumping, and so forth. Both the Disney and the Marriott organizations have offered plans to turn the lake into a recreational area again. Developers have drawn up plans for suburban housing in the hills of the south shore. One particularly ambitious plan envisions converting Antelope Island—connected by a causeway to the shore—to a "Living Great Basin Museum," and repopulating the island with the animals that roamed the Great Basin before the arrival of man. State Senator Haven Barlow is the principal booster for this project, which he conceives as "a tremendous tourist and recreational attraction," and "something that people could get enthusiastic about—seeing buffalo, elk, antelope, mountain sheep and goats, and a wide variety of birds all in their natural habitat. Driving anywhere else in the state you'll rarely see an elk, and never a buffalo." Visitors would be able to tour the game preserve from the south, and swim at the northern beaches. "Antelope Island's beaches are the best in the lake," says Senator Barlow.

But nothing can seem to overcome Utahans' innate antipathy

28

toward their lake. Bills for lake development in the state legislature get bogged down in committee, and nothing seems to happen. The beautiful lakeshore is still bereft of houses, hotels, or anything that would draw a human to it. The lake remains bare of sailboats, abandoned to the brine flies. Controversy over what to do with it has raged fitfully over the last twenty years, and the lake continues still and silent, except on stormy nights when huge waves gather. It has been noticed that every proposal or discussion of the future of the lake falls apart inevitably along religious lines (Disney vs. Marriott, for example). If it is a Mormon notion that is under consideration, the Gentiles are opposed to it, and vice versa. And so the rift between Mormon and Gentile—between Saint and Sinner—remains as wide as the Great Salt Lake itself, or as wide, at least, as Salt Lake City's wide, wide streets.

MIDWEST

4

Connecticut on Lake Erie

*I*n the new vernacular of citizens' band radio en-
thusiasts, it is known as "Junk Area," or "The Dirty City." From as
far west as Omaha, the call "Heading for the Dirty City, good
buddy," heard over the airwaves, means only one thing to CB-ers:
Heading for Cleveland—the city where rivers have been known to
catch fire and burn. Poor Cleveland.

But the elegant suburbs of Cleveland to the east of town—
Shaker Heights (now largely Jewish), Cleveland Heights, and the
rural, horsy towns of Hunting Valley, Pepper Pike, and Gates
Mills—are far from dirty. Though many of the old Cleveland
families—Mathers, Cases, Hannas, Humphreys, Gwinns—have
"escaped across the border to the Philadelphia Main Line," and
though the Rockefellers deserted Cleveland long ago, the families
who constitute what might be called the working wealthy are all in
the suburbs. But, like Grosse Pointe, the Cleveland suburbs have
managed to shrug off the city that spawned them, to blink at
Cleveland's squalor, and to concentrate, instead, on their own im-
maculateness. The great mansions still line the length of Shaker
Boulevard with an air of self-satisfaction so complete that the local
joke is: "Nobody really *lives* in those houses. You never see anyone
go in or out. There's never a sign of life from any of them."

Younger, more adventurous souls, meanwhile, have ventured
farther afield—into the rolling hills of Summit County, south of
Cleveland, where, oddly enough, it is possible to find a perfectly

preserved old New England village. It happened this way. When, in the eighteenth century, the Crown was dividing up territory among its American colonies, the colony of Connecticut felt cheated. After a certain amount of haggling, Connecticut was mollified by being given a wide strip of land along the southern shore of Lake Erie, stretching over 120 miles from the Pennsylvania border as far westward as Sandusky—three and a quarter million acres in area. This so-called Western Reserve of Connecticut remained technically a part of the New England state until as recently as 1800, when it was ceded to Ohio. The region was largely settled by Connecticut families, who established Western Reserve University in the town of Hudson, which had been settled by a Connecticut man named David Hudson (alleged to have been a descendant of Henry Hudson) and incorporated in 1799. Later, when the university moved to Cleveland, its handsome old brick buildings in Hudson, built between 1820 and 1840 and reminiscent of Harvard Yard, were taken over by Western Reserve Academy, a private college-preparatory school.

Western Reserve, both as a college and as a prep school, attracted the wealthy from Cleveland and nearby Akron, and in the years immediately following the Civil War, little Hudson became the "secret" retreat of Cleveland and Akron millionaires who had made money in steel, coal, and rubber products. Here they purchased and restored the quaint New England salt-box houses and Federal mansions that were charmingly clustered around a New England village green. Around the turn of the twentieth century, Hudson received a boon in the form of an endowment trust fund from a Cleveland coal tycoon named Ellsworth, who also erected a memorial clock tower to himself on a corner of the green. Mr. Ellsworth's gift was designed to preserve the town intact, but there were a couple of strings attached: All power lines had to be buried, and the town was to be dry. The former stipulation has been honored, but not the latter. Although Ohio has state liquor stores, the town of Hudson has one of the few privately owned liquor stores in the state.

Today, Hudson is still small—population around five thousand—and considers itself a very special place, where it is important to own a "century house," one that is at least a hundred years old. Its residents include remnants of the community's Old Guard—Mark Hanna once had a house there—who live on inherited money, and prosperous young executives who commute thirty minutes to Firestone and Goodyear in Akron, and forty-five minutes to Republic Steel in Cleveland. Life revolves around the Hudson Country Club and the one "social" bar in town—the Reserve Inn. The Daughters of the American Revolution have an active chapter there, and the Hudson Library Historical Society and the Garden Club are also socially important. Every year, the town turns out for the Annual House and Garden Tour, which is followed by an "ice cream social" on the green. There are no Jews and no blacks in Hudson (black day help is imported from Twinsburg, down the road) and there are virtually no Democrats. It is rumored that some people in Hudson feel that the National Guard did the right thing when it opened fire on students at nearby Kent State University several years ago, and a number think that a few more bullets sprayed around would have been a good idea.

As an Andorra and an anachronism—a New England village where a New England village has no real business being—Hudson, Ohio, presents a series of contradictions. Although most of its residents are wealthy, the town is said to be "a collection agency's nightmare" as far as the paying of bills is concerned. According to Mr. James Bonbright Anderson, who made his home in Hudson for several years, the town is "strait-laced, staid, and stuffy—and yet everybody is screwing everybody else. When I lived there, everybody was getting a divorce—including me." Not long ago, the head of the school board divorced his wife and married a neighbor across the street, whose husband married another woman, whose husband married the ex-wife of the head of the school board. For all its emphasis on New England quaintness, Anderson says, "Everybody was seeing a psychiatrist, everybody was smoking dope at parties, everybody was popping pills. One doctor—in order to keep a woman's husband from finding out about her pill habit—used to hide her prescriptions for them under a potted palm in the lobby of the movie theater." Hudson likes to use the words "peaceful," "serene," "charming," "Old World," and "quiet" to describe the community, and when freights carrying ore and coal thunder through town on the Pittsburgh & Cleveland line, people treat the noise as though it did not exist.

Outwardly, Hudson seems to present a solid, conservative front, with citizens toiling one for all and all for one for the betterment of the little community. Actually, the town is sharply divided within itself. The north side of town, for example, is the most desirable, with the east side of East-West Road coming next. (The two main thoroughfares, East-West Road and North-South Road, come together at the village green.) No one who is anybody would live in the south or the west part of town. As in many small towns, there is another wide social gulf between the men who belong to the Rotary Club and the men who belong to Kiwanis. "Rotary always attracts the bankers and the upper-management men," says one resident. "Kiwanis is for shopkeepers." It is impossible to belong to both. The Lions occupy a social level between Rotary and Kiwanis. There had always been a rift between the pupils at the public school and the day students who attended Western Reserve Academy, and when, not long ago, in an effort to be modern-minded, a Montessori school was established, it created a third division. The Akron Firestones helped endow it and sent their children there, and it became very chic to serve on the board of the Montessori school. Soon, however, along Hudson's thriving gossip grapevine word spread that the school was being used for other purposes and that its rooms had from time to time become the scene of after-hours extramarital carryings-on. Police interest was aroused and then for some reason faded. The school, meanwhile, became the target of teen-age vandals, of whom Hudson seemed to have more than its share.

Perhaps when a town such as Hudson becomes so enisled, so encapsulated, so inverted, so smugly proud of its architecture and unusual history, it loses all sight of reality. While maintaining its dreamlike "character," it begins to live the dream. How else can one account for the things that seem to go so wrong in enclaves like this? Why, for example, when a drug rehabilitation program called Head North was instituted for local high school students, did students from the third and fourth grades of the elementary school show up? Why did a respectable executive start painting murals on vans? Why don't Hudson people pay their bills? Why did an elegant "piping party," with Scottish bagpipers, end up with guests drunkenly trying to peer under the pipers' kilts? There has even been some odd municipal behavior. Though Hudson is known as a fiscally conservative, even tight-fisted, town—and a town where there are no buildings more than three stories tall—why did the town fathers splurge not long ago on an expensive piece of fire-fighting equipment with a snorkle that would extend eleven stories into the air?

Is it possible that living in a community that is too perfect, too controlled, can inflict a kind of paranoia on its citizens? Perhaps, in a town where everybody lives like everybody else, one tends to feel

36

like everyone else—anonymous—and people start to wonder who they are. One former resident of Hudson describes it as "a little like living in colonial Williamsburg, or Disneyland. I began to feel as though I had to get away to summer camp or something, to start making bird feeders and lanyards." Perhaps, in a community where everything is too rigidly standardized, where there is so little diversity, where there are no real problems, artificial or at least synthetic problems—such as drugs—must be created. In order to create the racial balance that it wanted, for example, Hudson's Montessori school had to import black students from Twinsburg. They have not done too well.

Perhaps it is dangerous to overidentify with a place, its history, its tradition, its architecture. When Levittown, Long Island, was first developed a number of years ago, from a handful of floor plans that were reversed from block to block, it was cheerfully predicted that Levittown would one day be a slum. But this has not happened. Over the years, the once stupefying sameness of Levittown houses has all but disappeared, as Levittown home owners have added to their houses, individualized them with landscaping, knocked down walls and added pools and patios. The "planned" look of Levittown is gone and, today, Levittown is a pleasant, prosperous middle-class suburb where many of the original owners still live and have raised their families.

While Levittown looked to the future, Hudson looks to the past. And the pretty little town—perfect in every detail that meets the eye, a little jewel—has been so admired that the experiment is being tried elsewhere. Eight miles west of Hudson is the little town of Peninsula, which, during Prohibition, was where all the local brothels were. Peninsula has old houses too, which had become run down. Now Peninsula is being restored, renovated, redecorated, and New Englandized—with quaint little Old World shops (a glass blower's shop, for example)—under the supervision of a young interior decorator whose work has found much favor with members of the Firestone family. The object is to turn Peninsula into another Hudson. Already people are saying, "Isn't it cute?"

But at least anything is better, as they say in Hudson, than living in Cleveland, a city that has become virtually unlivable—or Akron, for that matter. In Hudson, the trees are big and leafy, the fields are green and rolling, the houses are freshly painted, and the air is sweet.

Today, among other disasters in faraway Cleveland, the Republic Steel Company throws out iron oxide particles from its great smokestacks in such quantity that an entire stretch of Interstate 77, for miles around the intersection of 480, has been stained a bright, angry red.

Poor Cleveland.

5

Company Town

When the residents of Indian Hill—which, though some would argue the point, is generally conceded to be Cincinnati's most elegant suburban address—were meeting a few years ago to discuss plans for a new village church (Protestant Episcopal), it was assumed that there would be the usual heated arguments over design, choice of building materials, interior details, landscaping, and so on. To everyone's surprise, the proposed plans for the new church were quickly approved, with no serious objections from anyone.

Next on the agenda came the matter of the church burial ground, and suddenly the meeting was in an uproar. To some people it was inconceivable that a new cemetery should even be considered. As one resident put it, "We already *have* a cemetery. Everyone who is anyone has *always* been buried at Spring Grove."

Spring Grove Cemetery, located many miles from Indian Hill in a not particularly fashionable part of town, is one of Cincinnati's most enduring symbols. Furthermore, it is not a symbol of death but a symbol of substance and permanence. The reluctance to supplement—or, God forfend, part with—Spring Grove Cemetery is not an example of this conservative city's unwillingness to change, either. It is more an example of Cincinnati's fierce insistence on preserving the things it considers beautiful and unique and redolent of tradition.

Spring Grove was conceived as much more than a cemetery. It was to be a botanical and ornithological garden, complete with

39

lakes, ponds, winding lanes, hilltop vistas, and all manner of trees and flowering shrubbery. English nightingales and other exotic birds were imported for Spring Grove (only the waterfowl survived), and the vast acreage was laid out with the attention that might have been given to a great park. The imposing obelisks and mausoleums of granite and marble are arranged like pieces of monumental sculpture. In spring and summer, when Spring Grove is at its pruned and flowering best, it is one of the city's sights that Cincinnatians take out-of-town visitors to see.

Just as the city's famous Union Terminal, with its vaulting Art Deco façade and fountained avenue of approach, was designed to inform the arriving passenger that he was coming to a Very Important City, Spring Grove was designed to remind the departing Cincinnatian that he was leaving a Very Special Place. Within Spring Grove, there are divisions of class and money that are just as strictly maintained as within the city beyond. Old wealth is contained in one section, newer money in another. The city's German burghers, who were among the early Cincinnati settlers, have their own place, the German Protestants carefully separated from the German Catholics, as they were in life. The mausoleums of the best families have the hilltops with the best views, while modest graves of ordinary folk are confined to the less conspicuous slopes. The conscientious zoning of Spring Grove makes it quite literally a suburb for the departed.

Somewhat like "Proper Bostonians," with whom they are sometimes compared, the residents of Cincinnati are often called "The Serene Cincinnatians," and nowhere in the city can the serenity be better sensed than along the shaded gravel pathways of Spring Grove or along the dark, narrow, and spooky lanes that wind wealthily through Indian Hill. Of course, some things ruffle Cincinnati's composure *slightly*—such as when outsiders occasionally confuse it with Cleveland, or liken Indian Hill to Shaker Heights. As far as Cincinnatians are concerned, there is Cincinnati, and then there is the rest of the state. It also irks Cincinnatians when people—especially Easterners—mix Cincinnati up with Keokuk, Peoria, Muncie, or any other sprawling Middle Western metropolis. Cincinnati does not sprawl. It sits, sedately and complacently, in the basin that seems to have been carved out for it at the riverport, surrounded by green hills. Cincinnati, furthermore, does not like to think of itself as Middle Western. "I might call *Omaha* Middle Western," says one resident, "but after all, we border on

40

Pennsylvania. Would you call Pennsylvania part of the Middle West?" Emotionally, Cincinnati feels much closer to New York and Europe than it does to Chicago. And, next to clerks at Fifth Avenue stores who have difficulty spelling "Cincinnati" and routinely add an extra *t* when Cincinnatians use their New York charge accounts, the people who annoy Cincinnatians the most are those who telephone from the East and say, "What time is it out there?" "The same as in New York," is the tart reply. "We have always been on Eastern time." (Some forty miles west of Cincinnati, to be sure, the country goes on Central time.) If "serenity" can be envisioned mixed with a certain amount of edgy, chip-on-the-shoulder defensiveness, that would seem to sum up the city's overall mood.

Nowadays, with Union Station closed and obsolete—while the city struggles to find some use for the building, which is considered an architectural prize—the commonest approach to Cincinnati is from the airport. And to the first-time visitor, the physical appearance of the city often comes as a distinct surprise. All at once, around a hilltop curve and through a deep cut in the highway, the city's skyline presents itself, across a series of graceful bridges, as a cluster of solid, yet oddly delicate, spires and towers. The first thing one notices is that there are relatively few new high-rise buildings of steel and glass. The Cincinnati skyline has the appearance of having been there a good long time, which much of it has; it has a finished look. No booms from construction derricks slash across the sky. Cincinnati has had most of this skyline, pretty much as it is today, for the better part of fifty years, and it is in keeping with the city's nature that it sees no reason to alter, amend, or edit what is there. The new Kroger Building is an exception and, looking as though it had been built with squares of blue and white poster board and assembled by a kindergarten class, it is an embarrassment. Its design so offended the city fathers that Kroger, a supermarket chain, was forced to place its building several blocks away from the center of town.

Downtown Cincinnati is a tidy rectangle of no more than a dozen square, walkable, tree-lined blocks containing most of the city's shops, department stores, hotels, and restaurants. Roughly at the center sits Fountain Square, another of the city's proud symbols, with its elaborate Tyler Davidson Memorial Fountain, a forty-three-foot-high monument of ornamental bronze and porphyry, topped by "The Genius of Water"—a draped figure with arms outstretched in an attitude of invocation, from which the fountain's waters cascade. (Cincinnatians feel as strongly about Fountain Square as they do about Spring Grove Cemetery, and a suggestion several years ago that the fountain be moved elsewhere brought forth a great public outcry.)

Fountain Square is where downtown, daytime Cincinnati strolls and sits in the sun, where secretaries take their paper-bag lunches, where every important civic rally and demonstration takes place. It is Cincinnati's Hyde Park Corner and Place de l'Étoile. When streaking was in vogue several summers ago, Cincinnati's first streakers streaked shamelessly across Fountain Square. Fountain Square is the heart of the city, and it may be the single reason why the core of the city has not deteriorated as the centers of other cities have done. And yet, after five o'clock, Fountain Square and the streets surrounding it are almost deserted. Cincinnati is a town where almost everybody sleeps in one suburb or another.

As is the case in many cities, Cincinnati's best suburbs lie to the east, where commuting motorists will not have to face the sun when they drive to and from work. Here, in areas like Mount Lookout and Hyde Park, Cincinnati becomes a city where thousands of antique gas lamps still illuminate the streets, a city of large parks and splendid houses that perch on bluff tops and hillsides overlooking expanses of lawns and gardens, with sweeping views of the curving Ohio River. Cincinnatians take great pride and a not inconsiderable amount of pleasure from the river, along whose shores their city and its suburbs nestle. For here—at times, at least—the Ohio is still clean enough to be swimmable and the scene of boating and sailing parties. Mrs. Fred Lazarus III, the wife of the department store executive, and her friends can often be seen skimming up and down the river on water skis, or leaping from the decks of the Lazaruses' cabin cruiser into the cloudy water.

In Hyde Park, it is important to have a river view, and it is a great point of argument whether a downriver or an upriver view is better; some people, of course, manage to have both. Cincinnati's views may not be quite so arresting as those of San Francisco (like San Francisco, Cincinnati claims "seven hills"), and its grillwork may not be as elaborate as that of New Orleans, but it is certainly true that Cincinnati's suburbs must be counted among the prettiest in America. This is one reason why Cincinnatians—who admit that their summers are hot and muggy, that their winters are icy and damp, and that their springs are fraught with tornado warnings—insist that they would not live anywhere else. In fact, Cincinnati is so pleased with its suburban existence that even those who could well afford to do so rarely travel elsewhere. According to the *Summer Social Register,* only seventy-seven "social" families in *both* Cincinnati and nearby Dayton have summer homes or addresses elsewhere, the smallest number of any of the cities the *Register* registers. "When a Cincinnatian travels," as one woman puts it, "he is always looking forward to coming home."

Cincinnati, meanwhile, like Atlanta, is in many ways a one-company town. And just as Coca-Cola money rules along Paces Ferry Road, Procter & Gamble is the *éminence grise* of Cincinnati. Which suburb one chooses often depends on where one stands with P&G. If a man, for example, is in what P&G calls "middle management," he will likely live in Wyoming (no views). Higher Procter & Gamble executives will be found in Hyde Park, with views. The highest executives of all will be found in Indian Hill, where Procter & Gamble president Edward G. Harness lives in a large house, with a separate listing for "children's residence." People "waiting to get into Indian Hill" tend to wait in such cozy, folksy communities as nearby Terrace Park or "the perfect planned community" of Mariemont, a 423-acre development of look-alike Cape Cod houses designed, more or less, to create the atmosphere of an English Village, with a central green, winding streets, and Georgian Colonial shops with mullioned windowpanes. Mariemont looks as if it had been built all at once by a little old lady who liked chintz— which, indeed, it was: by the late Mrs. Mary M. Emery in 1922.

Glendale, however, is a suburb that has become almost exclusively Procter & Gamble, and Glendale people tend to see a great deal of one another and very little of the rest of Cincinnati. "Glendale," says one woman, "is a world unto itself." William Cooper Procter, the founder of Procter & Gamble, lived in Glendale, and ever since, the citizens of Glendale have been regarded collectively as "the Procter & Gamble people." The Procter & Gamble people, as far as the rest of the city is concerned, have no names. As one P&G executive, who, typically, refuses to be named, explains it: "At Procter & Gamble, there are no heroes. There is only the company itself. It is an unwritten rule that individuals are never singled out for attention or publicity. The individual is merely part of the team."

But at Procter & Gamble it goes even further than that. Not only are names and individuals underplayed, but the company itself does its best to keep *its* name out of the limelight. Reticence is the unspoken corporate motto. The job of Procter & Gamble's publicity department appears primarily to be to prevent publicity about the company. Old Mr. Procter, it seems, believed that corporate publicity was not just a waste of time, but actually dangerous. "Advertise the *products*," he used to say, "not the company that made 'em." To this day, the word "TIDE" blazes from the orange-and-blue detergent box, but only in the tiniest print can be found the words "Made by Procter & Gamble."

Cincinnati people are curiously ambivalent about what is called the "Procter & Gamble Presence." On the one hand, most Cincinnatians are glad to have the company headquartered there. Many of the city's greatest fortunes, though technically rooted in other forms of commercial endeavor, from broadcasting (Tafts, who started in newspapers) to machine tools (Emerys, who started as candle merchants), were substantially helped along by early investments in P & G stock. "On my grandfather's deathbed, he said, 'Never sell your Procter & Gamble,'" declares one woman. And certainly Procter & Gamble *fits* Cincinnati—a smooth, conservative, understated corporation which is run as efficiently and anonymously as the entire nation of Switzerland. P & G offers the safest of investments; throughout the Depression, it never passed a dividend. As an employer, it provides the safest of jobs. Once hired, a P&G person is seldom fired except for gross, repeated malfeasance. Just as there are no heroes at P&G, neither are there villains.

On the other hand, it is easy to laugh at Procter & Gamble, and there is a tendency to speak disparagingly and condescendingly of socially inbred and insulated little Glendale. "I don't know anybody there," says one woman, implying that Glendale people are not only faceless but not very interesting. Certainly, on the surface, Glendale is an unremarkable-looking township with not much in the way of beauty—or even beautiful houses—to recommend it. It has a bland, self-satisfied look, not unlike the bland façade of Procter & Gamble's downtown corporate headquarters—a low, flat, white stone rectangle that has been compared to a large cake of Ivory soap lying on its side—facing the blandest of little parks. It is easy, too, to poke fun at P&G's folksy, down-home, small-town ways. Though it is a multinational corporation, it still holds regular family picnic outings for its employees and their families and, each Christmas, delivers a gift basket of chicken and other goodies to each and every person on the payroll. At the same time, the company's influence on the city's life is vast and pervasive. If, for example, Procter & Gamble is unhappy with a school superintendent, it has ways of

44

seeing that he will be replaced. The two wary newspapers, the *Post* and the *Enquirer,* are careful not to tread on Procter & Gamble's toes. Not long ago, a local magazine, *Cincinnati,* purchased an article that, in part, was critical of Procter & Gamble. When the article was published, the offending material had been mysteriously excised.

The influence of Procter & Gamble on the city has not always been benign. Several years ago, the company decided that it wanted to tear down the old Wesley chapel on East Fifth Street to make room for its private park. As is usual when anything of historic worth in Cincinnati is threatened, Cincinnatians were up in arms. The Wesley chapel was the oldest religious building in Cincinnati, and had been in continuous use since 1831. President William Henry Harrison's funeral services had been held there, and John Quincy Adams had stood in the chapel's pulpit. When Procter & Gamble's demolition plans were announced, a group of citizens formed and obtained an injunction to provide a stay of execution. As the date of the expiration of the injunction drew near, a second injunction was sought and its supporters felt sure it would be forthcoming. Then, on midnight of the date of expiration, in a display of high corporate arrogance, Procter & Gamble sent in wrecking crews. In the morning, Cincinnatians woke to find their lovely old chapel gone.

Others have learned that dealing with Procter & Gamble can be frustrating. Lawyer Sidney Weil finds it off-putting that when the "Procter & Gamble people" go out, they never go out alone. "Whenever you have business to conduct with the company," he says, "you can never seem to deal with one man. There are always two—a second guy to back up the first. You feel hedged in a two-against-one situation."

Perhaps because of local attitudes like this toward the company, there is a noticeable ambivalence, too, in the way the Procter & Gamble people feel about themselves—a rueful smile when they identify their employer, as though it were necessary to apologize. To be sure, there is nothing particularly chic or glamorous about being in the soap business, and Procter & Gamble people tend to describe their jobs in terms of "market research" or "product development" or "regional sales." "Try to pin him down on what he really *does,*" says one man, "and a P&G man will rattle off corporate sales figures. He just won't *tell* you what he does. Sometimes I wonder if he really knows."

And perhaps this is why middle-to-upper-management Procter

& Gamble people have gravitated to the suburb of Glendale—like the company, a prosperous but hardly glamorous community. There, in the shadow of their late founder's house, they can mingle with each other, forget about what the rest of Cincinnati thinks—or doesn't think—about them, and console and comfort one another for the well-paid, job-safe anonymity of their collective lives.

6

Small Town

*F*or years, Mr. William Cooper Procter's company was noticeably non-Semitic, if not anti-Semitic, and even today, few Jews are found on high rungs of the corporate ladder. (In the company's early days, no blacks at all were employed except as janitors and messengers.) At one point, so a favorite Procter & Gamble story goes, the company was about to launch a new laundry product which, after much market research, it planned to call Dreck. Advertising plans, layouts, and schedules were drawn up to present Dreck to the American soap-buying public. Only at the last moment—and in the nick of time—was it discovered that *dreck* is a Yiddish word meaning "dirt." Hastily, the name of the new soap powder was changed to Dreft.

Meanwhile, though the rest of Cincinnati may chuckle at what goes on in Glendale and at P&G, it takes very seriously what goes on in Indian Hill. While practically all the residents of this hilltop community of great estates are wealthy, a number of the homes of the first settlers here reveal the more plebeian origins of the area and are still extensive, and working, farms, with barns and sheds and outbuildings. At Indian Hill cocktail parties, the talk is as likely to center around the current tomato crop as around the Dow Jones averages. Nearly everyone in Indian Hill, it seems, owns a tractor, and for years, tractor parties—with guests arriving behind the wheels of their machines—have been a summer tradition. "It isn't really gentleman farming, you see, it's more like playing at farming," explains one woman. Mrs. Edgar Mack (Mr. Mack's money is from malt which goes into Cincinnati beer) even has a slipcover for her tractor—a pretty flowered chintz that matches her china pattern. For her summer picnics, which have become something of a local legend, she slips the slipcovers on the tractor and on the wagon that is drawn behind it, and spreads the wagon with delicacies and drinkables. Her husband—in a blazer with a pocket emblem that says "Blome Road Tractor & Tennis Society"—then gets behind the wheel and drives the movable feast among the assembled guests while his wife, in a farmerette outfit, sits on his lap being hostessy.

Though Indian Hill tries to look countrified and old, it is really not that venerable a community. Originally, wealthy Cincinnatians lived on the west side of town or to the north, in the gaslit section called Clifton, where many old mansions still stand. (Today, Clifton has largely been taken over by physicians from the nearby hospitals and by faculty of the University of Cincinnati, whose campus is also nearby; it has become Cincinnati's "intellectual" suburb, and is appropriately dowdy.) Then Madison Road, leading eastward along the river, began to develop. One senior resident, Mrs. Russell Wilson, remembers when Madison was still a dirt road. And when Keys Crescent, one of the city's grander addresses, was first built just off Madison Road, Mrs. Wilson and one of her girlhood friends wrote "Stink Street" in the fresh concrete just outside the Crescent's entrance. Madison Road led into Hyde Park, where more big, imposing houses were built, particularly along Grandin Road, where they could command splendid river views. At the end of Madison Road lay Indian Hill—so named because an Indian burial ground had been discovered there—and in the 1920s, a group of wealthy Cincinnati businessmen formed a corporation, bought up some twenty square miles of farmland, and turned Indian Hill into the enclave of wealth that it is today. They added such standard accouterments as an exclusive country club—the Camargo—polo, fox hunting, golf, and a private police force.

Back in Hyde Park, however, along Grandin Road and its side streets—with the river on one side and the grounds of the Cincinnati Country Club on the other—there is little agreement that Indian Hill is the better address. "Is that Grandin Road group still going strong?" asked Alice Roosevelt Longworth, whose husband was a Cincinnatian, not long ago. It is, and people who live on or near Grandin Road consider themselves a breed both privileged and singularly blessed. They point out that Indian Hill, because of its

48

greater distance from the city, is a bit out of touch with things and, with its tractor parties, even out of touch with reality. They add that most of the city's movers and shakers—those not connected with P&G, at least—live in Hyde Park, on or off Grandin Road.

This is true. On Grandin Road are the Ralph Corbetts, for example. Corbett is the self-made multimillionaire who turned an idea for musical doorbell chimes into the giant Nu Tone corporation and whose Corbett Foundation has poured millions of dollars into the city to support its cultural institutions, particularly those in the field of music. (And in the process, some say, the Corbetts have managed to irk certain of the Old Guard families who *might* have been, but have not been, equally generous.) The Corbett name decorates dozens of prestigious boards and committees, but a part of Cincinnati will never quite forget that Ralph Corbett was born in Flushing, New York.

Hard by the Corbetts live various members of the large and wealthy Lazarus clan, whose Federated Department Stores include Bloomingdale's, I. Magnin, Rich's in Atlanta, and, in Cincinnati, Shillito's, the city's largest store. As far as Old Cincinnati is concerned, of course, the Lazaruses exist in a kind of limbo similar to the Corbetts'. Everybody agrees that the Lazaruses are *important*. Everyone *likes* the Lazaruses. Mr. Ralph Lazarus is frequently consulted on economic matters by United States Presidents. Mrs. Fred Lazarus III is unquestionably one of the city's two or three most important women. She heads the Ohio Arts Council, has her own television program, is into all sorts of civic and philanthropic doings, and is renowned as a hostess—particularly for visiting artists and performers with the opera, symphony, ballet, or theater. But Irma Lazarus was born in Brooklyn, and her husband's family was originally from Columbus. (Oddly enough, her identical twin sister, Mrs. Carl Strauss, may be on firmer ground; her husband's family, the Strausses, are Old Cincinnati.)

Clearly, Cincinnati is a place which attaches great importance to the length of time a family has spent in the city, and the oldest families have been there, almost literally, forever. Birthplace is stressed more than wealth, social position, or education, and a sharp distinction is drawn between people who "are Cincinnati" and those who "aren't Cincinnati" or are "from away." Mr. John Emery, for example, who headed Emery Industries, Inc., was one of the city's wealthiest manufacturers, benefactors, and an unquestioned business, civic, and social leader. It was his mother who gave the land

and developed the "ideal" community of Mariemont. For years, the 2,200-seat Emery Auditorium housed the Cincinnati Symphony Orchestra. Yet when it was suggested that John Emery be given the purely honorary title "Mr. Cincinnati," there were frowns of disapproval and reminders that "John Emery is *not* Cincinnati." By a fluke of timing on his parents' part, he was born in New York.

Mr. and Mrs. James Mixter *are* Cincinnati, however. They live today in the turreted Gothic mansion that Mrs. Mixter's great-great-great-grandfather John Baker built in Hyde Park in 1852. The Mixters' children represent the seventh generation of a family that has lived continuously in one house, which still contains the original high carved-plaster ceilings, chandeliers, floors, paneling, staircase, and even the original Oriental rugs that were woven long ago in Persia to fit the rooms. "How many New Yorkers or even Bostonians or Philadelphians know who their great-great-great-grandfathers were?" Mrs. Mixter wonders. "Well, there he is," she says, pointing proudly to the marble bust that stands in one of the twin front parlors.

The great Cincinnati families include the Hollisters (Mrs. Mixter was a Hollister), the Johnstones (married to Procter & Gamble Procters), Hamiltons, Sawyers (also married to Procters), Rowes, Warringtons, Kilgours, Gaffs, Chatfields, Hinckleys, Haucks, Swigerts, Keyses, Rawsons, Perrins, Deuprees (Procter & Gamble again), Andersons, Bailys, Kittredges, Wulsins, and Bergers. All are, without exception, conservative to say the least. Not long ago at a party, one distinguished guest exclaimed, apropos of nothing at all, "Dammit! We haven't had any freedom in this country since slavery!" They are also dizzyingly interrelated. "My husband's first cousin is married to her husband's niece," is the kind of explanation one hears here as to how families are connected.

Also in Cincinnati one must not overlook the Tafts, who have produced not only a United States President but a senator, Robert Taft, Jr., and a number of prominent Cincinnati lawyers and businessmen. Taft Broadcasting is a powerful force in the city, and the luster of the Taft name is enshrined in such institutions as the Taft Art Museum and the William Howard Taft School. Taft, Stettinius & Hollister is the city's most prestigious law firm. Even though Martha Bowers Taft, the senator's mother, is "from away," she is considered one of the city's *grandes dames*. And even though William Howard Taft could legitimately trace his ancestry back to the *Mayflower* as well as to King David of Scotland, it is typical of Cincinnati's lack of ostentation that the late President's son, Charles P. Taft, drives around town in an ancient compact with a canoe strapped to the roof.

Nor should one forget the rich Geiers, who run Cincinnati Milacron, Inc., manufacturers of machine tools. Mrs. Inga Geier is often cited as a prime example of how natives of Cincinnati keep their serenity even in moments of extreme crisis. At the outbreak of World War II in Italy, when Americans abroad were trying frantically to find ways to get home, a fellow Cincinnatian remembers spotting Mrs. Geier being driven through a crowded street in Rome by her chauffeur. Rushing over to her car, the friend cried out, "Inga, the war has started! We've got to get out of here!" Mrs. Geier replied, "Why don't you come over to my apartment later on for tea, and we'll talk about it.

There is also a strongly entrenched group of German-Jewish families in Cincinnati, most of whom live in or near Hyde Park. These include the Kuhns (related to Kuhn, Loeb & Co.), the Westheimers (some of whom have changed the name to Weston), the Friedlanders, Freibergs, and Seasongoods. The Ransohoffs are a problem. The name sounds Russian, and people like the Friedlanders say that the Ransohoffs *are* Russian. The Ransohoffs insist that the family is originally from Germany. There are also a number of old German-Protestant families, with names like Moerlein, Schmidlapp, and Kupferschmidt. All these families mingle freely on the social level although, as in most cities, country clubs have tended to form along religious lines. The Cincinnati Country Club in Hyde Park and the Camargo in Indian Hill are WASP-membership clubs. The Losantiville is the prestigious German-Jewish country club. The Crest Hills is the club for more recent arrivals from Eastern Europe who live in the almost entirely Jewish suburb of Amberley Village. In terms of the clubs, the members of the Fleischmann family (yeast) present something of an enigma. The Fleischmanns were originally Jewish, but a generation or so ago decided not to be. Today, they live in Indian Hill and belong to the restricted Camargo Club.

Archetypical of an old-line Cincinnati suburban family would be Mr. and Mrs. Charles Learner Harrison III. There have been Harrisons in Cincinnati for at least five generations, and the Harrisons can find two United States Presidents in their family tree—Benjamin Harrison and William Henry Harrison—along with a signer of the Declaration of Independence, another Benjamin Harri-

51

son. The first Harrison, Edmond, came to Cincinnati in 1814. His son, Learner Blackman Harrison, went into the grocery business where he made a tidy fortune, and became president of the First National Bank of Cincinnati. His numerous descendants are still prominent in the city today.

Charles Learner Harrison III is a pleasant-faced fellow in his forties, a partner in the stockbrokerage firm of Harrison & Company. His pretty wife, Molly, is also Cincinnati born—"though not from as illustrious a family as my husband's." Molly Harrison was a Maish, an old German family that dropped a *c* from its name (Maisch) at the time of World War I. As proof of the comfortable sense of continuity that old-line Cincinnati families develop, Molly Harrison points out that her children's friends are the sons and daughters of the people who were her own girlhood friends, just as those girlhood friends were the children of her mother's friends. "The daughter of the woman who cooked for us is a friend of my present cleaning woman," Molly Harrison says. "Even the servants here tend to stay with a family from one generation to the next."

Like a proper Cincinnati girl, Molly Harrison went to Miss Doherty's College Preparatory School, where Miss Doherty, in a pearl choker and with lorgnette, selected her young ladies for their pedigrees as much as their intelligence, and stressed etiquette equally with Latin. Because Cincinnati has—with its symphony, its opera, and its May Music Festival—long been a musical city, Miss Doherty's classes let out early on Friday afternoons so that the girls could attend the symphony. Which Molly Harrison did, accompanied by her mother and grandmother.

"We never traveled much," Molly Harrison recalls with a smile. "The feeling was that Cincinnati is such a pleasant place, so why should anyone go anywhere else? Women never went to New York or Chicago to shop. If they couldn't find what they wanted at Gidding-Jenny's, they had a little dressmaker run something up, or they made it themselves. If people left town for some reason, we always assumed that it was because of business or family—not simply for pleasure! It's still very much that way. We've never had a jet set here."

This is true, and what Cincinnati has instead might be called a *set* set. And it is an indication of how settled and secure Cincinnati society feels about itself that though an edition of the *Social Register* is published for the city, most Cincinnatians never bother to consult it. "It's been years since I've bothered filling out the little forms they send me," Molly Harrison says. "I don't even know whether we're still listed." (They are.) "I know who everybody is and what their maiden names were. The *Social Register* just isn't necessary. It's not like New York, where everybody seems to be trying to *prove* something and the *Social Register* is proof that you've arrived, I guess. Here you don't need any proof, any passport to society. Here we don't need our names in the society pages. There used to be a woman here named Dolly Cohen, who had a social secretary whose job it was to keep Dolly Cohen's name in the papers. We always rather laughed at that."

Not long ago, the Harrisons did a startling thing. They left their big, sprawling house in Indian Hill with its surrounding acres of lawn and gardens, and bought a small, picturesque Victorian house on a small lot in Terrace Park, which they proceeded to restore and remodel. It was startling because most people would consider a move from Indian Hill to Terrace Park a distinct step downward on the address scale. Most people in Terrace Park dream of moving to Indian Hill, not the other way around. "But," says a friend, "the Harrisons, being who they are, could get away with it. Leave it to Molly to make it suddenly look as though Terrace Park were chic."

For years, Cincinnati's suburban social seas were ruled imperiously by a small, indomitable woman named Marion Devereux, who, though she has been dead since 1948, is still talked about in hushed tones. She was the society editor of the *Cincinnati Enquirer* and, though her own social credentials were slim, the power she wielded was enormous. Cincinnati will be grateful if her like never appears again. Miss Devereux wrote windily and in prose of the lushest purple. No editor, furthermore, was permitted to cut or alter a word of what she wrote. Hostesses who kowtowed to her—and this meant regularly showering her with lavish gifts—were exalted in her columns, and those who dared to ignore her were made to pay for it.

Parties that were planned without Miss Devereux's permission, or to which she was not invited, were treated as though they had not existed, and those who gave them were labeled "social climbers." No debutante could be presented and no wedding could take place without prior consultation with the oracle. In return for snubs, real or imagined, Miss Devereux would write such items as: "Mrs. Hollister appeared last night at the Symphony in the same blue dress she has worn so often this season." Or: "Mrs. Anderson's

53

flowered hat looked just as fashionable at luncheon yesterday as when she first wore it seventeen years ago." One hostess who had the temerity to give a party without advising Miss Devereux got a telephone call in the middle of the night from the society editor, who said, "How dare you give a party without consulting me? Don't you know that I am the social arbiter of Cincinnati?" Thereafter, the woman was described in the *Enquirer* as a "social highway robber," and several years later, when the woman's three daughters were married, the newspaper ignored all three weddings.

Inevitably, considering Miss Devereux's exuberant prose style, her copy bristled with unintended double entendres, many of which were acutely embarrassing to the *Enquirer*'s editors. But again, not a word could be changed, and so readers were treated to such tidbits as: "Mr. and Mrs. Tom Conroy have been the center of many merry moments since their return from their honeymoon." Or: "Mrs. Ruth Harrison, whose toilet of black satin was relieved by a touch of ermine . . ." Or: "An hour of agreeable intercourse will follow this series of events, the membership being all cocked and primed to stay on to enjoy it." A typographical error in Miss Devereux's column could be disastrous, as in: "Mrs. Taft's pubic appearance last night was breath-taking, as heads turned in admiration," or: "At cockstroke, the lovely debutantes revealed themselves to their manly escorts." There were also times when, try as one might, no one in Cincinnati had the slightest idea of what Miss Devereux was trying to say: "In nothing to the Philistines are the May Festivals more intriguing than in the boxes and the Audience. Last night these themes of an corridor and foyer were paramount to the carnal-minded devotee of these two yearly events."

When, at the height of her power, Miss Devereux suddenly retired without notice, to become a virtual recluse—leading to speculation that she may have been, for some years, certifiably insane—she was replaced by Miss Jane Finneran, who had been her assistant.

Miss Finneran carried on in the great Devereux tradition. As her predecessor had done before her, Miss Finneran edited the Cincinnati *Blue Book,* which is still privately published and is considered a much more reliable guide to who is who in Cincinnati than the *Social Register*—since the *Register* is published "from away." Like Miss Devereux, Miss Finneran decided who could be a debutante and who could not. "I'm calling about Aurelia So-and-so," Miss Finneran would say. "I'm trying to decide whether to let her come out or not. Do you know her parents? Do you know who her friends are? I don't want any girl to come out who wouldn't be *happy* coming out." Miss Finneran, however, has retired, and no one with her authority has stepped forward to replace her—which, so far as Cincinnati society is concerned, is just as well—and society has gone back to its agreeable laissez-faire ways.

Cincinnati is also a city that loves gossip, and since it is a small place where everybody is not only related to everybody else but also knows everybody else, there is nearly always some new and juicy tidbit making the regular party rounds—such as when, several years ago, Mayor-elect Gerald Springer was discovered to have been patronizing a naughty massage parlor across the river in Kentucky, and had to step down. (He was caught because he unwisely paid for its services with either a personal check or a credit card; the stories varied.) Recently, too, there was a delicious public quarrel between Cincinnati's two leading civic ladies: Mrs. Fred Lazarus III and Mrs. Ralph Corbett, who live within hair-pulling distance of one another in Hyde Park. Irma Lazarus was reported to have said something to the effect that the Corbetts could afford to give $250,000 to the Symphony but were too cheap to buy a ticket to a performance. Patricia Corbett was naturally furious. The two ladies stopped speaking, their respective friends and adversaries fanned the flames, and the affair escalated to the point where *Women's Wear Daily* got the story and printed it. It took a letter from Ohio's then governor, John Gilligan, to get *Women's Wear* off the gossipy scent. But it required a third Hyde Park neighbor, Mrs. Leo Weston, to get the two women to kiss and make up; at her behest, they met to talk things over. For her role as peacemaker—as well as for her lovely old antique-filled house overlooking the river, her excellent food, and her bright chatter—Phyllis Weston has been elevated to the position of being considered one of Cincinnati's most important hostesses. Among other things, she was one of the first "social" Cincinnati women to invite blacks to her house for dinner.

Cincinnati thinks of itself as a city that is not easily ruffled, where everything will turn out for the best in the end, given patience, politeness, and time. But early in 1975, there was deeply disturbing news. Oscar Robinson and his wife, it was learned, had made an offer on a house in Hyde Park—and on Grandin Road, no less. Oscar Robinson and his wife are black. There was no question but what the Robinsons were exceptional people. Voted the National Basketball Association's Most Valuable Player, a former co-captain of the United States Olympic Gold Medal Team, a former guard with the Cincinnati Royals and, later, with the Milwaukee Bucks, listed in *Who's Who in America,* Oscar Robinson would have seemed a credit to any neighborhood. But still . . . he and his family *were* black. And it was *Grandin Road.* There was a great deal of agonized soul-searching over the prospect of having a black family move into an otherwise all-white neighborhood. People took sides. Hackles rose. Neighbors stopped speaking to neighbors. While all this was going on in Hyde Park, Indian Hill watched with a certain interested detachment, happy for the most part that such a crisis was not being faced in Indian Hill—yet.

Then, all at once, the problem evapoarated, blew away as though in a summer breeze. The Oscar Robinsons bought a house in another part of town. Like most problems in serene Cincinnati—like the feud between Irma Lazarus and Patricia Corbett and countless other controversies—this one had an ending that was happy and serene. For the time being, at least.

7

Pointes and Points

Old Mrs. Henry B. Joy of Detroit was determined to make it clear that her money was "pre-gasoline." To emphasize the point, for forty-four years, until her death in 1958 at the age of eighty-eight, she maintained—and drove herself—a 1914 brougham car that operated on electricity. The shiny little two-seater, which was unable to exceed a speed of ten miles an hour, was quite a sight around Grosse Pointe, where her neighbors (the Henry Fords, the Walter Chryslers, the John and Horace Dodges, the Ransom Oldses, and a great many brothers named Fisher) were all regarded by people like the Joys as "ex-bicycle salesmen who came in with internal combustion." Mrs. Joy's only concession to Detroit's automotive aristocracy was to permit her vehicle to be displayed at the 1957 Automobile Show. "I am very respectful of the age of my little car," she said at the time. "I have to treat it very carefully because it is very difficult to get parts."

Mrs. Joy was a Newberry, and the Newberrys are another old-line Detroit family that put down roots in the city early in the nineteenth century, long before automobiles were dreamed of and when, it seems, Detroit was a place quite unrecognizable in relation to what it is today. In the mid-1830s, for example, an English writer and social historian named Harriet Martineau visited Detroit and later wrote, in a book called *Society in America:* "The Society of Detroit is very choice; and, as it has continued so since the old colonial days, through the territorial days, there is every reason to think that it will become, under its new dignities, a more and more desirable place of residence." Miss Martineau's vision may not have been clear about Detroit's social future, and according to another Detroit historian, John L. Oliver: "We don't know exactly to whom La Martineau alluded." But he adds: "As the names of Newberry, Joy, Buhl, Alger, Barbour, Lothrop, and Hinchman begin to appear, our ears prick up and things begin to look more familiar."

Mrs. Joy was not at all the eccentric that she might have seemed—though she set some sort of record in Watch Hill, Rhode Island, by spending fifty-nine consecutive summers at her home there. Her husband was a dour sort, whose nickname was "Kill Joy,"* but Mrs. Joy was a perky little lady devoted to the Grosse Point Memorial Church—"I can't enjoy church until I get my gloves off," she used to say—and to the city of Detroit. At the time of her death, she was a member of a total of eighty-three civic and philanthropic organizations in the city, and she had never missed a meeting of a single one of them. Summers she was active in the Watch Hill Improvement Society, and "to keep fit," she regularly swam the choppy course around the Watch Hill lighthouse.

Her forebears were an equally doughty lot. The first Newberrys—the brothers Oliver and Walter—arrived in Detroit from the East as early as 1826, and went into the dry goods business. They prospered. Then they expanded into Great Lakes shipping, real estate, and lumber. They prospered further. They left no direct heirs, but their considerable fortune went to a nephew, John Stoughton Newberry, who, after graduating from the University of Michigan in 1847, went into partnership with a man named James McMillan in a firm that billed itself "Newberry & McMillan, Capitalists." He married Helen Parmalee Handy, daughter of the Truman Parmalee Handys, of the illustrious Cleveland family. Helen Newberry Joy was his youngest daughter.

Though Mrs. Joy was devoted to Detroit (if not to its motorcar millionaires) and to the suburb of Grosse Pointe, where she lived, she would doubtless be depressed at the sight of what Grosse Pointe has become in the twenty years since her death: high-rises and apartments in Grosse Pointe Shores, for example, and most of the big shorefront estates along Lake St. Clair torn down, broken up, and turned into much smaller, though still expensive properties.

*Mr. Joy was an early ham radio enthusiast whose specialty was picking up disasters from airwaves. From Treasure Hill, the Watch Hill estate, he was the first American to learn of the sinking of the *Titanic*.

58

Furthermore—and this would distress her most—Grosse Pointe has become a suburb that has turned its back, almost completely, on its parent city.

Detroit, it might be argued, could be an easy city for a suburb to shrug off. It has evolved into a metropolis with few of the "dignities" Miss Martineau envisioned for it. Even its gleaming new Ford-sponsored Renaissance Plaza, it has been pointed out, has the air of being an elegant, encapsulated city within a city—a group of buildings that seems to look inward upon itself, each building connected to the others by passageways so that occupants need encounter only one another without venturing into the street or facing the burgeoning indignities of the city beyond. In Grosse Pointe, where many Renaissance Plaza executives hang their hats, the sense of separation from the city is even more complete. One Grosse Pointe woman claims: "I haven't set foot in Detroit in years. The only time I ever see it is when I'm on my way to the airport."

It is true that Grosse Pointe is remarkably independent of Detroit. Everything the Grosse Pointer needs is right there in Grosse Pointe—in its shops, markets, movie theaters, restaurants, and, of course, its clubs. Charity balls are held in big Detroit hotels, and are subscribed to by Grosse Pointers, but they rarely attend them. The Detroit Symphony performs in the Ford Auditorium in Detroit, but Grosse Pointe usually has something better to do than attend. Plays and operas come to Detroit, but Grosse Pointers have either already seen them in New York or will do so later on. No one would dream of going to Detroit for dinner at a restaurant: "Why should we, when we have the club?" Detroit, in the minds of Grosse Pointe people, exists as a gray area where some men have to go for business, and from which they escape at night.

Actually, Grosse Pointe is not one town but five. Reading northward along the lakeshore, there are Grosse Pointe Park, Grosse Pointe City, Grosse Pointe Farms, Grosse Pointe Shores, and Grosse Pointe Woods. The five communities occupy a strip of real estate not quite six miles long and barely a mile wide. This narrow ribbon provides the addresses of some sixty thousand people, who live under somewhat crowded conditions but nonetheless comfortably.* The Grosse Pointes may not comprise the richest community per capita in the United States, but there are certainly more rich people here per square foot than anywhere else on earth.

*At a population density of one person per 300 square feet.

The first thing a newcomer notices is that Grosse Pointe, for all its reputation, is not really very pretty. Aesthetically, it would compare very poorly with Philadelphia's Main Line, with Santa Barbara, or even with Fort Lee, New Jersey. The terrain of Grosse Pointe is pancake flat. Lake St. Clair, really an arm of polluted Lake Erie, which the Grosse Pointes face and which periodically has to be banked with sandbags to keep it from flooding over them, is lead-colored and also flat. Grosse Pointe's streets, since there are no hills to traverse, run flat and straight and are laid out in a grid. Grosse Pointe houses, though large and frequently imposing, are of necessity close together. Neighbors can look into each other's windows and, because fences are zoned against, into each other's backyards. The shoulder-to-shoulder appearance of Grosse Pointe residences gives the place an air of tightness, compression, and restraint, as well as of conformity. Construction is of dark Middle West brick. The occasional "modern" house stands out starkly and uncomfortably.

Of the five communities, Grosse Pointe Farms is easily the best address. It is the roomiest and, with the Country Club of Detroit roughly at its center, has the most air to breathe. At the bottom of the status scale is Grosse Pointe Woods, the only one of the Grosse Pointes that has no lake frontage—and since so much of the land of Grosse Pointe Woods has been cleared for housing developments and apartment houses, there are no more woods in the Woods and hardly any trees. The other three communities hover somewhere between respectable and chic, with Grosse Pointe Park occupying a somewhat special position. The Windmill Pointe section of the Park is an area of large, well-tended, somewhat Mediterranean-looking houses which, several years ago, a television broadcast identified as the residences of a number of members of Detroit's Purple Gang. Indeed, many of the families in Windmill Pointe have Italian names, and the houses, with their gates and guardhouses, do rather resemble the one Marlon Brando occupied in *The Godfather*. At the time, the rest of Grosse Pointe was a bit ruffled by this publicity. "After all, they stick to themselves, they don't bother anybody," says one woman. There is also in Grosse Pointe Park a feeling that having members of the Mob as neighbors is a definite plus; they provide a certain protection, as it were.

Grosse Pointe has had a lot of bad publicity over the years. It has been depicted as a symbol of *nouveau riche* tailfin vulgarity, of the crassest kind of money snobbery and prejudice. Several years ago, for example, it was revealed that Grosse Pointe real estate people sold houses on a "point system," designed to keep "undesirables" out of the community. A prospective buyer, under the system, had to have a hundred points in order to buy a house in Grosse Pointe. If he was Jewish or black, that was ninety points against him from the start. Today, most Grosse Pointe people deny that such a system was ever in operation, or if it was, that they were ever aware of it. It certainly exists no longer, they say, pointing out that several—though not very many—Jewish families now own houses in the Grosse Pointes, and a few middle-class blacks have also moved into the area. If Jews and blacks have not been motivated to move to Grosse Pointe, it is because the country club—which, as in other areas like this, dominates the social life—still takes no black or Jewish members.

Grosse Pointe has also been accused of representing nothing but automobile money, as tasteless and chrome-plated as most annual models. And it is true that the fortunes of the local automobile companies play a large part in the lives of Grosse Pointers. Each year, the sales figures on new-model cars are watched anxiously, for whether a model year is successful or not will have a large part to play in the area's economy. The fluctuation of the automobile market, and of automobile stocks, affects everybody. Even the old "first-cabin" families such as the Joys, Newberrys, Buhls, and McMillans, who made their original money in other endeavors, have managed, over the years, to acquire automotive interests. "We all loaned money to old Henry Ford when he was first starting out," says one woman, "and he paid us off with stock in his little company. Nobody thought he'd be successful, of course."

And automobiles, as might be expected, are a popular topic of conversation in Grosse Pointe. The most frequent question the newcomer is asked is: "What kind of car do you drive?" (Needless to say, foreign makes are frowned upon.) Grosse Pointe tends to identify its citizens in terms of their automobiles: "She'll be driving a gray Seville," or "He drives a blue Skylark," or "Mine's the red Granada." (Also needless to say, it is a sin for an auto executive to drive a competitor's product; when Henry Ford was arrested for speeding in New York a few years ago, everyone was shocked—not by the offense, but by the fact that Ford was picked up driving a rented Chevrolet.)

Henry Ford II, a big, bluff, cheery, party-loving man, might pass unnoticed in the streets of New York, Philadelphia, or

Chicago. But when he appears in Grosse Pointe, he is very much a Presence, and people practically bow and tug at their forelocks out of deference to him. "The Fords are like royalty here," says one woman—though the royalty started out very humbly, just two generations ago, up on Detroit's Woodward Avenue, where "nobody" lived. The queen of the House of Ford is unquestionably Mr. Ford's mother, Mrs. Edsel Ford. When Eleanor Ford makes one of her regal entrances or exits, it is, according to a friend, "like the parting of the Red Sea" as people step aside to make way for the royal passage. Grosse Pointe is so obsessed with Fords—their whereabouts, what they're wearing, their divorces and love affairs, which ones drink too much—that scarcely a conversation can take place without some mention of them. The remotest relationship to a Ford is a sign of status. Mrs. Robert Kanzler is considered "terribly important" in Grosse Pointe, for example, because her husband happens to be Mrs. Edsel Ford's sister's son.

All the Ford talk in Grosse Pointe can be confusing, however, since there is not one Ford family in the community but three. The richest Fords are of course the royal Fords, or the "car Fords," as they are called. But far from poor are the so-called salt Fords—the John B. Fords and the Emory Fords—whose money comes from such enterprises as the Wyandotte Chemical Company and the Libbey-Owens-Ford Glass Company (soda ash from salt beds is used in glassmaking). Then there are the "old Fords," who would include the Frederick Clifford Fords; they, though not as rich as the others, have been around longer, and have prospered in such endeavors as law and banking. Frederick C. Ford's mother was a Buhl. The original Buhl was given a land grant by King George III in the 1760s, and not long ago, when a Buhl wanted to sell off some of the land, an elaborate search was made into the title of it. When no title could be found, Mr. Buhl grew exasperated. "Damn it," he said finally, "there *isn't* any title to that land; the Buhls just *took* it!" Mrs. Frederick C. Ford is an amateur genealogist and has made an ancestor search of her family, the Brushes—another first-cabin Detroit family. She discovered that the Brushes descend directly from Alfred the Great in the ninth century, so "old" would certainly apply to these Fords. None of the three Ford families, as far as anybody knew, was related to any of the others until the Frederick C. Fords' son, Walter Buhl Ford, married "Dodie" Ford, Henry Ford II's sister. This union created a family known locally as "the Ford-Fords."

Grosse Pointe started—as did Westchester County and the Philadelphia Main Line—as a resort, and the old first-cabin families built summer and weekend homes there. There was a logic to it. Detroit's rich used to live in large city mansions along Jefferson Avenue, and the Jefferson Avenue trolley line ended at the Grosse Pointe line. Beyond that was country, and Lake St. Clair was still clear and sweet, as the name implied. Immigrant French farmers, who gave the fat point of land its name, had small, rectangular farms in the area, and as these were bought up, one by one, by the rich, roads were built along the farms' borders, which accounts for the strict grid pattern of Grosse Pointe streets today. The French influence lingers in strange ways. A street with the odd name Kercheval is presumed to descend from the French *cours de cheval*—"horse path." The old rich built along the lakeshore places that were sprawling, comfortable, countrified, but not particularly grandiose. Life in Grosse Pointe was unhurried and informal. "It was lovely in the old days," says Countess Cyril Tolstoi, kin of the McMillans and the widow of one of Count Leo's nephews. The countess, whose house is now on a typically crowded Grosse Pointe street, says: "This place is all that's left of my grandfather's farm. His property ran all the way down to the lake, which is now I don't know how many blocks away. It was a long walk through the woods to the nearest neighbor's house. Now Grosse Pointe is so big and crowded that when I go to parties I hardly know anybody. I'm introduced to people I've never even *heard* of." The countess's butler pours a martini from a silver shaker and, as if to emphasize her remarks, the tinkle of a bell from a Good Humor truck can be heard outside her heavily curtained windows. And Mrs. Raymond Dykema, another old-timer, says: "There was a feeling of *importance,* growing up in Grosse Pointe in those days. As a girl, I would sit on our veranda and watch the ships go by and know that my father *built* them. They were *our* ships. It made one feel as though one were a part of the city and what the city was building and creating and contributing. That feeling is all gone now."

Then came Henry Ford, Sr., bringing with him the dawn of the Automobile Age. Quickly, in his wake, came the great automobile fortunes, and Grosse Pointe was in for a huge spate of castle-building—French châteaux, Norman keeps, Tudor castles, ducal palaces designed to outdo Blenheim. Gothic arches, gargoyles, crenelated rooftops, and flying buttresses abounded. During the first decade of the twentieth century it was estimated that the servant population of Grosse Pointe was thirty times that of the new gentry. Automobile money was big money, and it required a big show.

Today, most of the castles have fallen to the wrecker's ball. The few that remained along Lake Shore Road gave it the nickname "Widows' Row," since nearly all were owned by elderly widows who refused to bow to the winds of change. One of the last holdouts was the late Mrs. Joseph Schlotman (a salt Ford), whose house, a copy of a Tudor manor house, was complete with indoor fountains, greenhouses, and a ballroom with a private elevator. Mrs. Schlotman used to like to reminisce about the old days when she and her husband kept a huge yacht parked at the foot of the extensive lawn. "We used to have five miles of private fishing grounds on the Cascapedia River," she once said. Did she actually *own* five miles of fishing grounds? a visitor asked. "No, darn it, we didn't. You can't buy a river. You have to rent it," was her reply.

One of the last big places on Lake Shore Road which has managed to stand, undivided, in much the same state as it was originally conceived is the red brick Georgian mansion built by Roy Chapin, who was the head of Hudson Motors. It owes its life to the fact that it was bought several years ago by Henry Ford II.

"The automobile money took over, and then the automobile business brought more people," sighs one old-line resident. "They all wanted to live in Grosse Pointe because it was *the* place to live. They crowded in until now Grosse Pointe is simply bursting at the seams." A few Grosse Pointers have defected and moved northwest to the suburbs of Birmingham and Bloomfield Hills—where there is more space and air and, actually, hills. But Bloomfield Hills today means automobile money too—General Motors money, in large part. In the suburbs of Detroit, automobile money cannot be escaped. Only Detroit can be escaped. And the automobile-rich families enjoy pointing out that even first-cabin families such as the Joys have succumbed to automobile money. In the early 1900s, Mrs. Joy's husband, her brother, Truman Newberry, and a number of other local businessmen quietly bought controlling interest in the Packard Automobile Company and moved it from Warren, Ohio, to Detroit. "So much for your 'pre-gasoline' snobs," says one Grosse Pointer.

But Mrs. Joy held on to her electric.

SOUTH

8

The Country Club Set

"Jews and blacks are accepted everywhere here," says a Main Line woman, adding, with almost a touch of pride, "except, of course, the clubs."

The local clubs are five in number—the Philadelphia Country Club, the Merion Cricket Club, the Merion Golf Club, the Gulph Mills Golf Club, and the Radnor Hunt Club—and are strung out along the length of the Main Line. As they march westward from the Philadelphia Country Club (the least fashionable of the five), they are rated as increasingly exclusive and choosy, until one reaches the Gulph Mills Golf Club, where, they say, "someone has to die" before a proposed member can move off the waiting list; and "the dear old cozy" Radnor Hunt, which, as its name implies, is a paddock for wealthy members of the horsy set.

For years, America's suburban clubs have managed to lead an almost charmed existence. They were there, they catered to their members' athletic whims and fancies, they were restricted. The membership policies of the Gulph Mills Golf Club were no different from those of the Los Angeles Country Club—except that the Los Angeles Country Club restricts against Jews *and* movie people, on the assumption that they are one and the same breed. All over America, people who couldn't join the clubs accepted the situation matter-of-factly, while those who could, whose backgrounds and pedigrees were up to club acceptability standards, waited patiently to be invited. Whether one could—or wanted to—join a club remained a strictly personal and private affair. Clubs' policies went largely unquestioned. Freedom of assembly, after all, could be interpreted as freedom *from* assembly, and freedom of association as freedom *from* association. The feeling was: let people club as they choose.

Then, early in 1977, President-elect Carter announced that he "hoped" those in his administration would voluntarily withdraw from private clubs which had discriminatory membership policies, though he would not require that they do so. It was certainly an unprecedented statement in the history of American Presidents and Presidents-elect. All at once, membership in exclusive clubs became an intense public and political issue—private no longer. And it started with Griffin Bell, the man whom Carter had appointed as his attorney general, the highest-ranking legal official in the country. Mr. Bell belonged to two restricted Atlanta clubs—the Piedmont Driving Club and the Capital City Club—and after lamely complaining that he would lose something in the neighborhood of ten thousand dollars if he quit these clubs, Mr. Bell eventually did as he had been asked and resigned from both. Suddenly, a can of worms was opened in clubs all over the country, where, it turned out, the can had been lying about for a long time—particularly in Atlanta.

In the mid-1950s, for example, a group of German students had been brought to Atlanta as part of a student exchange program and, as a matter of course, was invited by the German consul general to the Capital City Club. During the visit, one student happened to ask, "Are there any Jewish members of this club?" No, he was assured—perhaps on the assumption that this was what he wanted to hear. An extraordinary scene followed. One student burst into tears, and sobbed that the reason the club excluded Jews was the same reason six million had died. What started as a polite occasion turned into a rout, with students and club members shouting ugly accusations at each other. At the time, Atlantans who heard about the episode were shocked. But Atlanta, a city that considers itself the queen city of the South and prides itself on its hospitality, up-to-dateness, and efficiency, soon pushed the incident into the bottom drawer of its memory chest, and went about business as usual.

Now, with Jimmy Carter in the White House, the city is in an uproar again, calling itself unpleasant names. In addition to Mr. Bell, Carter's ex-budget director, Bert Lance, turned out to have been a member of both the Capital City Club and the Piedmont Driving Club. He, too, elected to resign from both—again leaving the implication that membership in them ran contrary to the public interest. Did that mean, Atlanta wanted to know, that there was something *wrong* with its clubs? Suddenly Atlanta's Capital City Club began to seem the quintessential city club, and the Piedmont Driving Club, on the outskirts of town, the quintessential country club, encapsulating all the problems of the American breed.

The immediate reaction to the dispute in Atlanta was not breast-beating or agonized soul-searching, but—as in the case of the German students—almost total confusion. Was there, for example, an actual policy against Jews or blacks or both at either of the two clubs? No one, it suddenly seemed, was entirely sure. Both the Capital City and the Driving Club quickly produced copies of their rules and bylaws, proudly pointing out that nowhere, in the sections pertaining to membership, was specific mention made of race or religion. On the other hand, both clubs conceded that there "probably" were no Jews and certainly were no blacks in either club—but on the question of Jews there seemed to be some doubt. "I'm sure we have some Jews in the Driving Club," said Pegram Harrison, an Atlanta lawyer and Coca-Cola heir, "but I couldn't tell you who they are. Frankly, I've never thought much about it until now." Mr. James D. Custance, the Driving Club's manager, did not clear things up when he said: "Any member who would invite a Jew or a black into his living room could invite a Jew or black to the club." One wonders how many members of the club are the sort who would have Jews or blacks in their houses. Nor did the club's president, Frank Carter, a prominent Atlanta real estate man, help matters much by asserting: "The Driving Club only takes in members of fine old families."

In the confusion, all sorts of odd stories began to emerge. There was the case of Michael Peter Rich, the young scion of the Rich's department store fortune, and the great-grandson of the store's founder, Morris Rich. Michael Rich's father was Richard Rich, one of the city's great philanthropists. During the Depression, when the city of Atlanta was close to bankruptcy and was forced to pay its employees with scrip instead of cash, only Rich's of Atlanta stepped forward to say that it would cash the scrip. Depending on whom one talks to, Michael Rich has tried to get into the Driving Club one, two, or as many as a dozen times—all without success. The reasons given for his rejection vary. "He was a member of Sigma Alpha

69

Epsilon, which is a Christian fraternity," says one Driving Club member, "but we heard that some of his fraternity brothers didn't like him."

Both Morris Rich and Richard Rich were practicing Jews, but Michael Rich converted to Christianity a number of years ago and is a baptized Presbyterian. He married, furthermore, a Christian girl, the daughter of William S. Woods, who is nothing less than an honorary life member of the Piedmont Driving Club. For years, Rich and his wife used the facilities of the club, signing his father-in-law's name and settling accounts with Mr. Woods at the end of each year. "I was at the club so often, I'm sure a lot of people thought I was a member," Rich says. Then, in 1972, by his own account, Michael Peter Rich was asked to join the Driving Club for the first and only time. (One is *asked*—one does not ask—to join such a club.) His name, with a proposer, a second, and a third, went up on the bulletin board beside the front desk. Some weeks later, Rich was informed, regretfully, that his membership had been turned down. "They told me at the time that it was because I'd supported Andrew Young for Congress," Michael Rich says, "and I thought, well, that's as good an excuse as any. Of course I knew the real reason—my Jewish heritage."

In 1976, Rich and his wife were divorced. This means that as an "unmarried daughter of a member," Rich's former wife can enjoy full privileges of the Piedmont Driving Club, and so can her children. Rich himself, on the other hand, can enter the club only at the invitation of a member. "And I don't go there often," he says. "Ever since 1972, I've felt distinctly uncomfortable there, to say the least." When the Rich children, part Jewish, reach age twenty-one and become eligible for membership, will they be asked to join? No one knows for sure.

Michael Rich wryly remembers when, a number of years ago, his father was invited to join the Driving Club. "Are you changing your policy, or making an exception?" the senior Mr. Rich wanted to know. "We're making an exception," he was told. "Then I don't care to join," Mr. Rich replied.

More recently, there was the curious case of Rule 18 of the Driving Club's bylaws. Rule 18 covers "Persons Granted Club Privileges" who, though not members, are given full benefits of membership, and over the years, the Persons have included prominent local judges (though no Jewish judges), clergymen (though no rabbis), and, by tradition, the mayor of Atlanta. In 1970, however,

Rule 18 was revised to read: "No new Persons will be granted Club privileges as presently allowed under Rule 18 after April 1, 1970." What caused the raising of the drawbridge against new Privileged Persons in 1970? It seems to many Atlantans more than just a coincidence that this was the year Atlanta elected its first Jewish mayor, Sam Massell. And had Rule 18 not been revised to exclude Mr. Massell, it most certainly would have been when Maynard Jackson came to office a few years later.

Then there was the Leontyne Price incident. For years, the Metropolitan Opera Company has come to Atlanta, usually in late spring, and for years, one of the city's most glittering society galas has been the opening-night party for the opera company and cast at the Piedmont Driving Club. On the night, several years ago, when Leontyne Price was scheduled to open in Atlanta with *Tosca*, Mr. Rudolf Bing was privately advised that while the rest of the cast would be most welcome at the party, the star would not. Bing replied that if Miss Price could not attend, neither could anyone else. Disappointed party-goers were advised on opening night that there would be no party, "Due to the fact that the Clubhouse is undergoing renovations."

Reacting to stories like these, stalwart members of the Piedmont Driving Club spring to the club's defense with a variety of counterclaims. On the subject of restrictions against Jews, for example, there is what might be called the Eloise Pappenheimer Defense. "What about Eloise Pappenheimer?" is a stock response. There is also the Major John Cohen Defense. "Why, we've even had a Jewish *president* of the club," says one member. Major Cohen was president of the Driving Club from 1930 to 1932. But Mr. De Jongh Franklin, a prominent Atlanta attorney who is Jewish, scoffs at this and says: "Whenever the Driving Club is accused of anti-Semitism, they trot out John Cohen. He came in during the depths of the Depression, when the club was desperate for money and members, and he was only half Jewish anyway. Besides, he's been dead for years. So has Eloise Pappenheimer."

As for blacks being excluded from the Driving Club, members point to the Lester Maddox incident because it was Maddox, of all people, who first brought blacks to the club as guests. (It is widely suspected, of course, that Governor Maddox did this to embarrass the club, since he himself would have been among those least qualified for membership.) The episode took place when Governor Maddox and the Georgia Commerce Department were holding a luncheon at the club for the media, and when everyone sat down to eat, it was discovered with horror that the guests included two black television newsmen from Atlanta's station WAGA-TV. While guests watched apprehensively, the headwaiter rushed to consult with the maître d', who went for the assistant manager, who went for the manager. For several minutes, the four men stood about wringing their hands. Finally—perhaps because it seemed simpler not to make a fuss—they returned to their posts and the luncheon continued without further disruption. Through it all, Maddox seemed blankly oblivious to the situation he had created.

Finally, members of the Piedmont Driving Club defend their membership practices and policies by pointing out that there are at least two fashionable Jewish clubs in Atlanta—the Standard and the Progressive—which exclude Christians. If blacks wanted a club, the reasoning goes, they could form one of their own. There is also the downtown Commerce Club, which is completely integrated. (Originally an all-male affair, it has recently taken in about ten women members.)

But there is also some confusion about the policies of the Jewish clubs. "If a Christian wanted to join the Standard Club, I could get him in tomorrow," says Edward Elson, a prominent Jewish businessman. Not so, says Charles Wittenstein of the Anti-Defamation League's Southern Council. The ADL considers the Standard Club just as discriminatory as the Driving Club, though the Standard did recently admit one Christian husband of a Jewish lady member. "The Standard Club was formed in *reaction* to the policies of the Driving Club," says Mr. Elson. But this can't be right, either, because the Standard Club was established in 1867—in the beginning as a club exclusively for *German* Jews—twenty years before the Driving Club's founding in 1887.

One club that *was* established in reaction to the Driving Club was the Cherokee Club, but here again there were strange ironies. Several years ago, a group of young Atlanta couples impatient with the Driving Club's exclusive ways, got together and decided to form their own club. Among the founders were Mr. and Mrs. De Jongh Franklin and Mr. and Mrs. Lee Ross, who are also Jewish. All seemed to go well until the Cherokee Club was ready to send out invitations for membership. The Jewish families, the Rosses and the Franklins, who had helped organize the club, received no invitations. "It would never get off the ground if it weren't patterned after the Driving Club," their friends explained.

72

Now that the capital of Georgia has become nationally conspicuous, Atlanta's choosy clubs have become a local *cause célèbre*, and nearly everybody, pro and con, is up in arms on the subject. "Bob Lipschutz, the White House counsel, belongs to the Standard Club," says one Atlantan. He has resigned. Another says jokingly, "What if they took Bell into the Standard and Lipschutz into the Driving Club? Would that make everybody happy?" Most critical of the Christian clubs' policies, meanwhile, have been Atlanta's Jews. Important business decisions, the Jews claim, are made within the confines of the Capital City and the Piedmont Driving clubs—decisions which affect Jewish businesses, and yet about which Jews have no say. The Jews argue that the clubs put Jewish businesses at an *economic* disadvantage. At the moment, feelings are particularly bitter because Atlanta has been undergoing a sharp business recession, out of proportion to what has happened elsewhere in the country. "The fastest-growing city in the South," as it is called, has perhaps grown too fast. One enormous and ambitious office tower stands more than 75 percent unoccupied. "The world's tallest hotel," the staggering new Peachtree Plaza, is air-conditioning empty rooms. As far as some of the city's prominent Jews are concerned, the WASP establishment—and its clubs—are at least partway to blame.

But the most frequently heard complaint in Atlanta is: Why us? "There are thousands of clubs all over the country that have been restricted against Jews and blacks and Orientals and what have you for *years!*" says one indignant woman. "Why is everyone picking on poor little Atlanta?" What she says is of course true. But in the case of Atlanta, the situation is a little different. The position and the power of the Piedmont Driving Club—and, to a lesser extent, the Capital City Club—are somewhat special. The Driving Club is without exception *the* Atlanta Club. And how it achieved, and continues to wield, its immense social power in the city are worth examining.

To begin with, "Driving" has nothing to do with driving golf balls. The club has no driving range, and no golf course. It offers only tennis, squash, swimming, a men's health club, a number of dining rooms, bars, rooms for private parties, and a ballroom for quasi-public functions which has an unsupported ceiling so large that, not long ago, it fell down all by itself—fortunately late at night, when no one was around. The club was formed by a group of young, well-born Atlanta men who enjoyed driving their four-horse tally-hos through what is now a neighboring park, and was known as The Gentlemen's Driving Club. The original clubhouse has been much added to but most of the early building stands today. It is not particularly grand. Decorated in warm pastels and furnished with antiques and Chippendale reproductions and several fine Oriental rugs, it has an atmosphere that is intimate, cozy, old-shoe, and—well—clubby. Its smiling staff (mostly black) knows not only its members' names but also their preferences in food and drink.

Its members rave over the Driving Club's "marvelous" food. But a glance at its buffet table reveals nothing that is beyond country-club ordinary—or what might be called American Rich Predictable, the kind of bland and unsurprising fare that the wealthy eat and serve in their own homes: deviled eggs, cocktail onions, waterlogged lobster halves with Hellmann's mayonnaise, cold collapsed broiled tomatoes, peas, Parker House rolls, roast beef with rubbery Yorkshire pudding, sweet desserts ladled over with cherry syrup.

Strictly speaking, it has always been a men's club, though a group of women has been granted membership as "privileged widows." Wives and children of members are also given "privileges," but should a group of men wish to use a tennis court on which women are playing, the men merely step onto the court, say, "Thank you very much, ladies," and the women depart. A few wives of members have grumbled about this high-handed treatment, but most accept it as their mothers and grandmothers did, and regard it as just another of the club's traditions—quaint, but sacred. Some women actually defend it, saying, as one wife does, "After all, there are only a few hours in a day when a man can have time to play tennis. They deserve to have priority."

From the earliest days of the Driving Club, it has served as the scene of Atlanta's most gorgeous social events, topped by the annual Piedmont Ball, an invitation-only affair that benefits the Piedmont Hospital. For years, no Atlanta girl could be a debutante unless she was a daughter of a Driving Club member, and for years, the Atlanta Junior League was composed of wives and daughters of Driving Club members. Atlanta society says it has no use for a *Social Register*. The Driving Club membership list suffices. (For a while, the Social Register Association in New York published an edition for Atlanta; it was abandoned for "lack of interest.") Perhaps the most dazzling party in the club's history was the famous breakfast

74

tossed at the club in 1939, following the world premiere of *Gone With the Wind,* with Margaret Mitchell, Clark Gable, Vivien Leigh, and *le tout* Atlanta in attendance. (Hattie McDaniel and Butterfly McQueen were not present.)

As an example of the cachet membership in the club carries, an Atlanta woman was shopping recently for a gown to wear to the Piedmont Ball. "Shame on you for going to a party at a club that discriminates," said the salesgirl, who quickly added, "I'm only kidding. I'd give my eyeteeth to go to the Piedmont Ball! Even just to set foot in the club!"

The club has come, meanwhile, to represent an interesting axis of power in the city. The firm of King & Spalding is Atlanta's most prestigious law firm. (Griffin Bell was a partner in King & Spalding, as was Charles Kirbo, President Carter's old friend and troubleshooter.) King & Spalding drafted the Driving Club's original Petition for Charter, and remains the club's official counsel. In a city the size of Atlanta, such a law firm can become virtually a second city government, a law unto itself. There are three Kings and two Spaldings in the Driving Club today, and Kings and Spaldings decorate the boards of Atlanta's biggest banks. Hughes Spalding, Jr., is now a senior partner at King & Spalding. His brother, Jack Spalding, meanwhile, is editor of the *Atlanta Journal,* which, with the *Constitution,* is one of the two Cox-owned newspapers which serve Atlanta morning and evening. The publisher of both the *Journal* and the *Constitution* is a hot-tempered gentleman named Jack Tarver, another Driving Club member, and so it is not surprising that both newspapers have supported the club's membership policy, and opposed Mr. Bell's need to resign. In 1969, when Jim Montgomery, who was business editor for the *Constitution,* produced a story on discrimination in clubs, naming names and citing examples of how major business decisions in Atlanta were made within a tight-knit little group of members, hackles rose in the business community. Hackles rose even higher in Jack Tarver's office. After angrily telling Montgomery that he had embarrassed the paper, Tarver added, "Jim, I think you're getting stale." Montgomery was subsequently transferred from business editor to general-assignment reporting—which meant that his income dropped sharply, since he was no longer able to accept free-lance assignments. Montgomery got the message, and left the paper shortly thereafter.

Atlanta's most powerful society woman, meanwhile, is Mrs. Ann Cox Chambers, heiress to the Cox newspaper fortune, who has been a pivotal figure behind—among other things—the Piedmont Ball. Mrs. Chambers also provides what might be called the Coke Connection, linking the already great coalition of Atlanta forces with another giant power: the Coca-Cola Company. The two great Coca-Cola families are the Candlers and the Woodruffs—there are seven Candler families and two Woodruffs in the Driving Club—who live on large estates in Atlanta's grandest northwest suburbs (with other Coca-Cola money), on Chatham Road, Pace's Ferry Road, Normandy Drive, and Manor Ridge Drive. Two Candler brothers—Asa W. Candler and John S. Candler II—are lawyers in yet another powerful firm, Candler, Cox & Andrews, where, needless to say, Mrs. Ann Cox Chambers has close relatives. The Piedmont Driving Club, in other words, represents a four-sided axis of the press, society, and two large legal firms. It is a combination, Mafia-like in its interlocking complexity, that might seem rather difficult to beat. Not just millions, but *billions* of Atlanta dollars are represented here.

Efforts have been made, of course, to beat it, particularly by prominent Atlanta Jews, such as Edward Elson, who can produce a thick file of letters written to civic organizations urging them not to hold meetings and functions at the Driving Club. The club's claim that it is "purely social" is, he says, a lie. For several years, the Anti-Defamation League has been working to dissuade charitable and other groups from hiring the club's rooms for meetings, and it recently succeeded in having a convention of the American Bar Association reschedule a series of functions elsewhere. Jewish businessmen, aware of the Driving Club's strong power with the press, note that Atlanta newspapers show no reluctance to accept Jewish advertising. The biggest advertiser in the *Journal* and the *Constitution,* for example, is Rich's. If Rich's were to discontinue advertising on the issue of club discrimination, the papers would be dealt a severe financial blow. But this, Michael Rich says, would be "a negative approach."

A more serious threat may come from the Internal Revenue Service. At the moment, a number of the top banks, law firms, and corporations pay club initiation fees for their executives, and then deduct these as business expenses. It can be argued, therefore, that the United States Government is indirectly supporting clubs that discriminate. Of course, there are a number of ways by which corporations could get around an adverse IRS ruling. They could, for example, raise executives' salaries to cover club memberships.

But this could open them up to stockholders' suits. At least one Atlanta lawyer says that he could make a good case on such an issue before the United States Supreme Court.

Among the black community, meanwhile, there is less concern. Most Atlanta blacks would agree with Andrew Young, who feels that blacks have far more pressing priorities—better housing, schools, jobs, and so on—and that for a black to fret about not being able to join the Piedmont Driving Club is "silly." But at least one Atlanta black, Jesse Hill, the president of Atlanta Life and one of Atlanta's wealthiest and most respected black citizens, said recently that "the time has come" for blacks to storm what he calls "the last bastion of discrimination in America."

9

Rules and Regulations

Anti-Semitism and racial prejudice seem to billow in the suburbs, while they tend to lie dormant in the cities. Probably it is because who one's neighbor is and what he looks like become more important in the country than in the anonymity of a city apartment building; in the country, one's neighbor is more visible, you can see him come and go, watch how he tends his lawn and hedge and garden, and tell when his house needs paint. This is certainly why anti-Semitism and prejudice express themselves so readily in the American institution of the country club.

In Rye, New York, for example, the children's dancing classes were for years held in the gymnasium of Rye Country Day School—an upper-class enclave, to be sure, but one that was nonetheless a homogeneous mixture of Christian and Jewish children. (In fact, all Rye Country Day School students were invited to attend the dancing classes.) About ten years ago, however, the school decided that it was time to get out of the dancing-school business, and to concentrate its full efforts on educating the young in more important matters. The dancing classes—renamed, a little ominously, The Barclay Classes—moved to a new venue, the Apawamis Golf Club.

All at once, when invitations to the reorganized classes went out, it was apparent that the class would assume a somewhat different texture: only selected Jews or blacks were invited to attend. The club's rules, therefore, had taken over those of the community.

As one member put it rather blandly, "Well, those are the club's rules."

If there has been one result of the current brouhaha in Atlanta, it has been to cause club members everywhere to begin to come to grips with what their clubs really are. Up to now, institutions like the Piedmont Driving Club have been regarded, like Everest, as merely *there*, to be scaled by the most intrepid climbers. The clubs' rules and regulations have been shrouded in Himalayan mystery. How, for instance, does one get into a club like the Driving Club? Well, one must be asked, and one must be passed by a five-man board of directors. Is there a blackball? Absolutely not, said the club's manager, Mr. Custance. And yet the Driving Club's by-laws state that "One negative vote in the Board shall prevent election of any person proposed for membership." And the rules also state that it "shall be the duty of each member of the Club possessed of any information derogatory to the character of the member proposed . . . to communicate the same to the Board."

Membership in the Piedmont Driving Club is supposed to be restricted to one thousand men, and Mr. Custance speaks of a "long, long waiting list." It has been noted, however, that when a company of the stature of Coca-Cola, or a firm with the standing of King & Spalding, imports a new executive from out of town or appoints a new partner, these people become members of the club rather speedily. At this writing, the Driving Club roster consists of exactly 999 names, not including Mr. Bert Lance, but including Mr. Griffin Bell, who has resigned—plus a long list of nonresident members, honorary members, and "privileged widows." This would seem to indicate that the Driving Club has a vacancy right now.

There has been a lot of talk in Atlanta in recent months of the *morality,* as well as the legality, of private clubs that discriminate. Here, of course, is a knotty issue. At every level of society, and at every point in history, humans have tended to band together with other humans who bear similar physical characteristics. We tend to like people who *look* like us, and to feel distrustful of people who are "different" in appearance. This may even be an ancient, animal instinct. An experiment with infant monkeys, undertaken by Professor Harry Harlow of the University of Wisconsin, had some interesting results. A set of monkey "mother" dolls were made out of terry cloth and placed with the baby monkeys. If, it was noted, the doll mother looked like a real monkey—was monkey color, for example—the baby would cuddle up to it. But if the doll was the wrong color—say, purple—or if its eyes were sewn where its ears should be, the live baby would reject it in terror. Perhaps this is the real reason why we have clubs of any kind—to protect us from our deep fear of outsiders who are different, who have different noses, different cheekbones, a different-color skin, or different hair.

And yet, at the same time, clubs like the Driving Club have become objects of fear themselves. The Driving Club is feared by nonmembers and members alike. In Atlanta, it is astonishing to see how reverentially the club is treated, almost as though it were a supreme being in itself, and how fearfully its members react to any suggestion of change. "The club wouldn't like it," they say. And recently, when a visitor at the Driving Club asked to see the kitchen, the club member who was his host looked wary and said, "I don't think we're supposed to go in the kitchen. I don't think the club would go for that. I believe there's a rule." It is as though the club, with its rules written and unwritten, has developed a life and character of its own, has become a kind of deity—always capitalized—a Big Brother who protects but who also directs and overpowers, and dictates what its members do and think and say.

A thousand miles away from Atlanta, on the shores of Long Island Sound, stands the American Yacht Club, a prestigious club with an international membership. By tradition, the American Yacht Club—and its sister club in New York, the New York Yacht—have always taken in, as special honored members, skippers who have won the coveted America's Cup Race. But when Emil ("Bus") Mosbacher, Jr., became the first Jew to capture the coveted cup, there was a great deal of huffing and puffing at both clubs (eventually, he was taken in). Not long ago a member of the American Yacht Club was advised by another member—not by any official of the club—that it would "not be wise" to bring a visiting South Korean guest to dinner at the club. There might, it was suggested, be "objections." The party dined elsewhere.

On summer evenings, particularly on weekends, a feature of life at the American Yacht Club is "Picnic Point." Picnic Point is a rocky spit of club property that juts out into the water; from it, on clear nights, the Manhattan skyline can be seen twinkling in the distance. Picnic tables and outdoor fireplaces are provided for members and their guests, who bring picnic suppers there. Because space and tables are limited, it is necessary for picnickers to make reservations for Picnic Point. That is a rule that makes sense. Others are more difficult to understand. If, for example, a picnic-packer has forgotten to pack the salt, it is considered a great breach of etiquette

80

to ask to borrow the salt from another picnic table. Instead, one goes without the salt. Mrs. Robert Frisch, the wife of a Manhattan lawyer, was chagrined a while back to discover on Picnic Point that she had forgotten the butter for the corn on the cob. Her house was several miles away, and the grocery stores had closed. It was against the rules to borrow from a neighboring picnicker. Someone suggested that Mrs. Frisch step into the kitchen of the clubhouse, a few yards away, and request some butter from one of the staff. This was, after all, her club. Mrs. Frisch was aghast. "I could never do that," she said. "I'm sure that's against the rules. The club would never stand for something like that." Her guests ate unbuttered corn.

Will the situation ever change—in Atlanta, New York, or anywhere else, where country-club life is almost embarrassingly similar? Some people, like Atlanta's former Mayor Ivan Allen, think that eventually the barriers will fall. Ivan Allen, during his term as mayor, was often cited as a great liberal and proponent of black equality (though his critics note that he has never given up his membership in the Piedmont Driving Club). Mr. Allen thinks that the barriers will fall first, but gradually, for Jews, and "maybe someday" for blacks. He hopes so, he says.

Of course, the blacks of Atlanta, as in other cities of the South, have a special social problem, which most people don't like to talk about. Many of the families in the city's white establishment appear to have old ties with the black community. The Hamiltons, for example, are a prominent black family, and there are Hamiltons in the Driving Club. There are Yanceys in the club, and other Yanceys in Collier Heights, an expensive black suburb. There are Kings of King & Spalding; other Atlanta Kings produced Martin Luther King.

Most Atlantans appear to disagree with Mayor Allen, and think that nothing will change. The present controversy will result in opening no doors, nor will it create a reactionary wave of tougher discrimination. The club, as they say, "wouldn't go for" change. And the club is the Great Pumpkin, with a will and an impetus and a life—and very definite ideas—of its own. What must have seemed a charming and perfectly harmless notion in 1887 to fifteen young Atlanta dandies, who could remember the days of Scarlett O'Hara, young blades who squired their belles in their tally-hos, has become something they could never have imagined—a monster too mighty to be slain by mere mortals.

As one Driving Club member says: "We love our club, and we

like it the way it is. People criticize it, but we don't really care. It's part of our lives and it was part of our daddies' lives. Some of my best friends are Jews and some of my best friends are blacks. But the club is an extension of our living rooms, you see, and our living rooms are private, like the club."

To which a nonmember replies: "There are two questions I'd like to ask this friendly person. First, what is so secret in his living room that some of his best friends can't see it and, second, is he sure that some of his best friends are really his best friends?"

The club's president, Frank Carter, remains unfazed. "We've been criticized in the past and we'll be criticized again," he says. "We shrug it off. People can point fingers at us and call us all a bunch of snobs and bigots. They can print it in the *New York Times*. We'll discuss it for a day or two, and then forget about it. We'll just say, 'This, too, shall pass.' "

EAST

10

The Rockefellers on the Turnpike

*I*t might be stated as an axiom of American life that nothing ever turns out exactly as planned, and that the more monumental the undertaking, the more disastrous are the unexpected side effects. This has certainly been the case with the multimillion-dollar stretch of pavement called Interstate 95 or, more familiarly, the Connecticut Turnpike, which lines the New England seacoast, and which serves as the primary access to hundreds of thousands of New York commuter bedrooms.

The turnpike was preceded, more or less, by the Merritt Parkway. When the Merritt Parkway—running from the state's southwest border roughly eastward to just outside New Haven—was completed in the middle 1930s, everyone who saw it had to admit that it was something of a showplace of a road. It curved gracefully about and across the low hills, offering to the motorist sudden and surprising vistas. Its wide center malls were grassed and landscaped with a great variety of trees. For a few weeks each spring, the parkway blazed coolly with pink and white flowering dogwood and azalea. Each of its many overpass bridges was of a different design. The Merritt Parkway made entering Connecticut a particularly pleasing experience, and caused suburban Connecticut to appear to be a singularly pleasant place to live. State officials claimed the parkway was worth its cost in public relations value alone. It would, among other things, lure new money into the state.

Of course, while it was being built, there were the usual allegations of corruption. Highway department officials, it was rumored, had been paid off by wealthy estate owners in Fairfield County in order to ensure that the highway did not venture too close to their houses. In return for favors, other landowners had allegedly been advised in advance of the highway's intended path so that they could snap up land cheaply and then sell it, at high profits, to the state. And to be sure, when one studied the Merritt Parkway's gerrymandering course on a map, it did seem as though some of its pretty curves and digressions—it managed to avoid the rich "estate area" of Greenwich, for example—were not entirely arbitrary or aesthetic. Still, it was a handsome piece of roadmaking when it was finished, there was no denying that.

The years went by, however, and the Merritt Parkway did its job almost too well, tempting people in unexpected numbers from the city into the Connecticut suburbs, and it became inadequate. As automobiles got wider, the Merritt Parkway seemed to grow narrower. As automobiles traveled faster, the parkway, with its hills and turns, seemed to become slower. Friday and Sunday afternoons were the worst, with traffic jammed for miles as motorists struggled to get out of, or back to, New York on weekends. And so, in the early 1950s, as part of the Eisenhower administration's Interstate Highway program, construction on the new Connecticut Turnpike was begun.

The Connecticut Turnpike is a no-nonsense, no-frills affair—no dogwood trees, no planted center malls, nothing but concrete lanes and iron guardrails and blazing mercury lights and relentless toll booths spaced with gonglike regularity at intervals of roughly fourteen miles. The turnpike was designed to be flat and straight and fast, to whisk motorists from one end of the state to the other in less than two hours' time, including a stop for a Howard Johnson's hot dog. The turnpike played no favorites—enraging property owners whose homes and investments crumbled in its wake—as the old New Haven Railroad, which the turnpike roughly parallels, had not done. It plowed impartially through reproductions of English manor houses and through the steaming bowels of Bridgeport, taking with it tenements and tennis courts, destroying a mile of shoreline here and a three-hundred-year-old elm tree there with equal indifference. Today, the turnpike is over twenty years old, and it is still a tough, grueling road. The Merritt Parkway had banned trucks, which, as the suburbs burgeoned, demanding more goods and services, had also become an anachronistic notion. The turnpike welcomed trucks and truckers, not to mention buses, and the steady roar of the traffic it conveys can be heard, night and day, for miles away. Its stream of lights guides airplanes into La Guardia Airport from Boston. It's an ugly, utilitarian thing but, as they say, it gets you there and it takes you back.

To be sure, a number of city planners and environmentalists have questioned not only the aesthetics but also the economics of the whole thing. If the millions of dollars—at over a million dollars a mile—that were spent on the Connecticut Turnpike had been spent, for a fraction of the cost per mile, on refurbishing the rickety old New Haven Railroad line and its wobbling tracks, would not New Yorkers and suburbanites alike have been given a cleaner, safer, cheaper, and faster way of getting into and out of the city? But the voices of these visionaries have not been heard. Today, the dirtiest, most expensive, riskiest, but unquestionably the quickest way to go to and from the northeast suburbs of New York City is on the turnpike.

What the Connecticut Turnpike connects New York City to is a series of Fairfield County towns with pretty Old English and Old Testament names such as Greenwich, Stamford, Weston, Westport, New Canaan, and Darien. These Connecticut towns are generally considered to comprise New York's most desirable suburbs. Though there are pockets of suburban wealth in both New Jersey and on the northwestern shores of Long Island, neither "Jersey" nor "the Island" have ever managed to match the mystique of Connecticut's superiority and style; they have long been regarded as suburbs for the middle class, and "middle class," in New York terms, is sometimes another way of saying "Jewish."

For years, the queen of these Connecticut towns was unquestionably Greenwich, but the turnpike—as it has done to towns throughout the length of its route—has changed Greenwich considerably. Where it used to be a wealthy, countrified bedroom town—with winding streets and private lanes, no street lights and no sidewalks and a single shopping street—it is now a mini-city with hotels, motels, expensive restaurants, glass office buildings, apartment houses, and condominiums. But though many old Greenwich residents deplore the changes, there is at least one family who have lived there for several generations, who have become so cozily a part of Greenwich that they almost symbolize the town, and who have never seen any reason to live elsewhere: the Rockefellers. Turnpike or no, they stay.

There are two kinds of suburban Rockefellers, and there is a difference. There are the Tarrytown Rockefellers, whose vast estate-compound at Pocantico Hills is the largest privately owned property in New York's Westchester County. They are the Rockefeller Brothers—John D. III, David, Nelson, Laurance, and the late Winthrop—whom everybody knows about. Then there are the Greenwich Rockefellers, scarcely fifteen miles away from the others, in Connecticut, whom nobody has heard much of, which state of affairs suits the Greenwich Rockefellers perfectly. The Greenwich Rockefellers are sometimes called "the poor Rockefellers," though they are hardly that.

"People, when they refer to us at all, tend to refer to us as 'the other Rockefellers,'" says Godfrey S. Rockefeller, a tall, spare, scholarly-looking man who has the pronounced "Rockefeller nose." "But we've never been the ones for publicity the way the other branch of the family have. We're very private people. Of course, we used to be known as the Eastern Rockefellers, since my grandfather came east from Cleveland in 1867, long before John D. Rockefeller came."

Mr. Godfrey Stillman Rockefeller's grandfather was William Rockefeller, the older brother of the first John D. Rockefeller, whom everyone thinks of when thinking of Rockefellers. The two brothers could not have been more unlike. John D. Rockefeller was skinny, parsimonious, pious, and abstemious. For two generations in the John D. branch of the family, liquor was never served or consumed in any household. They had few friends, and life revolved around the family and the Baptist Church. Years later, John D. Rockefeller, Jr., described in his autobiography the lonely austerity of growing up in Cleveland:

Our social life, looking at it from today's standards, was cramped. It centered on the church. We didn't have in Cleveland a social life that other children had. We didn't go to school and when children visited at Forest Hill they were apt to be the friends of Father and Mother. Everything centered around the home and the church and there was nothing else. Our prime interest in the Sunday school centered around the orchestra because we all played instruments, myself and my sisters. It was a sort of social group by itself. Otherwise we had no childhood friends, no school friends.

William Rockefeller, by contrast, was a big, jolly man who loved good drink and good times and was not the least bit churchly. He once commented that the best thing about Sunday was the sound of church bells ringing across a golf course. When he arrived in New York to represent his younger brother's growing oil interests, he was immediately taken in by—and in a sense became the leader of—the so-called Standard Oil Gang, which included Henry H. Rogers, and James Stillman of the National City Bank; Stillman became William Rockefeller's closest friend. In addition to his Standard Oil activities, William, along with Rogers and Adolph Lewisohn, put together the United Metals Selling Company in 1898. The company controlled, among other things, Anaconda Copper, and within a short time 55 percent of all the copper sold in the United States was being sold by the United Metals Selling Company. With his easygoing ways and great charm—qualities that permanently eluded his younger brother—William Rockefeller moved rapidly into New York society, and acquired a large summer place on the Hudson in fashionable Tarrytown. There, a few years later, despite the differences in their personalities, his brother John joined him, establishing for himself what would become the famous John D. Rockefeller family compound at Pocantico Hills.

In 1864, William had married Almira Geraldine Goodsell, and they had four children—William G., Emma, Percy, and Ethel, who later changed her name to Geraldine after her mother's middle name. All four embarked upon a social life that made their cousins' lives seem decidedly dour and gloomy. As one of William G.'s grandsons, another William Rockefeller, asserts, "There was never so much Baptism in our branch." And as John D. Rockefeller, Jr., wrote of his cousins: "We children didn't have what those children had and we used to notice the difference. They had a gay kind of social life, with many parties which we used to wish we could have." John D. Rockefeller, Sr.—or "Senior," as he would always be called—thoroughly disapproved of all this gaiety on the part of his neices and nephews. There were terrible rows on the subject of gaiety as opposed to piety and, already, a deep rift between the two branches of the family had begun to form. Finally, "to get away from his overpowering uncle," as William G.'s grandson puts it, William G. pulled up stakes in Tarrytown and moved across the state line to Greenwich, Tarrytown's rival as a summer resort. He was followed by his brother Percy, and the family rift was complete. It would remain for a hundred years.

William Rockefeller's children may have inherited their father's ebullience and sense of fun, but they also inherited some peculiarities that have tended to show up in both "lines" of the Rockefeller family. (For example, William Sr.'s and John D. Sr.'s father—still another William—was once indicted on a charge of having impaired the morals of the family's servant girl; he had to move, one jump ahead of the sheriff, with his family from Moravia, New York, to Owego, in another jurisdiction, to avoid going to jail; here, in a small, untended graveyard by the side of a country road, repose a number of early, unheralded, and perhaps best-forgotten Rockefellers.)

William Rockefeller's son William G., founder of the Greenwich branch, for another example, became a hopeless alcoholic, to the horror of his teetotaling cousins. Daughter Gerladine (née Ethel) was a beautiful and popular debutante who had a passion for animals—canines, in particular. Soon her passion began to seem more like an obsession. During her lifetime she owned literally hundreds of dogs. She married Marcellus Huntley Dodge, a grandson of the founder of the Remington Arms Company, and became a matriarch whom even her older brothers and sister dared not cross. She ran the Dodge family office and her husband, "Marcie," with an iron hand, and acquired more and more dogs. She built a huge estate, called Giralda, on hundreds of acres in Madison, New Jersey, and filled it with dark and heavy furniture and hangings, and she built a large and extraordinarily ugly mansion on the corner of Fifth Avenue and Sixty-first Street in Manhattan, and filled that with more dark and heavy furniture and hangings. Though she never spent a night in the New York house, she bought adjacent pieces of property as soon as they became available until she owned most of the north side of the block between Fifth and Madison Avenues, and the entire Fifth Avenue frontage between her house and the Knickerbocker Club on the Sixty-second Street corner. These lots she kept vacant, and let them become overgrown with weeds and scrubby trees—to provide a "woods" for her dogs, though the dogs never visited the New York house either.

For years, the Dodge mansion remained New York's mystery house—shuttered and locked and dark and forbidding, illuminated only by a faint light from behind a barred caretaker's window. The reason—often wondered about—for the erratic placement of exterior windows was that the entire top floor of the mansion had been designed for use as a kennel. Geraldine Dodge was odd, all right, but a personal tragedy made her even odder. Her only child, a son on whom she doted, was traveling through Europe with a fellow Princeton graduate when his car struck a tree and he was instantly

90

killed. After the accident, Mrs. Dodge began to withdraw. She secluded herself in her New Jersey house, and she and Marcie Dodge began to occupy separate houses on the estate, just far enough apart so that they could "see each other's lights" at night. Occasionally, they visited each other. Finally, her husband had her declared incompetent and made her his legal ward. After his death, she became the ward of her banks and lawyers. She lived on and on. For eleven more years, not a soul entered her Fifth Avenue house save her elderly caretaker, who had one dog for company. Mrs. Dodge died in 1975.

When the contents of Geraldine Rockefeller Dodge's houses went under the hammer in 1976, her possessions—including a collection of bronze animals and strange bronze hands—brought close to seven million dollars at Sotheby Parke Bernet. It was not, the auction house admitted, the intrinsic value of the collection that produced this imposing figure. Instead, the mystery and publicity surrounding the strange lady brought throngs of the curious to the auction held on her New Jersey estate, and made everyone want to go home with a souvenir of the riddle that had been Geraldine's life. Huge sums were bid for pots and pans, for her ancient hats and fur coats, and for Louis Vuitton trunks that had not made an Atlantic crossing in more than sixty years. Later, the New Jersey property itself was sold to the Prudential Insurance Company for use as a conference center. The Fifth Avenue property was sold for ten million dollars, and the house was razed in the early spring of 1977; a luxury apartment tower will rise in its place.

Geraldine's brothers, William G. and Percy Rockefeller, married two sisters, daughters of their father's best friend, James Stillman. William G. Rockefeller married Elsie Stillman, and Percy Rockefeller married Isabel Stillman. Both families remained in Greenwich, and each couple produced five children. The William G. Rockefellers had four boys and one girl—William Avery, Godfrey, James, John, and Almira. The Percy Rockefellers countered with four girls and one boy—Isabel, Winifred, Faith, Gladys, and Avery. All ten children grew up in Greenwich as double first cousins on comfortable estates on Lake Avenue, Mead Lane, and Middle Patent Road. The cousins remained remarkably loyal to Greenwich. William Avery, Godfrey, James, John, and Avery all married and established residences of their own in the community—Godfrey and his brother James in houses that are back to back. Faith Rockefeller married Jean Model and settled in

Greenwich, as did her sister Winifred after marrying Brooks Emeny. Almira defected when she married, and moved to Philadelphia. Isabel Rockefeller and William Avery Rockefeller tightened the family ties even further when they married Frederic and Florence Lincoln. Today, there are seven different Rockefeller families, all interrelated, all close, representing the third and fourth generations of the family who have favored the Connecticut suburb.

When William Rockefeller, Sr., died in 1922 at the age of eighty-one, he left an estate of close to $200 million and a will that was unusual in several respects. For one thing, in contrast to his brother John D., who gave away nearly $600 million to charity, fun-loving William made no philanthropic bequests whatever. He did, however, devise a will designed to keep his fortune intact as long as legally possible—"through lives in being plus twenty-one years," that is, through at least two generations, in a series of trusts, with distribution not to be made until the fourth generation. He left heirs, in other words, who had not yet been born. He made a single exception with his favorite son, Percy, who was left three quarters of his trust outright. Commenting on this arrangement a number of years later, in 1937, the *New York Journal-American* said:

William Rockefeller, extending his patriarchal beneficence into the fourth generation, has endowed his country with some fifty prospective millionaires in their own right—all but two of them had not yet entered this world when he left it and nearly half of whom are still unborn.

Nothing like this is likely ever to happen again. Inheritance taxes took only one fourth of William Rockefeller's estate. Today they would take three fourths of an estate that size, and the rates are more likely to be raised than lowered. So there probably will not be another such dynastic transmission of wealth.

Despite the "dynastic transmission," William Rockefeller's heirs have not displayed quite the talent at holding on to—and making more—money that their Tarrytown cousins have. Shrewd investments within the John D. Rockefeller line have succeeded in vastly increasing the original fortune. With the William branch, it has generally been the opposite. A myriad of costly divorces, for one thing, has taken a toll of William's estate. With the exception of Percy—who, as his father may have foreseen, had a knack for making money in Wall Street in both a rising and a falling market—the Greenwich Rockefellers have tended to have either bad luck or little flair for making money. As a result, none today is as wealthy as the patriarch might have hoped.

At the same time, the Greenwich Rockefellers have displayed some decidedly un-Rockefeller behavior. One girl married a man forty years older than she. Another created a stir in the newspapers while she was at Vassar by having her aviator boyfriend drop love letters to her from the sky. Godfrey Rockefeller startled the family by marrying a Jewess—or at least a woman who was Jewish by heritage. She was Helen Gratz, a baptized Episcopalian but also a member of the distinguished Sephardic family of Philadelphia, and a collateral descendant of the beautiful Rebecca Gratz, whom Sir Walter Scott used as his model for Rebecca in *Ivanhoe.*

When traditional Rockefeller Spartanism has been tried in the Greenwich branch, it either has been overdone or has backfired. One Greenwich Rockefeller third-generation son was angrily disinherited for failing to meet his father's boat upon the latter's return from Europe. Another received so little spending allowance while at Yale that he had to go to work in New Haven as a night telephone operator in order to eat. Still another Greenwich Rockefeller refused to build a swimming pool for his family until his daughter lost enough weight to look attractive in a swimsuit.

Even Percy, considered the family financial genius in the Greenwich branch, became the center of a certain amount of scandal following the great stock market crash of 1929. He had, it was claimed, made a lot of money in the falling market by selling "short"—selling, in other words, stocks that he did not really own but had contracted to buy at a future date, and probably at a much reduced price. There was a great public outcry about the short selling of stocks, though this had been a common Wall Street custom and remains one, under stiffer regulations, today. Percy Rockefeller was summoned to testify before the U.S. Senate Committee on Banking and Currency, which was investigating stock market practices. He defended his actions and affirmed that in the "tremendous depreciation" since 1929, he had lost many millions of dollars. He needed money, and he claimed that his short selling had netted him only $550,000, which, he said, was a "slight sum" compared with his "tremendous losses." But Percy was a jolly soul with a host of friends in and out of Washington, and he was given no more than a light reprimand.

The Greenwich Rockefellers have always favored Yale, while the Tarrytown Rockefellers have preferred Harvard, Princeton, and, in the case of Nelson, Dartmouth. And so the cool distance that continues to exist between the two branches of the great family is based on tradition, geography, and education—not to mention a certain discrepancy in bank balances. Over the years, at least two attempts have been made to mend the split with a huge catchall family reunion, but on both occasions, negotiations fell apart on the issue of venue. Naturally, the Greenwich Rockefellers wanted the gathering to take place in Tarrytown—"They have so much more room there," says one—at the estate most of the Greenwich group had never seen. But Tarrytown, which has always regarded Greenwich as family mavericks, not to say poor relations, demurred. And so most of the Greenwich Rockefellers have never met their Tarrytown cousins.

There are also differences in attitude and life style between the Greenwichites and the Tarrytonians. "Everything is very grand at Pocantico Hills," says Mrs. Godfrey Rockefeller, munching a peanut butter sandwich in the library of her big Georgian house on Mead Lane—typical of the cozy, informal Greenwich Rockefeller style. "Even the children's playhouse there is three stories tall. They've tended to concentrate on philanthropy, public service, and corporate finance. We're more interested in our homes, our families, and our pleasant lives. We've stayed out of the limelight." Staying out of the limelight involves a great deal of visiting back and forth between the Godfrey Rockefellers' and their Greenwich relatives' houses—Rockfields, the James Stillman Rockefellers' place just behind them, and cousin Avery's pleasant Wild Wings on Lake Avenue. Godfrey Rockefeller, a retired banker, is still an avid skier (a leg recently broken in a skiing accident will, he insists, not keep him off the slopes). He and his family keep a winter ski chalet in Mad River, Vermont—a chalet with its own private ski lift. "Whenever anybody thinks of Rockefellers, they think of the John D. branch," he says a trifle wistfully. "But we've accomplished things too. It would be nice if someone acknowledged us once in a while. But most people, except here in Greenwich, don't know we exist."

Currently, the most distinguished of the Greenwich Rockefellers are probably James Stillman Rockefeller and his nephew William. James Stillman Rockefeller, the son of William G. and Elsie Stillman Rockefeller, is a Phi Beta Kappa graduate of Yale (1924). Married to the former Nancy Carnegie and now in his mid-seventies, he rose from a job with the brokerage firm of Brown Brothers & Company to the position of president, and then became chairman of the board of the National City Bank of New York. In the process he collected directorships of such prestigious corporations as National Cash Register, Kimberly-Clark, and Pan American World Airways. His son Andrew (Yale '51) lives nearby in Greenwich.

William Rockefeller, a hearty, husky bear of a man, is Yale '40. He is the son of William Avery Rockefeller, the grandson of William G. Rockefeller, the great-grandson of William Rockefeller, Sr., and the great-great-grandson of the William Rockefeller whom everybody on both sides of the family would prefer to forget, who allegedly toyed with a servant girl and yet who sired sons who would make the name Rockefeller internationally synonymous with enormous wealth.

When the present William married his pretty wife, Molly, his mother said to the bride, "You realize that you will have twenty-nine first cousins living in Greenwich." At first, Molly Rockefeller thought that her mother-in-law's comment was made out of a sense of family pride. She soon realized, however, that it was intended as a warning. Perhaps because of this, the young William Rockefellers defected from family tradition somewhat and settled in a large old house on Grandview Avenue in nearby Rye—"where you can walk to the station, walk to Rye Country Day School, and walk to the hospital." William Rockefeller says: "It wasn't just all the relatives, but as far as we were concerned, Greenwich had just gotten too big. It may sound snobbish to say so, but when I was growing up the people who composed Westchester and Fairfield County society were a very small group. Everybody knew everybody else. We dated girls from Larchmont, Pelham Manor, Greenwich, and Darien. But as these towns get bigger they get more isolated and self-contained. I grew up in Greenwich when Greenwich was nice. But now every time a company promotes a man to a big spot, the place he wants to move to is Greenwich, and all the big old places get broken up to make room for the new people. But Rye, because of its location, is different. It's on a peninsula, so it can't get bigger. There's just no more land."

Bill Rockefeller remembers when, growing up in Greenwich, there were really two kinds of Greenwich society. "There were the people who lived in the city and came to Greenwich for the summer, and there were the people, like us, who lived in Greenwich and went away for the summer. The two groups never met." For years, Greenwich Rockefellers have been summering in the Adirondacks near Saranac Lake (while the Tarrytown Rockefellers summer in Seal Harbor, Maine), where great-grandfather William

95

Rockefeller—"who was a great sport"—bought a large tract of land and built an elaborate "camp," with separate buildings for dining, cooking, sleeping, etc. The family has managed to hold on to much of the acreage, and Bill Rockefeller, his brother Frederic (Yale '47), and his sister, Mrs. Miles J. McMillin, the wife of a Wisconsin publisher, and their families share several of the numerous cottages. "It is a bit clannish, I admit," says Bill Rockefeller. "We sit on the porch and watch the kids."

Bill Rockefeller is a partner in the prestigious Wall Street law firm of Shearman & Sterling, and serves on the boards of a number of worthy institutions, including the Miriam Osborn Memorial Home (for elderly women) and the Sloan-Kettering Cancer Center. He is a past president of the ASPCA, and is currently president of the Metropolitan Opera. He used to do much more, until one of his three daughters ("No sons, much to my father's eternal disappointment") asked at the dinner table, "Which meeting are you going to tonight?" He was reminded then of a little ditty his mother once composed:

When to meetings I go,
With the greatest of skill,
I always contrive
To keep perfectly still.
For if I show interest,
Or seem a bit witty,
Wham, there I am,
On another committee.

Molly Rockefeller recorded this message in needlepoint on a pillow for her husband.

"People nowadays tend to give their children *things* instead of *time*," Rockefeller says. "I found I was guilty of the same thing. It burns me up to see the way people in Rye will give a kid a Thunderbird for his eighteenth birthday; the parking lot at Rye Country Day School is jammed with Thunderbirds. When I was a kid in Greenwich we had bicycles."

The youngest generation of Tarrytown Rockefellers—the so-called Cousins—have frequently claimed that it is an onerous thing to be born with the name Rockefeller. The fortune that John D. Rockefeller left is now so vast that it has a life of its own, a life that can crush the dreams or ambitions of mere human beings. Several of the Cousins in the John D. branch have tried to give their money away in order to attain freedom from its great weight. But it cannot be done. They are bound to their wealth by so many trusts and legal instruments that it is theirs to live with and deal with like a congenital disease. Some have talked of changing their names in order to be rid, in part, of the weighty connotation.

It turns out not to be easy to be part of the "poor branch" of the family, either, for somewhat different reasons. "It was very tough on the girls growing up," says William Rockefeller. "They were always being teased about their name. Their friends all assumed that they were enormously rich. Particularly after Nelson became governor, and all the facts about how rich that side of the family was came out in the press, my daughters couldn't understand why we weren't living on the same grand scale. They'd say to me things like, 'Why can't we buy it, Daddy—we're Rockefellers, aren't we?' It was a very tough thing for them to understand."

Perhaps that is why, now that they are grown, all three daughters are turning their backs on both Greenwich and Rye, on New York suburbia altogether, and have scattered in disparate directions. The oldest, Mary, is married and raising two boys in Chicago. The second, Edith, married to a sales executive with Boeing, lives in Seattle and works as a cartographer. The youngest, Sally, graduated recently from the University of Vermont, where she majored in forest management, and then headed for the great outdoors to work on reforestation projects.

When she was a student at the Oldfields School in Maryland, Sally Rockefeller encountered a classmate named Eileen Rockefeller. Eileen turned out to be one of David Rockefeller's daughters. "At that point, I'd never even met David," says Sally's father. Despite the century-old family schism, and the fact that, according to strict genealogy, the two girls were a full generation apart, they became friends.

Now that his daughters are grown and gone, Bill Rockefeller has a new project that greatly excites him. "After years of trying to get people to give me money," he says, "for Cancer, the Metropolitan Opera, the ASPCA, and so on, I'm finally in the delightful position of being able to give some money away." He has been made president of the Geraldine Rockefeller Dodge Foundation—appropriately, since he was one of the few people in the family who got on rather well with his despotic great-aunt. Since Geraldine Dodge's husband and son both predeceased her, her entire fortune was left to charity. The Geraldine Rockefeller Foundation will not nearly approach in size the massive philanthropic instruments created by the John D. branch, but with the sale of Giralda, the Manhattan real estate, the money achieved from the Parke Bernet sale, plus her own and her husband's personal fortunes, it will not be small potatoes by any means.

The final thrust of the new foundation has not been completely determined, but Bill Rockefeller feels that animals, for which Geraldine Dodge had such a passion, should be at least partial beneficiaries. Secondary schools, both public and private, will also benefit, along with programs such as Head Start, which help underprivileged children. The rest of the foundation's emphasis will probably be felt in New Jersey, where she lived, in education and in the arts.

"She may have been difficult," says Bill Rockefeller, "but she left a will that we're very proud of." It is a will that may help change the image of the Greenwich Rockefellers, and establish them as philanthropists in their own right.

As for Tarrytown, across Westchester County on the banks of the Hudson, William Rockefeller waves a jaunty hand from his home on the Sound, and says, "Anyone with any sense knows that summers are cooler on the Sound than they are on the river."

11

Troubled Darien

Each of the Connecticut suburbs has attempted to cultivate a personality and an aura of its own. Greenwich, despite the fact that many of the old estates have been razed and subdivided, still likes to think of itself as providing the grandest Connecticut address. Farther up the line, wealthy and conservative Southport regards itself as "what Greenwich used to be." Westport is "swinging"—artistic and liberal, popular with advertising and other media folk. Woodsy Weston is quieter, more family-oriented. When choosing a Connecticut suburb, one is supposed to take these differences into consideration.

Then there are the two pretty, well-manicured towns of New Canaan and Darien. New Canaan—to people in Darien, at least—is regarded as elegant but stodgy. It is a town preferred by dowagers and wealthy retirees. It is comfortably isolated. It is far from the Connecticut Turnpike and, by train, must be reached by a special spur of the New Haven tracks (which dead-end at New Canaan). Darien is considered a livelier, more fun-loving, party-going town for younger, upwardly mobile families. But Darien also lies hard by Exit 13 (a number which the superstitious find ominous) of the Connecticut Turnpike, and thereby hang many of the town's recent problems.

It used to be that the Darien Police Department had little to do besides quiet an occasional noisy party or domestic argument, and ticket cars without parking stickers at the railroad station. "Our main excitement was helping get pet cats out of trees," says a member of the Darien police force. But in the twenty years since the turnpike opened, the population of Darien has doubled, from 11,000 to 22,000. Most of the big old houses remain, but they have become crowded in by smaller, less expensive houses, many of them built for corporation executives stationed in the New York area for two- or three-year periods. There is much more turnover in real estate than there was a generation ago. Though it used to be that everyone in Darien "knew everybody else," this is now no longer the case, and long-time Darien residents now encounter strange faces in the shops and supermarkets. In the last ten years, twenty-one new commercial buildings have been built in the town, and the number of employees who commute into and away from Darien each day has doubled to three thousand. Two new motels have opened, bringing in transients for the first time.

There are still the small expensive shops along Darien's main street, but there are also new shops, restaurants, and bars where both the atmosphere and the customers are somewhat less refined. In 1975, Darien had its first murder in more years than anyone can remember—a triple homicide in a barroom brawl. A year earlier, the town had its first bank robbery and, shortly afterward, its first street holdup. The incidence of shoplifting and bad-check passing has climbed alarmingly, along with break-ins and residential burglaries. Home owners who never used to lock their doors when they went out are now installing elaborate burglar alarm systems, and shops and banks now scan customers with mirrors, sheets of one-way glass, and closed-circuit television cameras. Because of the town's easy access to the turnpike, trucks now turn in to the quiet, tree-shaded streets at night and park in front of empty houses, and within hours, burglars will have removed everything of value. Darien has now learned of the "specialty burglar," who may choose to go only after silver, or jewelry, or paintings, or furs, or hi-fi components, or Oriental rugs.

The local newspaper used to print routinely, as social items, details of residents' vacation plans. Editors have been told to discontinue this, and to print nothing until a vacationer returns. The news that Mr. and Mrs. So-and-so are departing for their winter home in the West Indies would almost certainly guarantee the arrival of a burglar's truck the following night. Though the town is proud of its fast and efficient police force, many residents are even hesitant to notify the police when they plan to be away. The fear is that the police, in their "dealings with criminals," may let a fact slip out that would lead to a burglary. The owners of expensive and expensively decorated houses used to be delighted when magazines like *House Beautiful* and *House & Garden* wanted to photograph their gardens or interiors, along with floor plans. "Now," says one woman, "I'd have to think twice about letting anyone into the house to take pictures. When something like that is published, it's like a blueprint for a burglary." (Friends and relatives of Mrs. Cornelius Vanderbilt Whitney were shocked when she published a book of pictures of her daughter's dollhouse—a detailed and miniaturized room-by-room version of the Whitneys' Kentucky mansion: for twenty-five dollars, a burglar could have an itemized catalogue of the house's costly contents. In Darien, the opening of houses to tours on behalf of a charity was once a popular fund-raising technique. Today, the best houses in Darien refuse to participate in such tours. "It's a shame," says one woman. "The only people you can get to show their houses are the ones where there is nothing pretty to see."

Another indication of what has happened in Darien is that the number of requests for "bank escorts" has climbed steadily in the last twenty years, reaching 1,085 last year. "It used to be that a local merchant just strolled over to the night depository of his bank at the end of each business day and made his deposit," a member of the local police force declares. "Nowadays, he asks for an armed escort from us."

To cope with the climbing crime rate, Darien has increased its police force to thirty-five, and a policeman's starting salary, which formerly was $3,800 a year, is now $13,000. Darien police used to be trained in a desultory fashion, and were not even instructed in the use of firearms. But now each officer must qualify weekly at the department's new indoor firing range with a standard .38 caliber revolver. Some officers have been taught bomb-disposal techniques and how to use tear gas and high-powered rifles, as well as to conduct ransom negotiations with kidnappers. Merchants, meanwhile, have been attending police seminars on credit card fraud, dealing with shoplifters, and how to spot a phony check.

While Darien feels that most of its crime comes from "outside," there is a new kind of criminal in the town that is even more disturbing: the young offender who is a member of Darien's old, proud establishment. The owner of one of Darien's snappier ready-to-wear shops describes the following incident: "A sixteen-year-old girl was in the store the other day, and I saw her pick up a fifty-dollar cocktail ring, look at it, and drop it in her purse. I know the girl, and I know her parents. So I telephoned her mother and told her what had happened. The mother immediately began screaming at me and telling me that her daughter would never do such a thing. She told me that she intended to close her charge account with me. Later, the girl's father called me and said that not only would his family never do business at my store again, but that if I tried to press charges against his daughter he'd sue me. So what can you do when something like that happens—lose a fifty-dollar ring or lose a customer who spends a couple of thousand dollars a year in your store? I wrote the parents and apologized for everything. I even sent the girl's mother a bottle of perfume."

Of course, it would be wrong to assume that a town like Darien is experiencing anything like a crime wave, nor is what is happening there much different from what is happening in suburbs all over the country, where, last year, as statistics from the Federal Bureau of Investigation show, serious crime increased 10 percent. Darien residents insist that their shaded, manicured streets are still for the most part safe, and that their rolling green hills along the Connecticut shore provide an unusually pleasant and comfortable place to live. They point to the fact that neon signs and outdoor advertising have been kept to a minimum, and that the old Boston Post Road which runs through the center of town still has an agreeable, New England look. They would live, they say, nowhere else. But the presence of crime has made Darien edgy, and added an uneasy note to the town's formerly leisured, sneakered, casual mood. Complacency has given way to a certain nervousness and wives cast worried looks at husbands when, in the night, the family dog sits up and growls at the door. The possibility of crime—or at least the interruption of peace of mind—hangs in the air as persistently as the distant drone of traffic from the turnpike. It is something unwanted and unexpected that the turnpike has brought to little Darien.

Becky Thompson graduated from Darien High School in 1965. A year earlier, a young man named Michael Valentine, leaving a teen-age party where he had had much to drink, was driving his date, Nancy Hitchings, home when his car struck a tree. Nancy Hitchings was instantly killed, and suddenly Darien was the center of unpleasant publicity. The parents of the youths giving the party were arrested for serving liquor to minors, and Becky Thompson's senior year at high school was spent with New York reporters roaming the school grounds looking for more stories about the rich, decadent, "swinging" youth of Darien. "It was also the year the police started making pot busts," Miss Thompson recalls. "Everybody was convinced that the youth scene in Darien was full of drugs, sex, and depravity. Actually, drugs had never been the real problem. The real problem was alcohol. Kids would swipe it from their parents' liquor closets, bring it to school parties, drink it in cars or even on the school bus."

Growing up in Darien was, for someone like Becky Thompson, a somewhat confusing experience. On the one hand, she was imbued at an early age with Darien's mystique of being one of the nicest places in the world to live—nicest, and most socially acceptable. "I was always convinced that the farther you got from New York on the New Haven Railroad, the better your address became," she says. "I was sure that we had it all over those New York suburbs down the line." She was also impressed with "the prettiness of the town," and the public school system. "I know the schools were superior to what you could find in other places," she says. "At Darien High, I was a slightly above average student. But when I spent my sophomore year with an aunt in Columbus, New Mexico—the only place in the United States to be invaded by a foreign power: Pancho Villa—I was at the top of my class."

Socially, however, it was another story. "There were cliques that started in grammar school, and that went right on through high school. They were cliques based on how much money your parents had, what kind of cars they drove, how big a house they lived in, whether they belonged to the Wee Burn Country Club and the Noroton Yacht Club, or Woodway, the poor man's club. The cliques were based on how well kids dressed, how much spending money they had, and what parties they were invited to. There was one section of maybe fifty Cape Cod development houses on Allen O'Neill Drive, cheap houses put up in the 1950s. Nobody associated with the Allen O'Neill bunch. There was also a tremendous amount of bigotry in the school—against Jews, but mostly against blacks. There was a handful of black kids, mostly the children of domestics, and nobody paid any attention to them; they were like invisible. There were a couple of Jews, but I was told that Jews had a hard time buying property in Darien. They had to go to Stamford or South Norwalk. Then there was the Tokeneke group, from the rich families on Tokeneke Road. They were a world unto themselves. By high school, most of the Tokeneke group went off to private boarding schools. The rest of us simply never saw them again. They disappeared."

Becky Thompson's parents were neither of the Tokeneke group nor of the Allen O'Neill bunch, but were somewhere in between. Miss Thompson grew up in a medium-sized house on a one-third-acre lot on Phillips Lane, modest by Darien's standards. Her father, now retired, was a design engineer, who commuted daily to New York. Her parents were Democrats, which marked them as oddities in the predominantly Republican Darien community. "My father always felt a little out of place in Darien, I guess," she says. "Actually, he had an excellent job and earned a fine salary, but it didn't seem fine enough for Darien."

To be betwixt and between, neither rich nor poor, in a town like Darien is not easy. "I used to walk along Tokeneke Road and look at all the beautiful houses," Becky Thompson says. "The Lindberghs' big place, for example. It made our house on Phillips Lane seem awfully small and pitiful. When I got a summer job as a cashier at Stoler's store, it was because I wanted to earn some money, but at the same time I knew that it was the lower-class kids who did this sort of thing. I grew up feeling that I—and my parents—just didn't fit into Darien, that I couldn't compete with the best kids because they wore more expensive clothes. I felt inferior, and I'm sure I grew up thinking that we were a lot poorer than we really were. I suppose that's why, after college, I left. My impression is that the rich kids come back to Darien, get married and settle there, and join the Wee Burn Club. It's the kids like me who leave."

When Becky Thompson comes back to Darien these days to visit her parents she tries, in a sense, to forgive it and to see it in its prettiest light—the tree-lined streets, the scarcity of neon. On a recent visit, she found the town still talking heatedly about the new nursing home, which was the center of a bitter zoning battle (it was opposed by many, first, because it was a nursing home and, second, because of its height: a full three stories), and which was built despite the editorial opposition of the *Darien Review*, a conservative publication generally against all forms of change. She was pleased to discover a new Darien paper, the *News*: "livelier, *somewhat* less Republican, and filled with more than just bridal announcements and social notes." Her parents and their friends were also talking excitedly about a neighbor's house on Phillips Lane that recently sold for $101,000. Though the house has only three bedrooms and one and a half baths, such a price makes it begin to sound like a rich person's dwelling and has the Thompsons thinking that their own house may be a rather valuable piece of property. "When I go back now, Darien doesn't seem *quite* as pretentious a place as it used to seem," Becky Thompson says. "But it is a pretentious place."

"Pretentious" is not really the right word with which to assess a town such as Darien which longs to be taken as a quiet, pretty town where people can lead quiet, pleasant, safe, and almost unnoticed lives—unless, of course, a conscious effort to appear as unpretentious as possible is, in itself, pretentious. Darien is certainly not pretentious in the sense that Las Vegas or Beverly Hills is pretentious, with vaulting marble façades concealing an essential shabbiness and poverty of spirit. But if beauty is in the eye of the beholder, what is the nature of the eye that beholds? If Darien, Connecticut, could hold a mirror up to its residents, what would it see? A certain amount of playacting, perhaps—a conspicuous attempt to be inconspicuous. The rich have always ached (or claimed to ache) for privacy, for anonymity, for shelter; at the same time, they cannot bear to be unheeded or overlooked. This ambivalence—this uncertainty whether to flaunt or to hide—is possibly too subtle and complicated for an "outsider" to grasp.

105

12

The Lively Art of Commuting

*W*ealthy residents of the New York suburbs are often spared the ordeal of commuting. Edgar Bronfman, for example, the head of Seagram's, solves the problem of getting to the office by having his private helicopter pick him up on his lawn in Yorktown and whisk him over the treetops to Manhattan. John D. Rockefeller III simply spends a good deal of time at home in Tarrytown, where he operates a two-hundred-acre farm. But for most suburbanites, commuting is simply a daily fact of life which, as they say, goes with the territory.

Because of New York City's size, its commuters probably travel greater distances—and spend more time and money traveling— than do those of any other city, with the possible exception of Los Angeles, which is another story. It takes a New York businessman anywhere from half an hour to an hour and a half to get to or from a good suburban address, and it costs him anywhere from seventy-five to a hundred and fifty dollars a month to do so. Obviously, a New York commuter has special problems which require special solutions.

The word "commute" has several meanings other than to travel with a commutation ticket. To commute also means to exchange or convert, to substitute one form of obligation for another, or to revoke a penalty and impose another that is slightly less severe—the death penalty commuted to life imprisonment, for example. In the case of the New York commuter, at one time or another all these definitions apply. Few New Yorkers would go so far as to say that they enjoy commuting. But most would agree that commuting is a price worth paying, a punishment less harsh than city living. Furthermore, just as a well-run prison must have regulations, so must well-organized commuting operate according to certain rules. Seasoned New York commuters know the rules by heart and seldom give them any thought, abiding by them automatically. To newcomers to the New York commuting scene, the rules at first seem mysterious and baffling.

First of all, in addition to not smoking in the "No Smoking" car, the conscientious commuter knows that talking is unwelcome almost anywhere in the train. On an airplane, it is perfectly acceptable to speak to your seatmate, but on a commuter train it is a breach of etiquette. The reason is simple. On a plane, you will probably never see your fellow passenger again after you deboard. On the 7:58 out of Larchmont, your fellow passenger may be your neighbor, whom you have seen and will see far too often. Most commuters, while commuting, are loners. From the window seats, they will gaze resolutely at the passing countryside. On the aisle, they will bury themselves in newspapers. If a commuter recognizes a friend or neighbor coming down the aisle, he will do his best not to show it. The same rule applies while he is standing on the station platform waiting for the morning train. A newcomer to Greenwich commuting says: "At first I couldn't understand it—how coldly people acted on the platform in the morning. I'd met a fellow at a party one night and had a great conversation with him. The next morning, I saw him at the station and went over to say hello. He just gave me a little nod and turned the other way. I thought: What the hell is this? But now I see that commuting is just a different scene." It is different because, as a more experienced commuter puts it: "If you strike up a conversation on the platform, the chances are you'll still be talking when the train comes in. That means you'll have to get on the train together, and *that* means you'll have to sit together. Next thing you know, you've got a regular commuting buddy who'll be sitting next to you every morning of your life. Of course, there are some commuting buddies who always sit together, who've been sitting together for years, but they're the exceptions."

On trains that are usually less than filled to capacity, it is acceptable to put an overcoat or newspaper on the empty seat beside you, to compose your face in a generally stern and unfriendly expression, and hope that no one will stop to ask, "Is this seat taken?" If

107

someone does stop and ask the question, of course, commuter etiquette requires that you relinquish the empty seat. On crowded trains, meanwhile, it has never been necessary for a gentleman to give up his seat for a lady—even an elderly or a pregnant one—unless she happens to be a neighbor or a close friend. After all, the argument runs, the man has spent his day hard at work at an office. The woman has probably come from her hairdresser or a matinee.

Commuting, most long-time New York commuters have discovered, is a kind of art, involving techniques and skills that must be learned as one would master any other craft. It is not, for example, a good idea to look too cheerful, either while waiting for the train or riding on it, out of respect for other commuters who may well be depressed. One develops, as one commuter puts it, an all-purpose expression: "a kind of loose half-frown, a vaguely dissatisfied grimace." To avoid attracting unwelcome attention or acquiring unwanted companionship, the commuter learns to stand on the suburban station platform in a way that makes him look somehow smaller and in a sense nonvisible, the shoulders hunched under the topcoat collar. A newcomer to a New York suburban town must earn the right to display any form of personal idiosyncrasy. Before he can alter his clothing from what is considered the standard, center-vent New York business norm—can appear at the station wearing a beret, for example, or flared trousers, or a too-loud tie—the new commuter must establish his place in the social pecking order. Only then—and then only gradually—can he dress to conform to his individual style. The business commuter who is not only a newcomer but who also seemingly "doesn't care" about his appearance will be quickly noticed and regarded as a pariah, and this could go against him when he wants to join the country club later on. To make enemies among one's fellow commuters is, as one man says, unnecessary. Mr. Harry Ireland, a Manhattan advertising executive who for years commuted to New York from Rye, discovered to his horror one morning as he waited at the station that he had inadvertently put on a left shoe of one color and a right shoe of another. He hurried home to change, missed his train, and was late getting to the office, but at least no one noticed his apparent "eccentricity."

Every commuter quickly develops his own routine by which he makes use of, or copes with, his commuting hours. In addition to the window gazers and newspaper readers, there are the briefcase workers. It is never permissible to speak to a briefcase worker during the journey except, possibly, at the very end, when a "Well,

108

here we are" will suffice. This is true even if the briefcase worker should happen to be a neighbor or a close friend, and it is to avoid such conversations that neighbors and close friends are always careful not to sit beside each other on commuter trains. Even those seated across the aisle from, or behind, a briefcase worker are expected to refrain from speaking. And if you have *been* talking to a briefcase worker, the moment he reaches for his briefcase it is the signal for the conversation to terminate. Most briefcase workers, however, open their briefcases immediately upon boarding the train.

The nap-taking commuters compose another group whose privacy is obviously not to be violated. To be sure, many nap-takers do not really nap, just as many briefcase workers will admit that they are not really working. Pretending to sleep is just another defense against the possibility of intrusion. On most commuter trains, there is also a bridge-playing group, which usually confines itself to a particular car, or to one end of a particular car. The train conductor carefully arranges double banks of seats face to face on whichever train he has learned to expect bridge players. He will also provide tables of sorts—squares of pasteboard to rest on players' knees—and playing cards, and he expects to be tipped for this service. In the bridge groups, conversation is restricted to bidding. Each bridge foursome usually has its regular, and favorite, group of seats which it considers "reserved," and therefore privileged—even sacred. The unwary, or green, commuter who sits in one of these special seats will be informed that it is special, and will be asked to move elsewhere.

Individual commuters also "reserve" seats for themselves on their regular trains going to and from the New York suburbs. A man may perpetually choose, say, the third window seat from the door on the shady side in the second car from the front of the train. This becomes, over the years, "his" seat, and his fellow commuters, who become aware of his preference, respect it. Not long ago, on the 8:18 from Rye, a long-time commuter boarded the train, to discover that his regular seat was occupied. He demanded that the occupant remove himself. The occupant, politely pointing out that there were many vacant seats in the car, demurred. What followed was a terrible scene in which the two well-dressed gentlemen hurled insults at each other until finally the conductor was called to settle the matter. Wringing his hands, he pleaded with the interloper, saying, "I know there are other seats, but Mr. Caldwell has been

109

taking this train for years and this has *always* been his seat!" Commuting patterns, when interrupted, can have effects that are downright traumatizing.

The commuting crowd changes, meanwhile, as the day progresses. On the earliest trains are the bright, eager young junior executives, clear-eyed and efficient, who will be at their downtown desks at the crack of nine or even earlier. The early trains fairly throb with youthful determination and ambition and high seriousness of purpose. The later trains convey an older, more secure and leisured mood and group of passengers. These are men who have successfully scaled the corporate and professional ladder and have found a comfortable place near the top. They are no longer in a hurry, and if they are not at their desks or in their board rooms by ten o'clock, the desks and board rooms will wait for them. But look carefully at the faces in this group, and some will seem less serene than others. This is because some of these men in the late-morning crowd are actually out of work and are headed into Manhattan for interviews. They will spend the afternoon, perhaps, in a movie theater. On Wednesdays, the late-morning crowd is special: ladies heading for early luncheons in town, followed by matinees. Then, in the late afternoon, still another group commutes from the suburbs: black domestics going home to Harlem.

The evening bar car is, of course, a world of its own—beloved by the regulars, shunned by others. Crowded and noisy, with miniature drinks served in plastic glasses at two dollars apiece, the bar car is the only car on the commuters' train where social intercourse is encouraged, or even tolerated. Commuters jostle each other for a spot at the bar, shouting orders; friendships are struck up here, but there are also, as in any bar, heated arguments and, on more than one occasion, fistfights. The bar car is a kind of rowdy prelude to the suburban cocktail hour, which in some cases begins in the suburban railroad station, where wives wait for husbands with glasses, flasks, and buckets of ice. The "driving home drink"—or the d. h. d., as it is affectionately called in suburbia—can be hazardous. Several years ago, a Rye housewife was killed when her car went out of control pulling out of the station parking lot; she had been turning the wheel while, at the same time, trying to hand her husband a martini.

For years, the most elegant way to commute to and from suburbia was in the private club cars—the most stylish, and the most mysterious. The club cars' membership policies were secret and their rules were unwritten. Formidable black porters guarded their entrances and exits and only members were admitted. Window shades were drawn closed for privacy, and the club cars were coupled to the end of their trains so that members—who paid as much as one thousand dollars for the privilege—could sit in comfortable parlor-car chairs undisturbed by ordinary commuters. There were two exclusive club cars on the Penn Central's New Haven line: the Rye-Greenwich car and the Southport car. On the western side of the county there was the Mount Kisco car. Memberships in these private-car associations carried great cachet, and were often passed down from fathers to sons.

In 1976, however, Connecticut's Governor Ella Grasso decreed that what amounted to restricted clubs had no place traveling on rails designed for public transportation, and the club cars were put back into ordinary service. Rye, Greenwich, and Southport members are still up in arms about Mrs. Grasso's action, and are fighting to get their club cars back—so far without success.

But at least one suburban club car remains: on the Erie-Lackawanna Railroad's line from Gladstone, New Jersey, to the Hoboken, New Jersey, pier, which carries passengers from the moneyed Somerset County suburbs of Bernardsville and Summit. For more than a hundred years, the 8:18 morning train out of Gladstone, which returns at 6:10 at night, has been known as the "Millionaires' Express," and its private club car has remained a bastion of upper-class exclusivity. Only members, their wives, and a limited number of guests—for a fee—may enter the Gladstone Car. The curious are turned away at the door by James Moore, who has been the car's porter since 1955. Though the car's exterior windows are as dirty and soot-stained as those of all the other cars, it is widely assumed that, behind the drawn green shades, the interior is luxurious. Actually, a guest on the Gladstone Car would be disappointed, for its furnishings are decidedly Spartan. The present car dates from about 1908, when it was an ordinary open-vestibule coach pulled by camelback engines, and its fittings date from roughly the same era. Two rows of white-painted wicker veranda chairs face each other down the length of the car, and Mr. Harry Young of Gladstone recalls seeing the same chairs, or their counterparts, when he was a trainman on the line in 1916. Foam-rubber cushions were added several years ago, and in 1975, the cushions were re-covered in a tweedy material when the Erie-Lackawanna raised the club car's rental. "Unnecessary," sniffs Mr. Seymour Hall of Oldwick, New

Jersey, the Club Car Committee chairman, who, like other members, reacts unfavorably to change.

The car's lighting is provided by a double row of incandescent ceiling bulbs shielded by fluted glass shades of the Art Deco era, and Harry Young remembers when these were gaslights. Brown-flecked carpeting and teak-paneled walls with small inlaid designs add meager touches of luxury. One luxurious detail—though some might consider it a necessity since the car's windows will not open—is air conditioning, though it is air conditioning of a 1935 variety. On hot days, before the car departs, two men slide three-hundred-pound cakes of ice into bunkers underneath the car. Water runs over the ice and into pipes, and a fan above the ceiling blows air over the pipes and into the car through ducts. This archaic system works fine, James Moore says, "as long as the ice is clean." Dirty ice causes the pipes to clog, and then the entire system must be flushed. The ice now costs twenty dollars a cake, and on the hottest days, as many as a dozen cakes may be required. These costs and others may one day spell the doom of the Gladstone Car. In fact, when the Erie-Lackawanna goes completely into diesel operation, which is expected to happen by 1979 or 1980, it is assumed that the club car will be declared obsolete. Meanwhile, the only significant renovation occurred as long ago as 1956, when the old restroom commodes were replaced with flush toilets.

Ordinary commuters on the line would also doubtless be surprised to learn that liquor is not and has never been served in the club car. In the morning, after each member is seated with his *Wall Street Journal* or *New York Times,* Mr. Moore comes through the car with glasses of ice water. On the evening run, he may heat up the water for tea, warm some soup, or serve soft drinks and cookies, for which members reimburse him at the end of each month. Mr. Moore is the members' custodian, guardian—and alarm clock, gently rousing sleeping commuters when the train comes to their stop. During the day, when the car stands locked and empty on a siding in Hoboken, there is plenty to do, Moore insists: polishing glasses and emptying ashtrays, doing personal errands or shopping for members, and endlessly repairing the ancient wicker chairs with tape, nails, and baling wire from his toolbox. Mr. Moore, one of the last of a breed, says he has been with the railroad longer than anyone in Hoboken.

The Gladstone Car is both exclusive and sexist. It is divided into

112

two sections: one for men, who may smoke, and one for women, who may not smoke. The women, mostly widows of members, accept this rule, which dates back to the turn of the century, when, of course, it was unladylike to smoke. Today, there are seventy-six members of the Gladstone Car, most of them from the Somerset Hills area, and nearly all of whom knew each other before joining the club. There is a waiting list, and prospective members are requested to supply two letters of recommendation from members. Dues in the club presently run two hundred dollars a year, plus the cost of first-class Pullman passage. Still, no more than thirty riders use the car on a regular basis, meaning it is nearly always less than half full. The decline, according to committee chairman Hall, is attributable to the fact that people are transacting more business away from New York, that former members are moving away or retiring, and that the economic crunch has been responsible for several dropouts. But, men like Mr. Hall are devoted to their club car. "It's comfortable, it's private, there's room to move around, and you're always guaranteed a seat," he says.

The atmosphere in the Gladstone Car, however, is not particularly clubby. As in ordinary commuter cars, conversation is discouraged, and with so many empty seats, members tend to sit apart from one another. Members nod briefly to one another as they enter and seat themselves, and then they retreat into their newspapers or briefcases. There is no camaraderie, no laughter. After all, commuting, which can consume as much as ten hours of a man's week—more than a full business day—is not a joking matter. It is a serious business. It is something that a man must do if he is to enjoy the suburbs. It is the price one has to pay, and one pays it as one pays one's monthly bills, grimly, with efficiency, and with strict adherence to the rules of Free Enterprise in a Capitalist Society. Commuting is a business.

Several years ago, a man who had been standing on the station platform in Scarsdale, New York, waiting for his morning train, suddenly collapsed of a heart attack and died. The stationmaster summoned a police ambulance. The ambulance arrived, and the man's body was covered with a gray blanket, lifted onto a hospital stretcher, carried into the ambulance, and driven away. Some three hundred commuters stood on the Scarsdale platform while all this was going on. No one looked in the dead man's direction. No one commented on the man's identity. No one, in fact, lifted his eyes from his newspaper, or changed his expression from that "loose half-frown." Occurrences such as this, the expressions seemed to say, are certainly unfortunate, even disruptive of a set routine, but commuting must go on regardless.

13

Three Ryes

*I*n Rye, New York, on a balmy June night, the students of Rye High School were presenting Rodgers and Hammerstein's *The Sound of Music.* The auditorium was filled with proud and expectant friends and parents. The boys and girls had worked hard on their material, and had rehearsed for many weeks. So had the stage and lighting crew, and the musicians. The members of the football team had been convinced that it was *not* effeminate to serve as male dancers and chorus boys. A white girl had been persuaded to accept a black youth as a dancing partner, though not without difficulty. She seemed to feel that she had been singled out for an unpleasant task, and that the assignment carried with it a certain loss of social status. Still, as she danced she smiled bravely.

The sentimental and familiar music and lyrics ("Climb ev'ry mountain . . . ford ev'ry stream . . .") contained no surprises, the voices for the most part were thin and untrained, and the performances were decidedly amateurish. And yet the youth and good looks and innocent enthusiasm of the performers on the stage—the pink-cheeked boys, and the girls with their clean, swinging hair—managed effortlessly to create the illusion that one was seeing and hearing something wonderfully fresh and new. It was as though the musical had finally, and quite accidentally, found the perfect cast and company to perform it. By the time the curtain fell on the first-act finale, the audience was moved to tears and the houselights came up with such a golden rush that it was possible to be suffused

115

with a feeling of awe and faith in the promises and prospects of today's young people.

During the intermission, however, excited whispers brought news of an episode that had taken place during the performance, and within fifty feet of the auditorium. A thirteen-year-old girl, taking advantage of her parents' absence at the play, had pinched a bottle of vodka from their liquor closet, drunk most of it, and then passed out in the grass. A group of high school boys, who had also been drinking, had taken this opportunity to unbutton her shirt and pull down her jeans and panties. They had not raped her, exactly. They had "fiddled" with her, and finally, tiring of this, they had run off and left her, unconscious and half naked, lying under a bush. There a cruising policeman had spotted her and transported her to a hospital where she was being treated for alcohol poisoning and was having her stomach pumped out.

Immediately, the girl's distraught parents left the auditorium for the hospital (which was able to release her the following day). The news had an unsettling effect on the rest of the audience as it lingered in the lobby waiting for the bell to signal the beginning of the second act. Most of them knew the girl and her parents. Her parents were not quite of Rye's elite, but ranked socially somewhere between the elite and the middle class. They were, as they say, people who were *known*. Their daughter, meanwhile, also had achieved a certain reputation. She had already been involved in one or two minor scrapes, and it was rumored that she had experimented with drugs—LSD and marijuana, at least. The group she hung out with was generally considered to consist of the town's troublemakers.

During the second half of the play, despite the energy of the young performers, the audience was subdued. At the final curtain, they clapped politely but perfunctorily, then hurried home to their own children.

Many people find the two-sided nature of suburban life disconcerting. On the one hand, there are comfort and space and ease and money. In Rye, as in other well-to-do Westchester County communities, it is commonplace for parents of children too young to drive to open charge accounts with one of the two taxi companies in order that the children can go to and from school, and visit their friends, without mothers and fathers having to act as chauffeurs. No one stops to ask whether this might be "spoiling" the children; it is simply a matter of practical convenience. But in Rye, as in other

116

such towns, there are also parents who simply cannot afford such luxuries.

"Rye is a town of people waiting to move on to Greenwich," is one statement frequently made here, but this is not entirely true. Rye has many families who are quite content with Rye, and have no ambitions to achieve a grander Connecticut address. Rye money is quiet, conservative, a little inbred. Out on Milton Point, it lives in large, well-tended houses overlooking Long Island Sound, and the possessors of this subdued wealth are bankers, insurance company executives, lawyers, stockbrokers, a sprinkling of advertising executives. Lesser money lives prettily, on smaller lots, in Indian Village (so named because the streets there have Indian names), or in Loudon Woods. These might be called the New Guard as opposed to the Old, and the gap between the Old Guard and the New is almost unspannable. Nowhere was the division more apparent than when, strolling together toward the 5:23 out of Grand Central, Mrs. Ralph Manny (Old Guard) and a neighbor (New Guard) chatted pleasantly until Mrs. Manny reached the door of the (now discontinued) Rye-Greenwich private club car. There, with a polite handshake, they parted, and Mrs. Manny entered the private car. Her friend moved on to one of the cars used by the general commuting public, where no reserved seat or Pullman porter waited. The same division was apparent on the night of the performance of *The Sound of Music*—the good kids (of "good" families) singing and dancing wholesomely on the stage, and the "bad kids" on the street outside: the longhairs, the pot smokers, and the girl found in the shrubbery with the empty vodka bottle.

In a real sense, Mrs. Manny represents the values of the Rye Old Guard. A sedate, pleasant-faced, white-haired lady, she moves with an air of polite self-assurance, never obviously condescending, everywhere in the town. The Mannys are listed in the New York *Social Register,* and are members of the American Yacht Club, the New York Yacht Club, the Colony Club, and the Huguenot Society. Elizabeth Manny is also a member of the Daughters of the Cincinnati. Several years ago, she helped found a local charitable organization called the Twigs. The Twigs started as a small ladies' sewing circle, and now has expanded to the point where there are a great many Twig groups (the idea being that each is a twig of the central branch). The Twigs toil chiefly for the United Hospital in Port Chester. One must be invited to join the Twigs. When it was pointed out not long ago that there were hardly any Jewish women in the

Twigs, it was pleasantly suggested that the Jewish ladies might like to form their own little Twig, and perhaps call it something else, like Tendril or Rootlet. The suggestion did not meet with enthusiasm. Mr. and Mrs. Manny are unusual, furthermore, in that they own their own club—the Shenerock Shore Club, a private beach club on the Sound.

Like many old-line Westchesterites, Mrs. Manny is distressed by the "Bronxification" of Westchester, the steady collapse of what was once rolling farm country, then became a leisured land of summer estates, and is now just another New York suburb with "a Jewish tinge," with high-rises, shopping centers, fast-food outlets, and motels. She is proud of the fact that the stretch of the Boston Post Road which runs through Rye is, with Darien's, one of the two remaining sections of the highway that have not become completely commercialized. And yet, at the same time, there have been incursions of industry into Rye—an Avon Products distribution center, for example. A hotel chain has built the huge new Rye Town Hilton—though "Rye Town" is technically Port Chester. (If you hear someone say he is from "the Town of Rye," you know he is trying to make his address sound better than it is; real Rye is the *City* of Rye.) Mrs. Manny deplores what she calls "the eleven little houses" that went up across the street from her tennis court when a large property was broken up—"little houses" which nonetheless sell in the $70,000 to $120,000 range. But, in the next breath, she glances at the still intact estate that lies behind her house and remarks: "When that place is broken up it will be a nice little piece of change for somebody." As is the case everywhere in America, the Old Guard is torn between a reluctance to see things change and the "nice little piece of change."

The people, meanwhile, who live in the "eleven little houses" and in hundreds of others like them are, of course, the newcomers—fresh from the city or perhaps, upwardly mobile, from a less fashionable suburb closer to New York. Their wives have not yet been asked to join one of the Twigs. They have not yet been invited to join the Apawamis Club, the Yacht Club, or the Manursing Island Club—the elite summer beach club—and have had, perhaps, to content themselves with membership in the Shenerock Shore Club. (Oddly, though the Mannys own it, they have never attempted to make it stylish and appear to regard it as mostly a business investment.) These people compose, as it were, a second Rye.

There is also a third Rye, in an area near the center of town loosely referred to as Grapple Street. Grapple is a street of run-down houses where a number of black families—many of them domestics—live interspersed with some low-income Italians. Neither of the other two Ryes pays too much attention to "the Grapple Street gang," as they are called, beyond assuming that the Grapple Street gang are troublemakers and that it is dangerous to go there at night.

A fourth group in a community like Rye might be said to consist of the small fraternity of local merchants and retailers who supply goods and services to the wealthy commuter community beyond and who serve an economic—but hardly a social—need. In Rye, this group would include bookish Mr. Goddard Light, the proprietor of the Lighthouse Book Store, and Mrs. Mary Seymour, whose Seymour Electric Company sells everything from light bulbs to small appliances. Both are popular tradespeople. Both are pros-perous, intelligent, educated, and well-traveled. Mrs. Seymour, for example, winters regularly in Florida. But socially, an enormous gap exists between the Rye merchants and their patrons. Mrs. Seymour's customers call her "Mary"; she addresses a customer as "Mrs. Smith." Perhaps because she knows too much about her customers' bill-paying habits, she would never be invited to join one of the important country clubs or be asked into a Twig. Possibly for this reason, most Rye business people prefer not to live in Rye.

The Rye public schools, meanwhile, have frequently been ac-cused of being elitist—of extending their major teaching efforts to the sons and daughters of the country-club set, who are probably college-bound, and of ignoring the others, the Grapple Street gang in particular. (In casting *The Sound of Music*, the lead parts seemed to go to the children of "nice Rye families," while the single black was in the chorus line.) Rye educators defend this on the basis of maintaining high scholastic standards, and boast that Rye High School prepares youngsters for college as well as any New England prep school.

Rye Country Day School is elitist by design. As a private school, operating within walking distance of the public high school, it is another local symbol of the gulf that exists between the wealthy and the less well off in the community. There is almost no social inter-mingling between the students of Rye Country Day and the public school students. In the old days, when Rye Country Day girls wore uniforms and the boys wore RCDS blazers, the division was more

119

noticeable and more bitter; there was marked animosity between the "rich snobs" at Country Day and the "poor slobs" at the public schools. Today, students of the two systems simply ignore each other. For many years, Rye Country Day offered education only in the primary grades, one through eight. After that, Country Day graduates generally departed for private boarding schools in New England. Several years ago, however, the then headmaster of Country Day, Gerald LaGrange, instituted a program to extend the school to the secondary level, turning it into a full-scale college preparatory school. This put Rye Country Day into direct competition with such redoubtable schools as Exeter and Andover in terms of preparing youngsters for Ivy League colleges. And this also meant that in order to attract students of Ivy League caliber, Rye Country Day had to look outside Rye. The school began recruiting students from all over Westchester and Fairfield counties.

Today, students at Rye Country Day arrive by bus from as far away as Stamford and Tarrytown, and many of the Thunderbirds in the parking lot bear out-of-town and out-of-state license plates. Rye parents, including William Rockefeller, note sadly that Rye Country Day is no longer "indigenous to Rye." This situation separates, isolates more dramatically than before, the Rye Country Day youngsters from the rest of the town.

An even sharper distinction, socially, exists between the members of Rye's country clubs and residents who have not been asked, or cannot afford, to join. Rye's is a country club society. If one is not a member of one of the three fashionable clubs—the Apawamis, the American Yacht, and the Manursing Island (and many families belong to all three)—one is very much out of things. Everything of importance—including the children's dancing classes and the summer day camps—is either club-sponsored or club-connected. For young people who are not members of the clubs, there is almost literally nothing to do. There is a public beach, but it is frequently closed because of pollution. There is an amusement park, but its admission, its parking fee, and its rides are expensive. There is no museum, no concert hall, no bowling alley, and no movie theater. The various churches have attempted programs for young people, but because church-connected endeavors inevitably become sectarian, they have not been outstandingly popular. Most teen-age mischief—the teen-agers say—results from sheer boredom.

Several years ago, concerned about youthful drinking, vandalism, and so forth, the City of Rye asked the Rye High School

120

pupils to draw up a list of things they would like the city to provide. A student committee was formed, and a list was diligently drawn up. Some of the requests were patently impractical (free marijuana provided by the city). Others (free public tennis courts) were sensible, but would have been expensive to provide. One (an area of city land set aside for drag racing) sounded both reasonable and cheap. At least one was pathetic: a suggestion that the public library be kept open for a few hours on Sundays so that young people, in school throughout the week, would have more time to use it. The city fathers took the students' requests under advisement. Nothing was done.

Of course, people of Mrs. Manny's generation and social position find it hard to understand why so many of Rye's young people are restless and getting into trouble these days. Her own two daughters grew up successfully in Rye and were never found in drunken stupors under hedges, nor has anything remotely like that happened to those of her grandchildren who are growing up in Rye right now. She can remember stories of how, years ago, the young sons of two of Rye's oldest and proudest families—they were young Roger Sherman and his friend Stuyvesant Wainwright, Jr.—used to go out at night and rip up the trolley tracks that were being laid along Peck Avenue. But that wasn't considered vandalism. That was just larking, and besides, it was done with a good deal of old-fashioned patriotic Rye spirit. "Everyone" was objecting to the trolley line's being placed in such proximity to the old Apawamis golf course.

Old Guard Rye tends to blame the winds that have ruffled Rye's once peaceful waters on "all these new people"—that second world that has moved in and built eleven little houses where one huge one used to stand. As for the little girl with the vodka bottle, that episode, though shocking at the time, has pretty much vanished from people's memories. More pressing concerns have taken its place, such as the recurring threat that an immense new highway bridge will be built between Oyster Bay, Long Island, and Rye, which, if it comes, will certainly alter Rye's pretty shoreline and carry off, in its wake, a number of fine old houses. As one woman says of what happened that long-ago night during *The Sound of Music,* (and the woman is *not* Mrs. Manny, though Mrs. Manny might agree with her): "That family wasn't a real Rye family. They were new people who came here from somewhere else. Before coming to Rye, they'd lived, I think . . . in an apartment, if I'm not mistaken."

121

14

The Grandeur That Was

*I*t is likely that the American suburbs achieved the status
for which they were intended sometime during the first decade of
the twentieth century, long before the present era of suburban sprawl.
In the early 1900s, no one of consequence actually *lived* in the suburbs.
They summered there, or spent weekends there. The suburbs were
essentially composed of second homes for the American rich.

From Detroit, the wealthy families who lived along Jefferson
Avenue went out on private trolley cars to Grosse Pointe for
weekends and holidays. It was considered a major trip. From Cleveland, families looked forward to a few carefree weeks away from
home in faraway Shaker Heights. From San Francisco, trunks were
packed regularly for train rides to "the Peninsula," which was still
synonymous with "the country"; and from Philadelphia, society
journeyed westward to the resort hotels which the Pennsylvania
Railroad had built along what it called the "Main Line of Internal
Improvements of the State of Pennsylvania."

The fashionable New York suburbs—in Westchester and Fairfield counties, on the North Shore of Long Island, and in northern
New Jersey—were similarly, in those days, resort communities,
devoted purely to leisure. The popular way to get to Westchester
from New York, for example, was by steam-driven yacht. Clearly,
times have changed. But it is important to remember that though
today some Westchesterites may speak of others as "nouveau," in
those days everyone was nouveau.

Before the Civil War, Westchester County was simply farmland. In fact, before the railroads began opening up the grain fields of the Plains states and the West, Westchester County was the East's granary, and its primary crops were wheat, oats, and corn. Then came the Civil War, and the great economic boom that followed it. This was the period—the 1870s and 1880s—when most American fortunes of any size or fame were made. Suddenly the rich of the burgeoning cities demanded second, country homes, and following the lead of the English gentry, it seemed necessary that these take the form of castles and manor houses, often complete with moats and private chapels.

Just why the new New York rich singled out Westchester County and the North Shore of Long Island for their castle-building has never been clear. Westchester, for example, is not, in many people's eyes, a place of singular scenic beauty. It has no mountains, nor is it rich in significant hills which command sweeping views. Its beaches are inferior, and there are no lakes of any impressive size. It has been argued that the best suburbs of most cities lie to the east of their parent towns, the theory being that commuters prefer to drive to work in the morning, and return at night, without having to face the rising or the descending sun. But Westchester is more to the north of New York than to the east, and besides, in the early 1900s, no one "commuted" to Westchester anyway. The most logical explanation is that as the railroads' proliferation encouraged the development of agriculture in the Middle West and West, the farmers of Westchester County languished and declined, and it was possible for the rich to buy up large tracts of property cheaply.

In any case, during the twenty years that followed the Civil War, Westchester County became castle poor. "The average size of a Westchester estate," it was reported in the 1880s, "is sixty-five rooms, not including servants' quarters. For staff, fourteen rooms are generally required." By the 1890s, the rich being the competitive lot they are, sixty-five rooms seemed scarcely adequate and architectural excesses became commonplace. In Tarrytown, for instance, General Howard Carroll built Carrollcliff on top of one of Westchester's few bona-fide hills. From it, on a clear day, General Carroll could view both the Hudson River and the Palisades beyond, plus a bit of the Manhattan skyline. (Today, Carrollcliff, which houses the offices of an investment banking company, has an unimpeded view of the Cross Westchester Expressway.) Carrollcliff was a line-by-line replica of a Rhine castle, and its baronial dining hall had a table that could seat eighty, which it often did, with a liveried footman behind every other chair. Several years ago, one of Carrollcliff's linen tablecloths found its way to a local hospital, where it was cut up to provide sheets and pillowcases for twenty beds. An American flag flew from the top mast of Carrollcliff's tallest tower. Its stars were the size of manhole covers and it weighed, when folded, forty pounds. Meanwhile, nearby, John D. Rockefeller was building Pocantico Hills, with a private police force, fire department, and post office. The bill for household servants there ran to thirty thousand dollars a year—in an era when a good maid could be got for two dollars a week.

The castle-builders of Westchester did their best to harness nature and to bring the landscape to its knees, creating grottoes and vistas and artificial lakes, streams, and waterfalls. Not all these attempts were successful. When Benjamin Holliday built Ophir Farm in Purchase (which later became the summer home of publisher Whitelaw Reid), he wanted, as he put it, to surround his house with "a private prairie." On his seven hundred and fifty acres Mr. Holliday placed a large herd of elk and an even larger herd of buffalo. But the elk jumped his fences and the buffalo broke them down, and the neighbors, understandably, complained. A similar neighbor problem presented itself to the first owner of Belvedere in Tarrytown, which later became the home of liquor magnate Samuel Bronfman. When a vast underground sprinkler system to water the lawns of Belvedere was turned on, it reduced the water pressure of the entire surrounding area to zero. A compromise was reached, and the owner of Belvedere agreed not to turn on his sprinklers during morning hours when gentlemen on neighboring estates might be shaving.

Hard by Belvedere, Jay Gould built Lyndhurst, a huge replica of a French château surrounded by seven hundred acres of lawns, gardens, greenhouses, stables, and other outbuildings. On Gould's death, the estate passed to his daughter Helen, who was by then Mrs. Finlay Shepard, and who continued to maintain the place on a lavish scale. Mrs. Shepard not only added a colonnaded swimming pool, but hired her own private lifeguard as well. Lyndhurst became the headquarters for what Mrs. Shepard called her "pet charities," which included a "crusade against Mormonism" and an attempt to halt Mohammedanism by having hundreds of thousands of Holy Bibles printed and distributed throughout the Middle East. As far as her household was concerned, on the other hand, rigid economy was the watchword. Her four children—all of whom she had adopted at once when she was in her late forties—received only fifty cents spending money apiece per month. Of this, five cents a week was to go into the Sunday school collection plate, and another five cents was for the church collection. This left each child with exactly a dime a month to do with as he pleased.

When Mrs. Shepard died, without having stamped out either the Mormons or the Mohammedans, Lyndhurst passed to a second Gould daughter, Anna, who had married, first, Count Paul Ernest Boniface de Castellane, and, second, "Boni" de Castellane's first cousin the Duc de Talleyrand-Perigord. The Duchesse de Talleyrand was, if anything, more eccentric than her sister. As though Lyndhurst were not large enough, the duchesse began buying up parcels of adjoining property as they became available, so that eventually Lyndhurst consisted of dozens of houses. Once she had bought them, however, the Duchesse de Talleyrand seemed to lose interest, and left them, empty and unmaintained, to fall into ruin and disrepair, much to the displeasure of her neighbors. But when they tried to approach her on the subject, they inevitably found themselves stopped at the gate by armed guards. Letters to the duchesse went unanswered, the telephone calls were not returned. For several years, it was a matter of local speculation as to whether the mistress of Lyndhurst was really there, or whether she had actually died within the walls of her fortress. The servants, it was whispered, had stashed the duchesse's earthly remains in the walk-in refrigerator in order that their wages would continue to be paid by the banks and lawyers who handled such mundane matters. Then, at last, the duchesse officially died. For a while, it looked as though Lyndhurst would surely be broken up and the house would go under the wrecker's ball. But a foundation came forward to save the estate, and today it operates as a museum and can be visited by the public for a fee. It is almost unique in that it is one of the few of the Westchester mansions, built to last for untold generations, that still remains intact. The Lyndhurst Foundation adds to the revenues it needs to pay for the considerable expense of upkeep by renting the house to motion picture producers, who find it a useful setting for horror movies.

Dr. Charles Brace, who made millions in patent medicines in the days when there were no income taxes, was another who built a house "to last a thousand years," in nearby Irvington-on-Hudson. His daughter, Mrs. Harold Scott, who lived to be a very old lady, used to like to reminisce about the great house and the way things were in that long-ago perfumed age. "Oh, those were days like none that will ever come again," she used to say. "The house was built of Westchester granite that was quarried right on the property. Father was so proud of that house—it's gone now, of course. At Father's house, dinner was at seven. And that meant not two minutes *after* seven, but *seven*. If you were early, you waited outside the door until the clockstroke. The gentlemen wore white tie, and the ladies long gowns. The ladies took their wraps to the downstairs cloakroom, and the gentlemen took theirs upstairs. In the gentlemen's cloakroom, white envelopes were arranged on a silver tray, with a gentleman's name on each envelope. Inside was a card with a lady's name on it—the lady he was to take in to dinner. That way, you see, a lady never knew which gentleman would escort her, which made it exciting, and the gentlemen were careful not to spend too much time during cocktails with the ladies they were escorting. When the ladies and gentlemen gathered downstairs, there were cocktails, but none of this "What'll you have to drink?' business. Father liked a Jack Rose cocktail, and so that was what was served. The butler came in with the tray—one Jack Rose for each guest. He was followed by the parlormaid with a tray of canapés—one apiece. No one would dream of asking for a second canapé, much less a second drink!

"In fifteen minutes, dinner was announced. No one would think, either, of carrying an unfinished cocktail to the dinner table. There was always sherry with the soup. At the table were printed menus and place cards; the menus outlined the courses through the appetizer, soup, meat, salad, cheese and fruit, dessert, and coffee, with, perhaps, a sherbet course somewhere in the middle to clean the palate. Dinner lasted for at *least* two hours. Really, I don't know how we managed to eat so much! It was a day of gracious living, and when you look at the way people do things now! Cocktail parties! Father would have died of horror if he'd seen a cocktail shaker in the drawing room. It was a kitchen implement."

It was an era so accustomed to entertaining on the classic, grand scale that hostesses were unfazed by situations which, today, would unhinge the average society woman. There were, for example, two prominent Brown families in western Westchester—the Franklin Q. Browns and the Walston H. Browns. One evening, the Frank A. Vanderlips (he was president of the National City Bank) got their Browns mixed. Instead of arriving at the Walston Brown's, where they were expected, they appeared at the door of the Franklin Q. Browns, who were having a quiet evening at home. Mrs. Franklin Q. Brown, however, sensing that something of the sort had happened, rose to the occasion magnificently. Murmuring to the Vanderlips that she was delighted to see them, and that dinner would be *en famille,* she then had a quick word with her kitchen staff. Within fifteen minutes, both couples were seated at a place-carded table for a six-course dinner with four wines. The Walston Browns, of course, spent the evening wondering what in the world had happened to the Vanderlips, while the Franklin Browns assumed that they had invited the Vanderlips and forgotten to put it on their calendar.

A great feature of this turn-of-the-century social life was the Afternoon Drive down Broadway in Tarrytown, a ritual that had been copied from similar promenades in such resorts as Newport and Saratoga. The Afternoon Drive was taken with huge seriousness and ceremony, and to appear on the drive was a mark of social status. Virtually all Westchester society turned out in full fig for these drives in good weather, sitting stiffly and erect in coaches-and-four. The horses wore silver harnesses and were driven by blue-coated coachmen with silver buckles, buttons, and brocade, high silk hats with black or red cockades, white gloves, white trousers, and patent-leather boots with blue or pink tops, everything polished to a gleam. On these splendidly important drives, Vanderbilts and Fields and Goelets, Schwabs and Rockefellers and Archbolds and Whitehouses, smiled distantly and bowed politely at one another, as gentlemen tipped tall silk hats at the ladies. Mr. John Archbold, who, like Mr. Rockefeller, was "in petroleum," was one of the more imposing figures, boasting not only one coachman but a second "on the seat," whose job was merely to help the Archbolds in and out of the carriage. Mrs. Jennie Prince Black, who wrote a chatty book about Westchester in those days, recalled seeing Alexander Hamilton II daily during the Afternoon Drive. "He always sat along in the rear of his barouche, a small figure wrapped in a gray plaid shawl. . . . He never seemed to notice anyone or to change his expression of solitary boredom." Mrs. Black also commented on the presence of "an interesting visitor"—Winston Churchill, "the novelist."

Two spinsters, the wealthy Wendel sisters, Miss Ella and Miss Rebecca, kept a large summer place in Tarrytown, which they shared with their aging bachelor brother, J. G. Wendel. The Misses

127

Wendel always dressed alike, in patched and tattered black dresses whose fallen hems trailed in the dust, and in matching black sailor hats which were secured to the ladies' heads with wide elastic bands beneath their chins. Though the Wendel sisters were not twins, it was difficult to distinguish Ella from Rebecca, and adding to the problem was the fact that they often spoke in unison. Despite their odd appearance and behavior, the Wendels were from a fine old New York family, listed in the earliest edition of the *Social Register* as well as in its predecessor, the *Elite Directory*. As an indication of their social prominence, they were allowed—long after New York City had passed an ordinance banning the keeping of large livestock in Manhattan—to keep their cow, Bossie, in the rear garden of their town house at 442 Fifth Avenue. In Westchester, each sister drove her own team of horses, with a groom seated at her side. At the same time, they were notoriously thrifty. Once, when a friend who had not seen them for some time asked of their whereabouts, the sisters chorused, "Why, we've been busy mending the saddle blankets for the past six weeks!"

When, eventually, their horses died, the sisters refused to replace them. Nor, long after other forms of transportation had become more fashionable and convenient, would they travel any other way; wherever they went, they went on foot. Nor was any other kind of traffic permitted to enter their estate. A visitor to the Wendels' estate who arrived by automobile was obliged to leave it at the gate and negotiate the long gravel drive on shank's mare, as the ladies did. One day a grounds keeper noticed Miss Ella Wendel walking up her drive carrying her little dog Tobey and in an attitude of some distress. When the grounds keeper asked her what was wrong, she explained that Tobey had got a piece of gravel wedged in his paw. The grounds keeper removed the bit of gravel from the troubled paw and remarked, in passing, that if the Wendels would have their drive paved with concrete, similar mishaps could be avoided in the future. "Excellent idea!" cried Miss Ella. She immediately telephoned a contractor, and within a few weeks, the drive was paved. When the contractor presented Miss Ella with the bill—for twenty thousand dollars—she opened her shabby purse and promptly paid him, in cash. Several years later, Tobey—a mongrel no more prepossessing in his appearance than his mistresses—achieved national celebrity as "the world's most expensively maintained dog." It seemed that the Union Club had offered the Wendel sisters five million dollars for their Manhattan dwelling in order to build a clubhouse. The Wendels turned the offer down. It was not, they said, that they minded selling the house; they could not bear to give up the backyard garden. It was needed as a run for Tobey and, of course, for the cow.

Those few men who, for business reasons, needed to commute from Westchester to New York on a more or less regular basis did so, needless to say, in a grand manner. The late Mrs. H. Stuart Green (a Browning, whose family founded Browning Fifth Avenue stores, formerly Browning-King) used to reminisce about the days when her father commuted to the city on his hundred-foot steam yacht, the *Gracemere,* named after the family's Tarrytown estate. "Father and a few of his friends would gather at the pier in the morning," Mrs. Green would recall. "They would go aboard the *Gracemere,* where breakfast was served and the morning newspapers were waiting for them. Then they'd cruise down the Hudson to New York. It was slow, but it was wonderfully leisurely and relaxing—such a pleasant way to go to business." After her father's death, Adelaide Browning Green kept the Tarrytown estate (though not the yacht), or at least as much of it as she could. Gradually, the surrounding grounds diminished through the steady attrition of real estate development and offers too lucrative to refuse. Eventually, she and her husband moved from "the big house" to "the little house"—not really little, though it had been intended as a guest cottage.

Sitting on her terrace overlooking Tarrytown—with the new high-rise apartment houses, the fast-food outlets, the smoke of industry that has moved there, and the hum of traffic on the new Tappan Zee Bridge, which connects Westchester with the interstate that leads to Albany "and God knows where else"—Mrs. Green liked to recall that long ago, more naïve, almost forgotten time. "It was wonderful," she would say. "It really was an escape to come up here, a beautiful dream. This was where it all started, you know, in this Hudson River Valley. There was nothing"—with a disparaging wave of her hand toward Rye and the other eastern suburban towns along the Sound—"over *there.* Tarrytown was *Tarrytown,* and Ardsley was *Ardsley.* These were towns that *meant* something. The Ardsley Club was founded here—in 1896, just eight years after golf was first introduced in this country; one of the very first golf clubs in America. And the founding board of governors of that club— John D. Rockefeller, J. Pierpont Morgan, Cornelius Vanderbilt,

Chauncey Depew. There were giants in the land in those days, believe me. What's more, they were *gentlemen,* and their wives were *ladies.* People were kind to one another in those days. I sit here and wonder where it went, and when it began to go. I try to tell my grandchildren about it, and they can't believe it ever was. Sometimes *I* wonder if it ever was. Perhaps"—a wistful look would come into her eyes—"it was simply all too beautiful to be true."

15

Nil Admirari

"They never give you anything to *eat* in Boston. Here, we serve marvelous dinners—terrapin fins in sherry sauce, wonderful lobsters, smoked salmon flown in from Scotland, crown roasts of pork, that sort of thing. In Boston, you're lucky if you get a cup of clear soup and a bit of tired fish. The food—that's the main difference between Boston and the Main Line." This was a Philadelphia woman describing what she felt sets the Main Line apart from Boston. Philadelphia inevitably compares itself with Boston—never, perhaps self-consciously, with the city in whose shadow Philadelphia lies: New York. Possibly this is because Philadelphians, like Bostonians, consider themselves an older, better-grounded aristocracy ("New York is all pretty much come and go, isn't it?" asks the same Philadelphia lady), with a strong continuity of traditions, breeding, and manners. Philadelphia and Boston, along with such cities as Charleston, Savannah, and Cincinnati, are known to their citizens as America's Heirloom Cities. The fine things are not only there; they have *always* been there and, the assumption is, they always will be. In these cities, doing the Right Thing is natural because it has been bred in for generations. But in Philadelphia, Philadelphians feel, the Right Thing is more natural and more firmly bred in than anywhere else—particularly when it comes to food.

The Philadelphia Main Line is often accused of having so narrow a view that it takes in only itself. Indeed, this sometimes seems to be the case. Several years ago, the late Miss Anna Ingersoll ("When a Biddle gets drunk he thinks he's an Ingersoll," is the local joke) was eager to discuss with a friend a new novel that had appeared that year, called *The Philadelphian*. "What did you think of it?" she wanted to know as she sat in her granite mansion in Penllyn. The friend hesitated, and then said that he found parts of the tale difficult to believe. "The opening, for instance," he said, "where the Philadelphia society girl marries a proper Philadelphia boy. They go to the Bellevue-Stratford to spend their wedding night, and there the girl discovers that her husband is impotent. She becomes hysterical and rushes out of the hotel and down Broad Street into the night. Then who does she meet but an Irish construction worker who had flirted with her in the past. She goes with him into an empty construction shack that just happens to be handy, they make love, and, from this encounter, she gives birth to the hero of the book. Her husband, meanwhile, has also run out of the hotel, into his fast sports car, and gets himself killed in an auto crash. I found all this a little hard to credit."

"Absolutely!" cried Miss Ingersoll. "Nobody would spend their wedding night at the Bellevue-Stratford!"

The Philadelphia Main Line has often been cited by architects and city planners as one of the most beautiful of American suburbs. Of course, the physical beauty would not be apparent to the casual motorist driving westward along Lancaster Avenue between Overbrook and Paoli, the Main Line's technical limits. On Lancaster Avenue, the Main Line's main artery, the developers have laid a particularly heavy hand, and the street is awash in neon, which advertises the motels, silver-domed diners, gasoline stations, and automobile showrooms that are interspersed with prison-like highrise apartment houses and morticians' studios. But beyond all this—and not very far beyond—lies a particularly gentle countryside of hills, twisting streams, waterfalls, and meadows, with roads winding narrowly under tall trees, past moss-covered rocks, fern-choked creek beds, sudden ponds afloat with ducks, and houses of brick and local stone gracefully designed to accommodate, and not quarrel with, the landscape. There is no doubt that much of the Philadelphia Main Line is pleasing to the eye.

And yet, ironically, and unlike Westchester County, the Main Line was not "discovered" by the rich of Philadelphia. The rich, in fact, were virtually forced to settle there. The Main Line, among fashionable American suburbs, may be unique in that it was coerced into fashionability. Also, for all Philadelphia's claims of continuity and age, the Main Line is a relatively new suburban area, barely a hundred years old. The area was conceived, designed, and developed in the 1870s and '80s by the Pennsylvania Railroad as a hard-nosed real estate venture. The railroad was not interested in aesthetics. It was interested in making money. When it began pushing its tracks westward along its "main line," it was naturally eager to develop passenger and freight business along the way. To encourage this, the railroad built a chain of large and reasonably glossy resort hotels along the route, just as Henry Morrison Flagler was to do, a few years later, with his Florida East Coast Railroad, creating such places as Daytona Beach, Palm Beach, and Miami. The Pennsylvania Railroad then, in its advertising and promotion, declared that these hotels were fashionable. They weren't. Philadelphia is a city that is slow to change its ways. At the time, Philadelphia society, by tradition, lived in either Society Hill or Chestnut Hill, both well within the city limits. Philadelphia snubbed the Main Line, and stayed put, summering, as it always had, in Northeast Harbor, Maine. The resort hotel business seemed doomed to failure. Then the railroad decided to use a little muscle. Applying the kind of pressure that only a large corporation can, it urged its top executives to build expensive homes along the Main Line in order to give the area some cachet and chic. The railroad had become a great social force in Philadelphia, and many wealthy Philadelphia families—whose money came from other endeavors—held large blocks of railroad stock. The railroad applied pressure on its shareholders, too, until the message was clear: Build on the Main Line and help tone things up. And so, reluctantly, almost begrudgingly, the rich of Philadelphia began packing up and moving to the Main Line, which, at the time, seemed terribly far from the Philadelphia Club and the Cotillion.

It was not long, of course, before the Main Line towns, as in other suburban areas, arranged themselves in a well-defined pattern of social stratification, with some addresses better than others. Bryn Mawr, Villanova, and Haverford became the three most fashionable places, in that order. Gladwyne, however, can, according to one Philadelphia woman, "be either-or." There is a great—some say the greatest—amount of wealth concentrated in Gladwyne. But Gladwyne, as some people point out, "is a little bit Jewish." On the Main Line, Radnor is considered "very nice" ("Very nice is another way of saying filthy rich," says one Main Line resident), and so is

Wynnewood, where the Walter H. Annenbergs have their large spread, which makes Wynnewood a little bit Jewish too. Bala-Cynwyd is to Philadelphia what Palo Alto is to San Francisco and what Stamford is to New York—sort of fashionable, but not really all that fashionable. Much of Bala-Cynwyd has become an extended shopping center. Poor Narberth, meanwhile, is at the bottom of the social pecking order. "Narberth just never *did* have any style," says one woman. Penn Valley, on the other hand, is regarded as "a very nice young community," but Penn Valley has a heavy cross to bear. It must use "Narberth" as a postal address. Wynnewood was dealt a similar blow by the Postal Service a while back when it was announced that mail could no longer be addressed to Wynnewood but had to be designated "Philadelphia, Pennsylvania, 19151." The town of Devon, many people feel, would not make a particularly good address if it were not for the famous Devon Horse Show which takes place there every year, and draws the fashionable from all over.

Wayne is a problem. It is considered "not a good social address," but the people in Wayne would live nowhere else. Wayne people stress the "friendliness" of Wayne, and call it "the friendliest town on the Main Line." To be sure, a great many Wayne families tend to see a lot of one another and tend not to mingle with non-Wayne folk. "It's a nice, *family* sort of place," says another Wayne resident. And a movie exhibitor who operates a number of theaters in the area says: "It's very strange. A Walt Disney movie—and I mean a *terrible* Walt Disney movie—that laid an egg all over town will break box office records in Wayne." Perhaps this is because the big, comfortable old houses in Wayne appeal to young couples with small children. Or perhaps it is because, as the rest of the Main Line says, "Wayne is just hopelessly square."

"Old Maids Never Wed And Have Babies, Period," is the phrase one is supposed to commit to memory in order to know the sequence of the stops on the Main Line's Paoli Local out of Thirtieth Street Station: Overbrook, Merion, Narberth, Wynnewood, Ardmore, Haverford, Bryn Mawr—with "Period" standing for Paoli, at the end of the line. Between Bryn Mawr and Paoli, the phrase is somewhat more outrageous: "Really Vicious Retrievers Snap Willingly, Snarl Dangerously. Beagles Don't," for which the acrostic is Rosemont, Villanova, Radnor, St. Davids, Wayne, Strafford, Devon, Berwyn, Daylesford.* There is some justification for

*In Westchester County, one can keep track of the station stops by memorizing: "When the pie was opened, the birds began to cry, 'Larchmont, Mamaroneck, Harrison, and Rye.'"

the preponderance of Welsh, or Welsh-sounding, names on the Main Line: a small group of Welsh Quakers farmed the area before the Pennsylvania Railroad moved in. But most of the communities—Narberth, Radnor, Wynnewood, Bala-Cynwyd, Berwyn, and so on—were given their Welsh names rather spuriously by the railroad, which thought that this made the area sound quaint and Old World and therefore chic. Since then, private builders, developers, city planners, estate owners, restaurateurs, and shopkeepers have added to the Welshification process with names of their own devising—either lifted arbitrarily from the map of Wales or invented and made to *sound* Welsh—until today almost everything on the Main Line that does not appear to commemorate a member of the Continental Congress has a name that is Welsh-like.

But though the Main Line may have been created by artifice and public relations, it has now become extremely serious and solid. And for all its diversity and contradictions, there is a uniformity of feeling on the Main Line, a consistency of tone. Also, though some American suburbs have almost managed to insulate themselves completely from their parent cities—as, say, Grosse Pointe, Michigan, appears to have fully seceded from Detroit—the Main Line towns are always conscious that they are a part, and an important part, of that historic good gray entity that is the City of Brotherly Love and the Cradle of Liberty. There are attitudes and aspects of the Main Line that seem indigenous not only to it but to Philadelphia as well. "The most astonishing thing to me about the place," says one woman, "is how many people move here from other parts of the country, and begin acting exactly like 'old' Main Liners. They begin to dress Main Line and talk Main Line and think Main Line." This, of course, is due to the towering influence of the Old Guard of Philadelphia society—the Ingersolls, the Biddles, the Robertses, the Morrises, the Wisters, and so on—upon the rest of the populace, and to the tremendous respect in which the Old Guard is held. One New York man whose Main Line friends are newcomers to the area said not long ago: "There's a funny Main Line practice, have you noticed? The minute you arrive, they pile you into their car and take you on a tour of the best neighborhoods, pointing out all the houses of all the rich people they don't know." Old Guard Main Line society is, of course, quite aware that its style and behavior are being studied. This gives the Old Guard a sense of purpose, duty, and responsibility. It *must* set the tone and point the way.

"My God!" said one young woman the other day. "My daughter's started talking with that Main Line accent. She's picked it up at school. She's even started using Main Line words, like 'yummy' and 'super.'"As for the accent, Mrs. Hugh Best of Wayne calls it "Philadelphia paralysis," or "Main Line lockjaw," pointing out that it is not unlike "Massachusetts malocclusion." Mrs. Best, who was raised in Southern California, recalls that when she first moved to the Main Line, a native said to her: "My dear, you have the most beautiful speaking voice. I can understand every word you say!" And another parent swears that in her daughter's elocution class at the Shipley School the children were taught to speak correctly by clamping a pencil tightly between their jaws and then saying what they had to say.

Some observers have noticed a slight improvement in Main Line *couture* in recent years, and give the credit to such New York stores as Bonwit Teller and Lord & Taylor, which have opened Main Line branches. But the rule is still "Nothing flashy, nothing low-cut" when it comes to women's clothes, and the Main Line uniform still relies heavily on the conservative services of Nan Duskin and Peck & Peck, with perhaps, for the adventurous, a touch of New York's Bermuda Shop. For spring: print cotton blouse by McMullen, cotton skirt; for summer, print cotton blouse by McMullen with a gold circle pin on the collar; for fall, cardigan sweater, pearls, tweed skirt; for winter, good black suit, pearls, mink jacket, and perhaps a little hat for lunch at the Barclay.

"Most of us have gotten a little better," says one woman, "but there are, I'll admit, a lot of women here who think it's all right to go to a dinner party dressed for golf." As for men, the Philadelphia banking and law community have always set the style, which is Brooks Brothers' best. "In dress, we're very English here," says one man. "A lot of men have their suits made in London and—well— you know how kind of funny English tailoring fits." Philadelphia lawyers and bankers are also respectably a little out of press, and since they set the tone, other Philadelphia men follow their example. One man, who is particular about his clothes (and buys them in foreign places like New York and Beverly Hills) and is partial to Gucci loafers, admits that he is teased and kidded by his business associates for "trying to dress fancy, like a New Yorker."

But even more distinctive than the Main Line speech and dress is the Main Line manner, which is often unsettlingly aloof and distant. Some attribute this to a certain shyness and a faint feeling that, *au fond,* Philadelphia is a somewhat second-rate city for which one must in the long run apologize. Others insist that it is just the opposite: snobbishness, and an intractable sense of superiority. One out-of-town houseguest who was taken to a series of Main Line parties recently complained that, while the food was indeed good—and perhaps better than that in Boston—he was never introduced to anybody. "Well," said his Philadelphia host, "the feeling here is that if you have to be introduced to people, you shouldn't have been invited—if you didn't know everybody already, you wouldn't have been there."

"How very *calm* all these people seem," said one young woman who was visiting the Main Line. Whether she intended this as praise, or whether she found Main Line calmness faintly off-putting, is hard to say, but since she was from New York, one suspects the latter. New Yorkers enjoy their rapid, competitive pace. A Philadelphian compares Philadelphia with New York this way: "In New York, everybody is so busy making money. In Philadelphia, we *have* made money." Others point out that in New York men rarely get drunk at parties; they're too busy doing business. In Philadelphia, on the other hand, men get drunk at parties rather a lot. Some even say that there is a palpable difference between the way commuter trains leave Grand Central Station for Westchester County and the way the Paoli Local leaves for Bryn Mawr. The New York trains start off with a jolt and a seat-shaking rattle, followed by a lurch, while all the lights flash off and on. The Philadelphia trains, they say, *glide* out of the station.

A curious negativism also floats in the Main Line air. "Oh, I don't think so," is apt to be the reaction to almost any suggestion. There is a tendency to run everything down a bit—other people, other cities, other parts of the Main Line itself. You may be invited to a club or restaurant where, you will be warned in advance, the food isn't very good—hardly edible, in fact. If you ask whether there isn't perhaps a better place, you will be told that yes, there is, but it is always so crowded that no one can ever get a table. You may be invited for a weekend on the Main Line but, your hostess will explain beforehand, you won't have a very good time; you'll probably be bored stiff; there's nothing to do. "It isn't like Beverly Hills, you know." Main Liners spend a great deal of time emphasizing what the Main Line *isn't*. "It isn't like New York . . . it isn't like Chicago . . . it isn't like Washington . . . it isn't like Wilmington. Wilmington is nothing except Du Ponts."

The Main Liner usually turns out to be against most things— most developments, that is, or anything new. He is against high-rise apartments, against public housing, against day-care centers, against busing, against newcomers—so contagiously that even new-comers who have moved into high-rise apartments quickly become against other high-rises and other newcomers. The Main Liner is strongly Republican, but when he talks politics, he is more anti-Democrat than anything else. When he talks about what is wrong in Philadelphia, it is in terms of what is even more wrong with New York.

But an even more pronounced characteristic of the Main Liner is his imperturbability. His composure is complete and nothing as-tonishes him or ruffles him. The Main Liner is proudest of his poise—of how, even in the most awkward moments, he can rise to the occasion grandly and with perfect aplomb. There are, for in-stance, an unusual number of Main Line stories—most of them surely apocryphal—of how well-placed Main Line ladies have dealt with underpants crises. If all the stories are true, something like Legionnaires' Disease must have affected the elastic in local panties, because panties seem to have descended with alarming frequency here, and always in important places: while standing in a receiving line at the Assembly, while walking down the aisle of Old St. David's Church (Episcopal) in Radnor, or while leaving the restau-rant at the Barclay. One story has the lady in question merely stooping to collect the fallen garment and putting it quietly in her purse while continuing to shake hands. Another has the debutante picking up the panties and handing them to her escort without comment. Another has her merely stepping out of the collapsed lingerie and signaling to a waiter to carry it away. All these under-pants stories are recited with a chuckle but also with respect for the lady in question's cool self-possession in a situation which would have reduced lesser mortals to crimson-faced embarrassment.

This *nil admirari* attitude often means that the Main Liner dis-covers something that he is very much against long after it is too late to do anything about it. It is characteristic of the Main Line that the huge shopping center in Wynnewood which contained, among other things, a large new branch of Wanamaker's was completed and open for business before a local group was organzied to oppose its construction. One woman, who resents the prevailing apathy to the continuing spoliation of the local landscape, says: "I swear that these old Main Line people don't even *see* what's going on around them. They think it's beneath their dignity to even notice such matters. One morning they'll wake up and see that it's happened—

that there just isn't any Main Line anymore. They live in their gilded ghettos, and if something ugly is going on next door, they simply draw their curtains, like ostriches burying their heads in the sand."

The late Mrs. Katherine MacMullan, a social secretary and party-planner who, for years, ruled the social seas of Philadelphia from a modest flat in the Rittenhouse Tower, once said: "The old money here just hasn't *stood up against* the new money the way it should have done." This is an interesting principle. Old money, in other words, should resist the invasion of new money—the kind of money that builds, and lives in, high-rises—as a principle of aristocratic rule. It is the incursion of "new money" into the Main Line, and the Old Guard's failure to fight back, that has brought down many of the old barriers of class versus mass. There ought to have been a law.

Other unwritten Philadelphia laws have fallen by the wayside. It used to be a law that you should "Never speak to a new neighbor until you have seen her wash hung out on the line. That way you can decide whether she is someone you want to know." Still another was: "Never speak to fellow passengers on shipboard until you are four days out." And another was: "It takes at least three generations before a family can be accepted here." Now people say: "Look at the Liddon Pennocks: they're new, but they're accepted everywhere. And what's more, he's a florist—he's in trade." It used to be that no Jews or blacks were welcome on the Main Line. But today, the Walter Annenbergs, who generously support the arts and who give splendid entertainments, are pretty much accepted everywhere, even though Mr. Annenberg's father spent a certain amount of time in a federal penitentiary. As one woman puts it: "Anyone who is worth ten million dollars or more ceases to be Jewish." The same rule may eventually apply to wealthy blacks, but meanwhile any number of well-to-do black families have moved to the Main Line without incident.

Society here, as elsewhere, has been for years involved in the business of creating enduring *families*—families bound by blood and common interest—and in building with these families an enduring community of wealth. But a camel has staggered into the tent: the newcomers. They cannot be overlooked. ("I'm really very anxious to meet some of these new people," said—anxiously—a mother of a debutante daughter, "but of course I want to meet *attractive* new people.") At the same time, the Main Line was several years ago

139

presented with a shocking statistic: roughly 30 percent of its young people, according to a study made at Villanova University, are moving out of the Main Line and to other parts of the United States. There are deserters in Main Line society's ranks. Actually, the percentage of deserters is not statistically larger here than in any other prosperous American suburb, but that does not console the Main Line, which always supposed that it deserved *special* statistics. It is a bitter pill to be told that what is happening everywhere is now happening here, on the Main Line: the young are flying from their golden nests.

But the inner, Old Guard Main Line is not all that alarmed by what the future holds. As Mrs. John Wintersteen—*very* Old Guard, whose collection of Picassos alone would make her a millionairess—put it not long ago: "In one form or another, there will *always* be a Main Line." And there are young people from her circle of friends who would seem to back her up. Not quite ten years ago, a nineteen-year-old youth named Alan McIlvain, Jr., was asked to write an essay which outlined his life's goals. McIlvain is an heir to a fortune which the J. Gibson McIlvain Company, one of the largest wholesale lumber companies on the East Coast and one of the oldest family-owned businesses in America, has been building for him and other McIlvains for nearly one hundred eighty years.

Young McIlvain's essay demonstrated that the Old Main Line Values were still alive and springing in at least some breasts. "I plan to enter the business in the tradition of my forefathers," he wrote. He went on to list his favorite pastimes, which included all the proper sports of a proper Main Line gentleman: hunting, fishing, skin diving, soccer, tennis, squash, and swimming, "in their designated seasons." (No football or baseball, mind you.) He also allowed that he was properly interested in young ladies in *their* designated seasons. He displayed a correct aloofness toward politics and politicians: "Though I enjoy trying to analyze political strategy, I would never seriously consider entering politics." Looking again, he said: "Besides just inheriting the business, I want to improve and utilize it to its benefit. I hope to exploit [*sic*] new fields, and exercise the knowledge I will have spent so many years receiving. I would also like to have a happy social life by marrying and settling down in the Main Line."

That was in 1968. And that is precisely how, and where, he has settled today.

140

16

Summer Camps

A suburbanite is probably lucky if he has a second home to go to in the summer, a "summer camp." A certain distaste for one's regular surroundings is maybe a healthy thing. A second home is a handy vent for anger and impatience: It's good to get away, good to get back, as the cliché goes. Only a few Cincinnatians go away for the summer; they're too content where they are. No one to speak of in Hudson goes away in summer. New Yorkers, on the other hand, who distrust their city as much as they adore it, could not tolerate the summer without the Hamptons, Connecticut, or the Jersey shore. Boston suburbanites troop off to the Cape, or to Edgartown, Chilmark, and West Chop on Martha's Vineyard. Main Line families gather at Northeast Harbor, Maine. Certain resorts, in other words, become suburbs of the suburbs.

Watch Hill, Rhode Island, is one of these suburban suburbs, and it is also, by conicidence, a suburb of the neighboring town of Westerly. Mr. and Mrs. Paul Myers, furthermore, are an exception to the rule—a Cincinnati couple who own a large house in suburban Hyde Park, with a swimming pool and extensive gardens, and yet summer regularly at this pocket-size resort. The Myerses' two teenage children, in fact, represent the fifth generation of Mrs. Myers's family who have summered at Watch Hill.

When Suzie Myers, an attractive woman in her forties who keeps a year-round tan, was a girl, only one event, as far as she remembers, disrupted the tranquillity of the otherwise long, sunny, and breeze-swept summer days. It occurred at the height of the Great Hurricane of 1938, when Mrs. Myers's Grandmother Anderson was visiting her friend Mrs. Shinkle and the ladies were having their customary afternoon of bridge. Presently Grandmother Anderson, consulting her watch, remarked that it was several minutes past the time she had instructed her chauffeur, Walter, to pick her up and take her home. While the storm raged on, and Walter still failed to appear, Mrs. Anderson became increasingly annoyed. There was a dinner party to dress for, and so forth. When Walter finally appeared, drenching wet and close to hysteria, he explained that not only the car but the entire garage containing it had been swept into the sea. "Nevertheless, Walter," Mrs. Anderson said crisply, "you must learn to be more punctual."

Watch Hill is that sort of place. Nothing much has disturbed its peace or ruffled its composure since the 1880s, when wealthy businessmen from Hartford, New York, and the Middle West began coming to Watch Hill for duck-shooting, and presently began building large, shingled summer homes for their families on this tiny promontory of land overlooking the ocean. (Watch Hill is the highest point of Atlantic coastline, they say, between North Carolina and Maine, and from it on a clear day there is a view of three states: Connecticut to the west, Fishers Island, New York, to the south, and of course Rhode Island.) Since then, little has changed.

The old-line Yankee names of the town fathers—names like Nash, Crandall, Vose, and Brewer—are still there, leading the year-round business community. So are the old-line moneyed-society names of the summer colony: the John S. Burkes (ex-B. Altman and Company), the Hunter S. Marstons (American Home Products), the Whitney Addingtons (Sears, Roebuck), the Hugh Chisolms, the Jack Heminways, the George Y. Wheelers, the Britton Browns, the Reginald Fullertons, the George Lauders, and Mrs. George M. Laughlin (Jones & Laughlin Steel). These are, as the Yankees say, "the swells," who still live in the big, drafty, unheated houses their grandfathers or great-grandfathers built, houses with cavernous basement kitchens and dining rooms served by dumbwaiters. Not long ago, "some real estate people named Murphy" built a modern house, but as Watch Hill says, "We don't know them." Other than that, Watch Hill, as a summer colony, has remained a pocket of Victoriana on the New England shore.

There are, all told, only 213 summer families in Watch Hill, and they are carefully divided into three categories. Not long ago, at one of the long procession of parties that dot the Watch Hill season, identification badges were passed out, designating which of the three sorts each person was. The most prestigious declared: "I Am Watch Hill," indicating that the wearer was *at least* a second-generation Watch Hill-ite. A second badge read: "I Married Watch Hill," for people who had made their way into the tight little enclave by the marriage route—as Paul Myers did when he married Suzie. A third badge read: "I Found Watch Hill"—for the newcomers. Though the badges were distributed as a party joke, they were intended to be taken with a certain amount of seriousness.

When one marries Watch Hill, and passes through its rigidly required initiation rites (joining the Misquamicut Club, giving and attending the usual number of parties and little dinners), one enters a rather special world. Sylvia Drulie discovered this when she married a prominent New York lawyer named John W. Mazzola. Before her marriage, Miss Drulie had an exciting career in Broadway theater and television, helping to mount shows with the likes of Robert Whitehead and Stephen Sondheim. When she married Mr. Mazzola, and Watch Hill, she settled happily into a summer life as comfortable and casual as a freshly washed Lacoste dress. But she brought along a few mementos from her glamorous theater days. Among her close professional friends in New York, for example, is choreographer Alvin Ailey, leading spirit of the American Dance Theater. Mrs. Mazzola had a number of photographs of herself, of which she was rather proud, dancing at parties in the arms of Mr. Ailey—who, of course, is black. And when Mrs. Mazzola started to hang some of her framed photographs on the walls of her Watch Hill house, her husband studied them for a while and then said, "Honey, I understand how you feel. But I'm afraid I really think—well, not *here*." The photographs were taken down.

Watch Hill's Victorian air is such that, at the Misquamicut Beach Club, one is not surprised to notice, as a silver-haired dowager rises from her luncheon table and disentangles herself from her chair, that under her dress she is wearing knee-length cotton bloomers. For this and other reasons, "Not here" was also the answer to the agelessly beautiful Rebekah Harkness, née Betty West, who for a number of years housed her Harkness Ballet troupe each summer in her huge Watch Hill mansion. Mrs. Harkness, the widow of millionaire William Hale Harkness, says: "Ballet started in palaces. Dancers deserve something equally good now. People in the arts function better if their surroundings are inspiring." But having what amounted to a hotel for dancers in the heart of their little principality was decidedly irksome for the rest of Watch Hill. Dancers, after all, are presumed to have unorthodox sexual tendencies, and there was much whispered talk of "orgies" *chez* Harkness. Besides, Rebekah Harkness once commented: "I don't really like rich people. They're bored—and boring." This did not sit well with the rest of Watch Hill, who, for the most part, are rather rich, and for years, Mrs. Harkness was Watch Hill's most celebrated social pariah. Finally, as a result of much social pressure from the neighbors, she put her Watch Hill house up for sale—first offering it, according to a wholly groundless rumor, to Rhode Island's Mafia, in an attempt at revenge. Perhaps to avoid any such outcome, the house was purchased by a syndicate of perennial and proper Watch Hill summer residents, and now—after a fire that did considerable damage—it is in the process of being extensively renovated and restored to its original elegance.

Watch Hill does have one real hotel—of sorts—in the handsome old Ocean House, dating back to 1906. But the top-floor rooms cannot be rented because the big frame building with its wide, rocker-filled verandas is considered too much of a firetrap. Fire has always been a threat to the community, and the tiny settlement was very nearly destroyed entirely in 1916, when a fire broke out in the old Watch Hill House hotel and started to spread to nearby houses. The flames were fortunately put out by a sudden downpour of rain, leaving residents with the firm belief that God somehow takes a special interest in Watch Hill—although the local water pressure remains today, as it has always been, too low. To this day, Watch Hill has no fire department. It has no school district. It has no sewers, hardly any sidewalks, only a handful of street lights. And it has no political voice in nearby Westerly, upon which Watch Hill must rely for all its services.

It has only one restaurant of any quality, the Olympia Tea Room—locally known as "The Greek's"—famous for bay scallops, lobster, high prices, and not having a bar. Why would anyone want to summer in a resort that has no fire department, no sewers, and one restaurant which has no bar? The answer is simply that Watch Hill has never had any of these things, and sees no reason why it ever should. What makes Watch Hill special, its residents feel, is that it has steadfastly refused to pretend that it is anything it isn't. It is, they say, a wonderful place for kids because there is absolutely no place for them to go, and no way they can get into trouble. Entertainment for Watch Hill youth is confined to planned activities at the club, and as a result, Watch Hill children tend to be every bit as proper as their parents.

What Watch Hill has also is a strong sense of continuity and family tradition. In Watch Hill, one is not permitted to speak of one's "family house" unless the house has been in the family for at least three generations. Watch Hill is proud of the fact that Misquamicut is the third-oldest golf club in the United States. "Downtown," at the end of Bay Street, Watch Hill's one shopping street, with its cluster of small, expensive shops, is a little merry-go-round said to be the oldest operating carrousel in America. For diversions, Watch Hill prefers cozy, family-oriented, old-timey things—like kite-flying contests, for example, with prizes awarded for "Distance" and "Endurance." There is an annual tug-of-war contest "for those over sixteen," and there are sand-castle-building contests, and contests for sand art, "using only what's found on the beach." There are clam-digging contests, with a prize going to the person who can dig up the biggest clam. Also, each year Watch Hill awards a prize to "The Most Harmonious Family."

In keeping with its prevailing mood, Watch Hill is perhaps proudest of its little Victorian chapel, with its natural wood interior and trussed ceiling, which has changed very little since its dedication in 1877. To be a member of the Watch Hill Chapel Society is a great honor. Near the altar of the chapel, above the organ pipes, mottoes in blue and gold read: ONE LORD—ONE FAITH, and THE CHURCH IS MANY—AS THE WAVES—BUT ONE AS THE SEA. In accordance with this, the chapel's eleven-o'clock service is Protestant (with Episcopal and Presbyterian clergymen presiding on roughly alternate Sundays), and two Roman Catholic masses are offered earlier on Sunday mornings. Since the chapel was dedicated to the performance of Christian rites, no rabbi has ever addressed a Watch Hill congregation. But this is no problem, since there are virtually no Jews in Watch Hill. When Watch Hill is labeled "restricted," however, residents take quick exception and point out that for many years Albert Einstein kept a summer home in Watch Hill and was treated fondly by the community. He loved to sail, but was a terrible sailor, and whenever he took his sailboat out, he regularly managed to run it up on the same rock, from which he regularly had to be rescued. Dr. Einstein, of course, was a famous physicist, and so may have been tolerated as a celebrated oddity.

Throughout the summer season, a series of visiting clergymen are invited to conduct the Protestant services at the Watch Hill Chapel, and these men are chosen for the social standing of their home parishes as much as for anything else. The late Reverend Arthur Lee Kinsolving, for example, retired rector of New York's elegant St. James's Episcopal Church—a man said to keep only two books on his desk: the Holy Bible and the New York *Social Register*—was a frequent visitor, and was scheduled to appear in the pulpit during the summer of 1977. When he died earlier in the year, a Watch Hill mourner at his memorial service in New York complained, "He had no right to do this without consulting us."

Other visiting clergymen are Reverend Ernest Gordon, chaplain of Princeton University, and Reverend Samuel Lindsay of the Royal Poinciana Chapel in Palm Beach. Not long ago, the visiting minister was Right Reverend John M. Krumm, D.D., bishop of the Diocese of Southern Ohio, who had such a fine time at the party tossed in his behalf the night before that he lost the notes for his Sunday sermon. He improvised, however, with a sermon titled "The Church of Your Choice." In his remarks, the bishop illustrated "choice" by pointing out that we all choose things. We choose husbands, wives, and so on. We are offered a wide choice of things to buy in television commercials. "We are urged to choose this make of car, this brand of toothpaste, this kind of mattress," said the bishop. At the word "mattress," there was an audible rustle in the congregation, and an outsider might have inferred from this that the bishop had used a dirty, or at least suggestive, word. After the service, the stir was explained when the bishop was approached by Mr. Claude Douthit, Jr. (a trustee and former president of the Chapel Society, and fourth-generation Watch Hill), who asked him, "I hope that remark about mattresses was not intended for me personally." Mr. Douthit's wife, the former Nancy Simmons, is an heiress to a mattress fortune.

Watch Hill takes its wealth casually, and even makes little jokes about it. When Paul Myers stated, in his wife's hearing, "I'd never marry a rich woman unless I really loved her," his wife said, "Why, darling, that's the sweetest thing you've ever said about me!"

Watch Hill is often spoken of in the same breath as nearby Newport, and nothing could annoy Watch Hill people more. Watch Hill, they point out, is simply *not* Newport, nor do the two summer colonies have anything at all in common—except, of course, wealth, and the fact that they exist in the same state.

"Watch Hill is *much* older than Newport," one Watch Hill woman says, and it is—a little. Newport reached its glittering heyday in the Gay Nineties and the Mauve Decade which followed, and when one thinks of Newport one thinks of liveried footmen, gold dinner services, old Mrs. Astor in her black wig and ropes of diamonds, pompous Ward McAllister and his lists, bitchy Mrs. Stuyvesant Fish, and effeminate Harry Lehr. Watch Hill never went in for any such nonsense, and regards Newport as a collection of gauche, pretentious, New York *arrivistes.* The gilded and marble palaces that are Newport's "cottages" bear no resemblance to the weathered, gabled, and shingled style of Watch Hill. It is almost bad form to mention Newport in Watch Hill, and most of the regular summer residents have never set foot in the place, though it is only a few miles away. Newport today is dismissed as "touristy," while the average tourist would find little to attract him to Watch Hill. There is only one road leading into town, and when there, the tourist would find himself in a cul-de-sac. "Watch Hill is to Newport what East Hampton is to Southampton," one member of the colony explains, meaning that Watch Hill's wealth is decidedly more old-shoe and unshowy. Unlike both Newport and Southampton women, Watch Hill party-goers do not show up in designer dresses and bedecked with jewels. In Newport and Southampton, divorces, lawsuits, alimony, and custody battles are the staples of dinner-party conversation. Watch Hill frowns on divorces, and prefers "harmonious" families. It disapproves of extramarital love affairs. By contrast, a Southampton woman says: "By the end of the summer, everybody's ready to go home. By then, all the feuds have broken out and all the love affairs have gone stale. There's nothing more to talk about."

(A summer resort that *is* close to Watch Hill in feeling is Northeast Harbor on Mount Desert Island, Maine, the suburb away from the suburbs that is most favored by Philadelphians. Rockefellers may hold sway over Seal Harbor, but Northeast, down the road, belongs to Philadelphia, and represents a coalition of Philadelphia's religious, educational, and social lives. For years, the rectors of Philadelphia's favorite schools, Groton and St. Paul's—Dr. Endicott Peabody and Dr. Samuel S. Drury—maintained summer homes there, along with most of the prominent Episcopal bishops of the East. When one marries Northeast Harbor, it is like marrying Watch Hill: it lasts. In 1899, for example, the late George Wharton Pepper spent the summer there with his fiancée and his

147

parents-in-law to be. "Thereafter," he wrote in his autobiography, "there have been only three summers in fifty-four years when we have failed to visit our beloved Mt. Desert." And when Mrs. J. Madison Taylor of Philadelphia died in 1952, it was noted in her obituary that she was preparing for her seventy-fifth consecutive summer at Northeast Harbor.)

Watch Hill has two rules, or Rules: Never try to outdress your hostess, and never try to flirt with her husband. As for dress, Watch Hill has one or two black-tie dinners per summer, but otherwise the evening garb for men is sports jackets and shirts with open collars, along with trousers by Lilly Pulitzer. (In Newport and in Southampton, it is possible to go to black-tie parties every night all summer long.) At the Misquamicut Club, the only daytime rule of dress is "No bare feet in the clubhouse," and this, the club's president points out, is more a matter of safety than of etiquette. As the late Mrs. John Heminway once remarked: "Here, it's so chic to be unchic that it's almost chi-chi."

This is not to say that Watch Hill isn't "social" in the party sense. Watch Hill loves its parties, and during the summer season, there is usually a party every night, and sometimes several. With all the parties to go to, there is a commensurate amount of drinking. A typical Watch Hill social day begins with pre-luncheon cocktails at the Beach Club, followed by lunch, followed by a nap in order to rest up for the pre-dinner cocktail parties and, later, the after-dinner drinking parties. Watch Hill has also established the tradition of the "dressing drink," or "d.d.," which is the drink you have while dressing for the cocktail party.

But otherwise Watch Hill contents itself with its tennis, its golf, its beaching and swimming, and its sailing. As in most resorts, a discernible social gulf exists between the golfers, who belong to Misquamicut, and the sailors, who belong to the Yacht Club. There is thus a "golfing group" and a "sailing group," and the two groups don't mix all that much. In between, there are always bits of insular gossip going around—such as the tale about the wedding of the daughter of a prominent member of the colony. The bride was visibly pregnant, and Peter Duchin, who was playing for the reception, led off the dancing with "Just in Time."

"Watch Hill is such a *relaxed* place," says one woman. "There's no *striving* here, no social climbing or competitiveness. There's never been such a thing as a 'social leader' here, nor does anybody want or aspire to be one—unless you want to think of us all as social leaders, each in his or her own way. There have never been any serious social feuds here, the way there always seem to be in Newport. If I'm not invited to a certain party, I don't feel I'm being slighted. After all, you can't ask everybody to every party. No one has to prove who he or she is, because we all know who we are, and many of our parents knew each other too. Of course, some people find it a little boring and inbred—after all, it *is* the same faces, pretty much, summer after summer. And some people, who want a more glamorous sort of thing, desert us for the Hamptons. But the rest of us wouldn't dream of spending summers anywhere else."

It is the relaxed air of unshakable imperturbability, they say, that has attracted so many nice people to Watch Hill. Even the transient guests at the Ocean House tend to be gently bred little old ladies who have been coming there for years and make no more noise than the clicking of knitting needles. It is Watch Hill's *niceness,* its sense of nineteenth-century gentility and *politesse,* that caused Mrs. Walbridge Taft (kin of the Ohio Tafts) to do what she did. When Mrs. Taft built a new garage next to her Watch Hill house, she became concerned that it blocked her neighbors' view of the bay. So she hired an artist, who painted a view of the bay on the side of her garage, complete with scudding clouds and a sailboat. Everyone loved Elizabeth Taft for that.

There are a few things that Watch Hill might like to see changed, but not many. Some people wish the resort had a good motel, since even the biggest homes overflow with houseguests. And a good restaurant that had a bar might be nice. Otherwise, most people would prefer to keep Watch Hill as it is for all time to come. But what of the youngest Watch Hill generation: will they want to carry on the long tradition, and continue to live a summer life out of another era? Apparently so. The Paul Myerses' two teenage children have been summering at Watch Hill with their parents for as long as they can remember, in the house, built in 1886, that has always been in the family and was handed down to Mrs. Myers from her great-grandfather William P. Anderson, the first president of the Misquamicut Club. The house stands on a large acreage of lawns and gardens overlooking a salt pond, a tall stand of beach grass, and the Atlantic Ocean. There is a guest cottage, and the pond teems with snapping turtles, which, like the Myerses, appear to have made this their home for generations and refuse to give it up. The main house, with its wide covered porches and its enormous basement kitchen, presided over by Goldie, the family cook,

149

has become one of the popular gathering places for Watch Hill youngsters, who sit around most evenings, talking and drinking a bit of beer and wine. "This house is a kind of magnet for kids!" says young Jamie Myers.

Mrs. Myers says: "Believe it or not, one of the things my kids talk about and argue about is which one of them is going to inherit the house. They couldn't care less about the house in Cincinnati. All they care about is Edgmere, and who's going to get it. I'm not altogether happy that they're already making plans for what's going to happen when I'm gathered to my Maker, but I suppose it's nice to know they feel that way about the house."

Just the other day, Suzie Myers relates, her daughter approached her and said, "Mom, isn't it true that this house usually goes to the *girl* in the family?"

WEST

17

"A Feeling of Separation"

*S*ingle women, it was agreed, should not move to Los Altos. Divorced and widowed women should move away as quickly as possible. The suburbs offer hostile territory to the unattached female. The occasion for these observations was what an earlier generation might have called a coffee klatsch—a morning gathering of five neighborhood women, the wives of a dentist, a drug company vice-president, a commercial artist, a United Airlines pilot, and a radiologist. But since the setting was California, the klatsch had a decidedly West Coast flair. Instead of coffee, the tanned and well-scrubbed ladies were sipping tall glasses of iced tea graced with sprigs of mint, in front of a garden table set out with watercress sandwiches, thin pralines, Monterey Jack cheese and biscuits, and strawberries the size of a child's fist. Of course there was a pool. "Everyone has a pool," said the drug vice-president's wife.

The "problem" of the single woman in Los Altos had come up because, it seemed, the single woman was the only serious problem that Los Altos faced. Los Altos is one of a string of pretty to prettier towns that dangle, like beads, along the old Camino Real as it winds down the San Francisco Peninsula—Burlingame, Hillsborough, Atherton, Redwood City, Menlo Park, Palo Alto, Mountain View, etc. Some of the towns—Burlingame and Hillsborough in particular—are quite grand, and politically quite conservative. Others, like Palo Alto with Stanford University at its heart, are considered more intellectual and liberal. Menlo Park is regarded as a somewhat substandard Palo Alto. Redwood City, Mountain View, and Sunnyvale are ranked below Menlo Park on the intangible social scale. Los Altos—socially about midway between blue-jeansy, pipe-smoking Palo Alto and marble-colonnaded Hillsborough—is a *cozy* town, a family town, a town of largish, well-manicured, but unpretentious California one-level houses with redwood-fenced backyards, gardens, terraces, barbecues, and the inevitable swimming pools. Because of the recent California drought, water to fill these pools must often be brought in, expensively, in large trucks. Lawns in certain areas which have had to ban the use of sprinkler systems may now be only hose-watered, leaving grass thirsty. It is a town that seldom bothers to lock its doors when it goes out of an afternoon. Entertaining here is casual, spur-of-the-moment, drop-in-anytime. "It's a town," as one Los Altan puts it, "where we all own good crystal, but almost never take it out." The air, for the most part, is clear, cool, and sunny all the year around—the Peninsula escapes San Francisco's chilly summer fogs—and smells of lemon eucalyptus.

This is shopping-center country. Nowhere on earth, they say, are more shopping centers more heavily concentrated than in this long, wide Santa Clara Valley. At latest count, there were 135 shopping centers between Palo Alto and San Jose. More are being built, and still more are on the drawing boards and in the endless dreams of the developers. They proliferate like suburban weeds. Where fruit orchards once stood, these new landmarks proclaim themselves with towering neon signs: Blossom Valley, Valley Fair, The Prune Yard, Oakridge Plaza, Seven Trees, East Ridge, and so on. East Ridge, in fact, is the largest shopping center on the West Coast, with 160 shops, eight banks, four department stores, and fourteen restaurants. Kathleen and John Stolp got married in an open-to-the-public ceremony on the mall of East Ridge, drawing an audience of thousands. It was a first, a milestone in the history of consumerism. Robert Redford filmed part of *The Candidate* in the East Ridge shopping mall, drawing even more spectators and potential shoppers. When the San Jose Symphony Orchestra performed Symphony No. 26 by the American composer Alan Hovhaness on the East Ridge mall, it drew an audience of over five thousand—the largest in the orchestra's history—even though most of the listeners had never heard of Hovhaness. Before, during, and after the concert, business boomed. Today, the shopping centers compete with

154

one another for "attractions" and "events," which range from wedding receptions, fashion shows, art shows, to cake shows, dog shows, and frog-jumping contests. "We try to create the atmosphere of small-town U.S.A.," says C. W. Rowan, West Coast manager of the Taubman Company, which built, designed, and operates East Ridge and fourteen other centers across the country.

In architectural style, the shopping centers run the gamut from California Ranchero to Hacienda Moderne to Adobe Op, and a map of the Santa Clara Valley shopping centers would resemble a well-planted minefield. They are larger, more numerous, cost more money to build, and consume more acreage than the Pyramids, and more people visit them each day than have ever visited Egypt. If all 135 centers were bunched together, their commercial space would cover thirty square miles, with over fifteen million square feet of shops surrounded by enough asphalt to provide free parking for 93,858 automobiles, and every year some three billion dollars changes hands in this vast bazaar. The shopping centers, which did not exist twenty-five years ago, are now a major part of the Peninsula's way of life. Some shoppers have their favorite centers. Others play the field, going from one to another. A great many people confess that they spend much of each day in this or that shopping center—not really to buy, but just to stroll, look at the changing window displays, and watch the other shoppers. These shopping-center wanderers, most of them women, are an increasing phenomenon as they move through the glassed-in malls, past fountains that flow out of futuristic sculptures, past reflecting pools, past tall indoor stands of tropical trees; up and down the automated stairways they travel, their eyes glazed as if in a hypnotic trance. Mrs. Babette Markel, who has made it her practice to visit each of the 135 shopping centers on a rotating daily basis, is typical. "Each one is like a different fairy tale," she says, "and every four months, when I start out all over again, there's nearly always something new."

Sociologists disagree about the social value of the Santa Clara County shopping centers. Dr. Thomas Tutko, a psychologist at San Jose State University, is enthusiastic. Shopping centers, says Dr. Tutko, "serve our individual needs for security and satisfy our needs for material objects to make us feel worthwhile. They provide the opportunity to show others that you've 'made it.' Shopping centers seem to combine old psychology with new psychology. The new psychology is that you need things that are convenient, all in one spot, in the hustle-bustle present philosophy of life. But more importantly, on another level, they epitomize the old family square. It's a return to the old marketplace, where the community really meets. We need a sense of protection and security. In the old days, we built forts." On the surface, of course, these observations seem somewhat contradictory. Is a shopping center more like a down-homey family meeting place or an armed encampment?

Donald Rothblatt, a Harvard University scholar of urban affairs who came to California a few years ago to study Santa Clara County's galloping shopping-center syndrome, has a different view. "Shopping centers offer a false sense of reality," Professor Rothblatt says. "They blur the focus on the human condition, don't accommodate the full range of people, and fail to provide a sense of centrality." Professor Rothblatt feels that any metropolis needs "a concentration of activity at the center which creates an intensity that is urbane. It captures the historical image we have of civilized man, and gives an identity—visually and spiritually." As for Santa Clara County, he says: "I have yet to find the essence of this place. It lacks identity, a sense of where you are. There's no *here* here."

The shopping centers, meanwhile, are distrusted by the more family-oriented Peninsula-ites. Because it is here that the unattached woman—the widow, the divorcee, the single girl—often plies her unsettling trade. Some of the merchandise that the shopping centers offer is human. The Peninsula used to consist primarily of bedroom communities for men who commuted back and forth to "the city," as northern Californians like to call San Francisco. Today, commuters represent a much smaller proportion of the male population. The Peninsula has become industrialized, particularly by electronics companies. In addition to branches of the big San Francisco stores and the dog-grooming shops and beauty salons, the shopping centers contain banks, insurance companies, brokerage houses, lawyers' and doctors' offices, where professional men who used to commute to San Francisco now find it more convenient to have their practices. The shopping centers contain bars and restaurants where such men have lunch or stop for a drink before heading home on the freeway, and the single women have learned that these are excellent places to encounter temporarily unfettered men. The men they find, of course, are often husbands of dutiful housewives in communities like Los Altos.

Without ever discussing it, therefore, the wives of Los Altos and communities like it have devised tactics designed to protect their property, and to make single women feel as uncomfortable and

156

unwelcome as possible. It boils down to an effort to keep the single woman from entering the community. Many home owners, for example, out of fear of neighbor pressure, will refuse to sell their house if the prospective buyer is a single woman. It also involves a not-so-subtle campaign to drive out the newly single woman, whether widow or divorcee. One recently divorced woman describes it this way: "It was really the Big Freeze. When it happened, I couldn't believe it. I suppose in any divorce, your friends choose sides. But I thought that at least my *women* friends would stand by me. Oh, they were loyal and sympathetic enough while I was going through the separation and the divorce—as long as I was still technically married. But the minute I had my decree, the phone stopped ringing. It was as though I'd become a nonperson. My neighbors stopped smiling and waving when we passed on the street. One woman, whom I used to think of as my *best* friend, now absolutely cuts me dead. I hear about her parties, parties I always used to be invited to, but I'm never asked. When I tried to ask her and her husband to dinner, she told me very coldly that they were busy, though I found out later that they weren't. At one party that I *was* asked to, none of the women spoke to me, and neither did most of the men. When they did, they were embarrassed and self-conscious, as though afraid of what their wives might say. I spend my evenings now doing things I never did before—going to lectures, concerts, or to the movies by myself. I refuse to go to the bars; I'm not ready for that scene. At home at night, I watch television, eat supper over the kitchen sink. I've read more books in the last six months than I did in twenty years of being married. I used to love this little town, but now I think I hate it. It's been terribly lonely. I've practically decided to sell the house and move to the city, though I don't know anyone there. My ex-husband, meanwhile, has taken an apartment in another part of town. And he gets asked out all the time!"

The ladies of Los Altos agree that suburbs like theirs are much kinder to the single male. "He poses no threat," one woman says. "And for some reason, an extra man at a party is much more welcome than an extra woman. An extra man is fun; an extra woman just seems in the way." But divorced women complain that this attitude is grossly unfair. "A man doesn't even have to be *attractive* to be invited to all the parties," the recent divorcee complains. "He can be a feeble-minded alcoholic homosexual with a wooden leg, and as long as he's recognizably *male* he's on everyone's list. I know of one man in particular who's such a bore and such a slob. He's always sloppy drunk before dinner is served, and has to leave half-way through the evening. But he's still the darling of all our leading hostesses!"

Somewhat less easy to deal with—even in towns like Los Altos, which, on the surface at least, like to project a sober, "unswinging" image, and boast of a high degree of quiet domestic stability—is the phenomenon of the marauding *married* woman. "I blame the Women's Lib movement," says one of the Los Altos wives. "A lot of women have decided that it's okay to be promiscuous—just the way it used to be considered more or less okay for men." Recently, Los Altos was abuzz with events in a nearby Peninsula town. An attractive woman in her middle thirties, the mother of three children, had had a brief affair. Afterward, she had decided to tell her husband about it. The result of this information was that he became impotent. As the woman explained it to her friends: "As long as he's impotent, I don't see why I'm not perfectly entitled to have some fun of my own. The other night, in a bar at East Ridge, I met a terribly attractive man. He said he was going to San Francisco for the weekend, and asked me if I'd come up and have dinner with him. I said I'd think about it, and he gave me his card. The next day, I decided, why not? and called him at his office. He asked me to meet him at the Bourgogne, which happens to be my favorite restaurant. We had a lovely dinner, one thing led to another, and I found myself back in his room at the Stanford Court. The next morning, I had breakfast in bed for the first time since my honeymoon."

This woman's friends are not sure what to do about these adulterous confessions. Her immediate neighbors, however, secretly hope that her behavior will lead to a divorce, and that she will get the house, sell it to some nice, solidly married couple, and move away.

The men of the San Francisco Peninsula, meanwhile, express doubts of another sort about the quality of the suburban experience, and what it sometimes does to human relationships. Allan Benjamin, for example, is a prosperous physician who lives and practices in the area—"Nowadays we only get up to San Francisco a couple of times a year"—and who recently, in his spare time, built a fanciful gazebo out of slender redwood strips to add another touch of gaiety to his already very pretty backyard. "There's a feeling of *separation* here," he says. "It's very hard to define, hard to put your finger on. It's a feeling of living apart from other people, even your closest neighbors. It's not just that you don't borrow your neighbor's lawnmower—everybody knows that you mustn't do that. It's a feeling that you have to leave them alone in other ways. For example, if you hear a woman screaming in the house next door, you don't run over, or pick up the phone, to see if she needs help. You think it's probably just a domestic argument: stay out of it, mind your own business. Of course, she could be being raped or murdered. Still, you don't do anything. Or if you see a police car pull up in front of a house on the street, you don't go out to find out what's the matter. You don't phone. That would be considered nosy. You don't ask questions. You sit it out. If, later on, the neighbor wants to tell you what the trouble was, he'll tell you. Otherwise, you never know." Not long ago, in one quiet neighborhood, a youth battled with his stepfather and broke the man's neck. Later, the boy boasted to his friends of what he had done, and how his stepfather's face "turned green, then white." In very little time, the whole neighborhood had heard about the episode. Everyone was shocked. Everyone was sorry. But no one mentioned it to the boy's mother, nor did she mention it to them. No one had gone to see the stepfather in the hospital. He might just as well have been off on a routine business trip. As far as the beleaguered family was concerned, it was a private, closed affair. As far as the neighbors were concerned, it might just as well not have happened. Close the door. It will go away.

Al Benjamin says: "As the suburbs have grown, they've separated more and more into tiny islands—each one cut off from the others, isolated from the others, and then separated again into islands within islands. The insularity becomes stronger and stronger." Perhaps, then, what Professor Tutko was trying to say was that in shopping-center country, a family meeting ground and an armed camp are now pretty much the same thing.

Indeed, it could be postulated that nearly all of California (with the exception of "the city") is a collection of islands in search of a common state of mind. (Los Angeles, in fact, has often been described as "a group of suburbs in search of a city.") California's growth has been suburban sprawl, and though each new California suburb looks much like all the others, no prevailing emotional force has appeared to bind them all together except, perhaps, the climate. Truly, California's communities waste a great deal of energy denigrating each other. Publisher Michael Korda, who has spent a good deal of time in the state, thinks all this is because when the west-ward settlement of the United States ran its final course, it encoun-tered the Pacific Ocean; it was stopped there and could go no farther. The pioneer spirit that had pushed across Ohio and the Great Plains, over the ordeal of the Rockies and the Sierras, came to rest at the beach. There, with a feeling of "Was it this that we were after?" it has been reposing ever since, disappointed, but too tired to go back. If California communities seem to lack separate iden-tities, and to lack a sense of commonality as well, this is perhaps why.

And yet at least one California community has managed to create a distinctive personality for itself, and that is Santa Barbara. Too far from both Los Angeles and San Francisco to be "influenced" by either place, Santa Barbara has set about determinedly to develop its own particular style. It is a style, furthermore, that resents and resists criticism from outside. Not long ago, for example, Santa Barbara was up in arms. There was only one topic of conversation on everyone's lips. (Normally, there are two topics of conversation on everyone's lips in Santa Barbara: rising real estate taxes and the more comforting phenomenon of rising real estate values.) The uproar was over a magazine article.

In its June, 1976, issue, *Town & Country* had published an article by Easterner Linda Ashland called "The Santa Barbara Style," consisting of a short text and many pages of photographs of wealthy Santa Barbarans enjoying their favorite pastime, Santa Barbara. It showed Santa Barbarans in their terraced, Italianate formal gardens, around their colonnaded pool houses and pools, in their opulent living rooms and bedrooms with *trompe l'oeil* walls painted to pro-duce, say, a likeness of the view from the Gritti Palace in Venice, in polo outfits and riding habits. It showed Santa Barbara suffused in sunlight with views of blue sea and skies and purplish mountains, and dressed in pastels of pink and blue and lavender, in Pucci pants and Gucci shoes. "Disgusting!" "Perfectly ghastly!" "Dreadful!" were some of the opinions circulating about Miss Ashland's article. But considering the obvious beauty of the setting which the article conveyed, along with the golden healthiness of its residents, it was hard to figure out what the fuss was all about.

Gradually, it emerged. While everyone agreed that Miss Ash-land had been correct in pointing out Santa Barbara's fondness for foreign cars—Mercedeses and BMWs in particular—what everyone objected to was the magazine's choice of people photographed to illustrate the article. What, for example, did Suzy Parker (formerly a New York model, now married to actor Bradford Dillman and living in Santa Barbara) have to do with Santa Barbara? How did Clifton Fadiman (born in Brooklyn, and Jewish) or Barnaby Conrad (a San Francisco transplant) fit into the Santa Barbara scene? Certainly *Hair* producer Michael Butler, sort of a millionaire hippie from Chicago who was once arrested for growing marijuana in his garden, was far from the typical Santa Barbaran; he had once entertained Mick Jagger. Most offensive of all, it turned out, was the woman whom the magazine had chosen to place on its cover, Mrs. Manuel Rojas, wearing chandelier emerald earrings to match her eyes. What did *she* have to do with the Santa Barbara style? everyone wanted to know. Chandelier emerald earrings are most definitely not the Santa Barbara style. The Rojases, furthermore, are considered *nouveau riche* (Perta Oil Marketing, Inc.) and originally came from, of all places, Beverly Hills. They settled in Santa Barbara as recently as 1974.

Santa Barbara is a community where literally hours can be spent discussing who is "typical Santa Barbara" and who is not. The typical Santa Barbaran, it is agreed, is "conservative." If, for conservative, some people read stuffy and smug, that is perfectly all right with Santa Barbara. Santa Barbarans feel that they have elevated smugness to the level of an art form. The typical Santa Barbaran goes in for espadrilles and tennis shoes more than for emeralds, which Mrs. Rojas was clearly shown wearing in broad daylight. The typical Santa Barbaran distrusts outsiders, and dislikes change. When the local Baskin-Robbins ice cream shop discontinued a flavor called Pralines 'n' Cream, the citizenry, who had grown fond of the flavor, picketed the establishment until Pralines 'n' Cream was restored to the inventory. Santa Barbara women like to boast that theirs was the last community in America to accept the pants suit. The typical Santa Barbaran is extremely town-proud and civic-minded. It has been said of Santa Barbara that it is a city of meetings, and that nothing can be done until at least one meeting has been called to discuss all the ramifications of whatever it is. At the same time, Santa Barbara is distrustful of city government, and prefers to leave any decisions affecting the city to its citizens themselves, who are believed to know what is good for them and what isn't. When a stretch of freeway was planned between San Francisco and the Mexican border, Santa Barbarans decided that they did not want traffic streaming through their community at seventy miles

161

per hour. They went to battle with the California State Department of Transportation and—though it took years—they won. Now Santa Barbara is the only segment of the freeway's six-hundred-mile length where motorists must keep a respectful speed and pause for traffic lights. When offshore oil spills began dirtying their beaches, Santa Barbarans met and formed an organization called GOO (for Get Oil Out). They took on some of the country's largest oil companies, and got them to clean up their operations.

Typifying Santa Barbara's attitude toward city governments is Miss Pearl Chase, who says: "People won't be inspired to help a community unless they are part of it. Government officials are really temporary. They come and go, and this constant turnover means that citizen organizations have far greater impact." Miss Chase is perhaps the most typical Santa Barbaran there is. She is immensely rich. Her family owned the vast Hope Ranch, which, not long ago, was sold off and subdivided to become one of the town's most elegant and expensive areas. But she lives in a Victorian house full of sagging furniture, old scrapbooks, and genteelly dusty clutter. When she goes out, she is always hatted, always gloved. If she owns any emeralds, she has never been seen wearing them. Though she is eighty-eight years old, and ailing, she is still regarded as one of the town's leading dowagers.

Change, of course, has come to Santa Barbara as it has everywhere else where the rich have tried to isolate themselves behind walls and gates and rolling lawns and gardens. Not long ago, for example, a rich and social wedding united two old-line Santa Barbara families. Shortly after the wedding, however, the young bridegroom announced his intention of undergoing a sex-change operation. And for years, the Little Town Club was Santa Barbara's leading social club for women. Founded in 1914, the club never served alcoholic beverages. But several years ago, a proposal was made that the club offer wine with lunch. In a surprising development, it turned out that all the older ladies were in favor of wine, while all the younger members were not. Eventually, the older group won out and wine was introduced, then liquor. "Now," complains one member, "it's so noisy at lunchtime you can't hear yourself think!"

"Oh, how Santa Barbara has changed!" complains one matron, Santa Barbara resident for over fifty years. "It used to be a simple, charming place. All the houses had blue shutters. We would eat at

El Paseo, standing in line with trays for the most delicious food. The annual Fiesta was beautiful. Now it's horrible. People used to have lovely parties; now we don't go anywhere. There was wonderful dancing at the Biltmore. Now it's part of a chain."

The change, the dowager feels, began during the Second World War. "There began to be a strong Fascist feeling here," she says. "There were a few men who were out-and-out Nazis. I remember one man who called 'Heil Hitler!' across a table, and another who said, 'Let us hope and pray that Germany wins the war.' One of those men is still around. During the war, it all became terribly snobbish and anti-Semitic."

But a more profound change occurred earlier, on the twenty-ninth of June, 1925, a date engraved on the memory of every true Santa Barbaran. That day, an earthquake registering 6.3 on the Richter scale rocked Santa Barbara. Trees thrashed about, the towers of All Saints' Church swayed, and the ground heaved in great waves. At least one Santa Barbara dowager, old Mrs. Cunningham—a Forbes of Boston—was killed. (One of the residents had a psychic butler, who foresaw the quake and removed all her costly vases, which were thereby saved.) The aftershocks continued for the rest of the summer, and before it was over, most of what had been old Santa Barbara had been destroyed.

Nowadays, in retrospect, the quake is usually referred to as "a blessing." Santa Barbara had, up to that time, developed somewhat haphazardly, without zoning. When the earth finally quieted, an architectural board of review was formed by a group of local worthies. Its purpose was to oversee the rebuilding of the town, and to see to it that it was rebuilt in such a way that it would be pleasing to the eye and would also have a certain architectural uniformity. The result was a vaguely Mediterranean mixture of Spanish Colonial and Mission Revival, appropriate to Southern California's history. Walls were of beige or yellow stucco, and roofs were of red or yellow tile. Bell towers and balconies and grillwork abounded. Santa Barbara's acres were strictly zoned. For obvious reasons, high-rise buildings were prohibited. These architectural, building, and zoning codes have been adhered to until this day, and have become a matter of intense civic pride. Right now, the city is in the middle of an intense dispute over the design of a new wing for the art museum, which proposes to depart, ever so slightly, from the Spanish Mission style. Though architects have found Santa Barbara's elaborate building codes and rules somewhat inhibiting, landscape architects have flocked to the area and have prospered creating the town's many pretty parks, malls, and private gardens.

Santa Barbara first came into existence in 1850, when it was incorporated by an act of the California legislature a few months before there actually was a state of California. But it was not until the late 1860s, in the post–Civil War days, that it had its real genesis. It began, like so many wealthy enclaves, as a seasonal resort. These were the days when so many families, rich from the war, began to cast about for new ways to spend and display their money, and to encapsulate themselves in luxurious redoubts where they would encounter only their "own kind." This overnight gentry—members of the Armour family (meat), the Mortons (salt), the Fleischmanns (yeast), the Hammonds (organs), to name a few—came largely from the East and the Middle West, and began to build imposing winter homes in the hills above the town. This was the era when golf, tennis, and polo suddenly became popular pastimes for the rich, and it was the dawn of the American country club. Many of the rich Easterners who came to Santa Barbara were, furthermore (or so Santa Barbarans like to boast), the black sheep of their families, and were encouraged to go to California by relatives who were just as happy to have them several thousand miles away. This accounts, Santa Barbarans say, for the relaxed and laissez-faire air of the place—less grand and pretentious than Newport, less formal and competitive than Palm Beach. "Here we have always just gone our happy ways," says one long-time resident.

The exclusive Valley Club was built, which is now the "Old Guard club," and then the Birnam Wood Club, which is considered the "New Guard club." The third country club, the Montecito, bought recently by a Japanese syndicate, stands lowest in the club pecking order and is considered "commercial." The Little Town Club established its quaint rules, such as "Six to a Susan." (For lunch, the club has tables for six, with a lazy Susan in the center of each table; it is against the rules to sample a tidbit from anyone else's lazy Susan.)

When an architect named George Washington Smith came to Santa Barbara, he quickly put his stamp on the place, doing for Santa Barbara what Stanford White did for New York and Long Island and Addison Mizner did for Palm Beach; he designed mansions in the preferred Spanish Colonial style with vaulted ceilings and the requisite bell towers, balconies, and courtyards. His flights of Mediterranean fancy were extreme, and he thought nothing of going to Spain and Italy to bring back boatloads of tiles, lanterns, shutters, and grilles to adorn his creations. It is said that when Harry K. Thaw (who murdered Stanford White) was released from prison, he visited Santa Barbara, and viewing a George Washington Smith house, commented, "I think I killed the wrong architect." Still, because there are only twenty-nine Smith houses in Santa Barbara, to own one is now a—if not *the*—major status symbol. And when, as rarely happens, a Smith house goes on the market, it is certain to bring at least $100,000 more than a comparable one.

One woman who still lives in the Smith-designed mansion she built in 1925 after the earthquake is Mrs. Angelica Schuyler Bryce, the widow of Peter Cooper Bryce, who, along with Harold Chase, Pearl Chase's brother, developed Hope Ranch. (Things tend to get somewhat inbred in Old Guard Santa Barbara, and it is important to remember who was a Hollister, who was a Meeker, who was a Poett, and so on.) The eighty-six-year-old Mrs. Bryce, who has always been known by her childhood nickname, "Girlie," is, along with Miss Chase and Mrs. Horace Grey, one of the grandes dames who for years have ruled the social seas of Santa Barbara. She actually worked with George Washington Smith on her house, helping him collect the antique hammered-iron hardware which was copied in Europe and brought to her estate, Florestal. On her fifty-five landscaped acres Girlie Bryce maintains what amounts to a private zoo, including forty-five peacocks and a sixty-year-old tortoise named Gappy, who is fed a diet of watermelon and fresh fruits imported from Hawaii. Gappy reciprocates by letting Mrs. Bryce's thirty-eight grandchildren take turns riding on his back when they come for visits. For all the splendor of her surroundings, Girlie Bryce complains: "Santa Barbara has gotten so big. If it gets any bigger it's going to be a horrible place."

Santa Barbara has gotten big, and now has a population of over 200,000. After World War II came Vandenberg Air Force Base, bringing in a sizable military contingent. Then came the University of California's Santa Barbara campus, and Robert Hutchins with his Center for the Study of Democratic Institutions, both of which not only added people but contributed what Santa Barbara considers an intellectual, think-tank atmosphere to the place. Dr. Hutchins's pronouncements from his lush hillside villa ("Mankind's intellectual power must be developed") are given much weight. Then came General Motors, bringing with it some hundred new families. The

General Motors people tended to stick to themselves, which was fine with Santa Barbarans, who said, "If you don't want us, we don't want you."

But, for the time being at least, Santa Barbara isn't going to get any bigger. For the last few years, Southern California has been undergoing an acute water shortage and now each Santa Barbara household has a water ration allocated on a complicated formula based upon past consumption, number of persons in the household, etc. If a Santa Barbara home owner exceeds his water quota, he is charged a penalty, even though there seems to be plenty of water to sprinkle golfing greens and to fill thousands of backyard pools. It was the water shortage that was given as the reason Santa Barbara declared a moratorium on new building some time back. But the real reason for the building moratorium, Santa Barbarans admit, was to keep out more new people. It has also had the pleasant effect of keeping Santa Barbara real estate values going up and up.

"Santa Barbara is an *international* suburb," says Mrs. Michael Wheelwright, the wife of a prominent landscape architect, and many Santa Barbarans would agree with her. It is true that many Santa Barbarans maintain homes elsewhere, and are always jetting from one part of the world to another. When Santa Barbara attempted to publish its own edition of the *Social Register* a few years ago, the enterprise collapsed after four editions—largely because most of social Santa Barbara is already registered in *Social Register*s of other cities. Foreign visitors also abound, including Baron Philippe de Rothschild, who customarily winters at the Santa Barbara Biltmore and swims daily in the Olympic-size pool at the adjacent Coral Casino (a members-only club for Santa Barbara residents, free for guests). And certainly, for all its suburban appearance, Santa Barbara is technically not a suburb of any particular city. It is too far from Los Angeles to be considered a commuting town—though some people, like Manuel Rojas, make the trip back and forth to business in private planes. It is no secret that San Francisco thinks little of Los Angeles, and that Los Angeles echoes these sentiments about San Francisco. But Santa Barbara thinks little of both Los Angeles and San Francisco. "I go to Los Angeles as little as possible," says one woman. "I sometimes go there for shoes from Saks." Santa Barbara thinks even less of the Los Angeles suburbs. Beverly Hills is dismissed as "mostly Jewish." And of mostly non-Jewish Pasadena, a Santa Barbaran snorts: "They have more smog in Pasadena than they do in Los Angeles!" San Francisco is also given short shrift. When a visiting San Franciscan mentioned, in the way San Franciscans have, that he lived in "the city," his hostess retorted, "I live in a city too—Santa Barbara!"

Santa Barbarans also point out that Santa Barbara actually has suburbs of its own. The old money lives in a coastal community called Montecito. New money has collected itself in the hills beyond, at Hope Ranch.

In fact, the word "suburban" is anathema in Santa Barbara, as it is becoming elsewhere in America. The word no longer has the pleasant, easy ring that it once had. Euphemisms have been tried. "We live in the *country*," is a popular one. A Santa Barbaran, of course, would say, "We live in *Santa Barbara.*"

Santa Barbara is one of the few remaining towns in the United States—Port Huron, Michigan; San Antonio, Texas; and possibly Greenwich, Connecticut, are some of the others—that, for whatever else it is or isn't, is still a *place,* its own place. It's a place where, as one woman describes it, "genteel people live—people who don't need to be justified by anything."

As for the rest of California, Merv Griffin, an unwilling transplant from the East, asserts: "It's nothing but polyester leisure suits, frozen yogurt, mood rings, Big Macs and fries, Cuisinarts, heated water beds, sharks' teeth on chains, and jogging"—little of which will be encountered in Santa Barbara.

CITY VS. SUBURB

18

The Price of Status

City planners bemoan the fact that the so-called flight to the suburbs has already begun to cause the death of the cities which spawned the suburbs. "We're moving out of the city for the children's sake," is the commonest excuse that is given, and it is true that the suburban migration has been led by the responsible, well-to-do, well-educated parent group in search of the grail of better schools—that is, by the people most able to bolster the tax bases of the cities. With these people gone, the cities become abandoned to the poor, the ill-educated, and the irresponsible. Tax levies for schools are voted down, and city school facilities deteriorate, while good teachers flee to the suburbs as well. Some cities have managed to solve the problem in part by annexation. The Ohio villages of Hyde Park and Clifton, which used to be separate townships, are now annexed to Cincinnati (though Indian Hill and Glendale have no intention of becoming annexed, and have resisted). This has helped the city's tax coffers somewhat. But a Cincinnati school-tax levy failed in 1966, and the schools had to give up their kindergartens. Currently, Cincinnati's police and fire departments—a community's first lines of citizen protection—are both in the throes of manpower cutbacks. Without protection and without good schools, what the city planners call the "responsible parent group" simply will not stay.

Dr. Margaret Mead has said: "People find it very difficult to face the problems which are confronting all cities today. Every city in

171

America is presently faced with going to pieces—letting suburban shopping centers develop until the downtown shopping area is destroyed, going in for the kind of urban renewal that means destruction [Cincinnati's Wesley Chapel?], breaking up neighborhoods to the point where there are no neighborhoods left, turning a city into what Newark is today." Dr. Mead can remember when Newark was a not unattractive city, and when Bamberger's was a pleasant place to shop. "But today," she says, "people who work at high levels in Newark come in through tunnels, then take elevators to their offices. They never go out in the street. That's the sort of place that's taken over by machine guns in the end."

To avoid such a direful end to American cities, Dr. Mead says flatly: "First of all, you need to give your citizens protection and good schools. They've got to know they can come and go in safety—that's basic. And you must have excellence in the educational system. If you don't, people are going to move out. After all, their children have only one life to live, and you don't sit around in a city and have your child's schooling wrecked." When reminded of the economic plight afflicting American cities today, which has forced cities to make drastic cuts in budgets for schools and for fire and police protection, Dr. Mead snorts: "Nonsense! It's ridiculous to wail about the financial state of the United States. This is the richest country in the world. We're just spending our money in the wrong places." To reverse the trend toward urban disintegration, Dr. Mead prescribes "a massive reordering of priorities" on both the local and the national levels: measures as diverse, and drastic, as redistribution of welfare services to keep the poor from "piling up" in the cities, an all-out effort to develop efficient mass-transportation systems, and diverting federal funds from arms expenditures to financial assistance for the cities.

Meanwhile, of course, the flight to the suburbs continues, and Dr. Mead foresees the day when the suburbs will fall prey to all the ills that now beset the cities. "It's already happening," she says, and it is true that towns—such as New Rochelle, New York; Stamford, Connecticut; Beverly Hills, California; and Shaker Heights, Ohio—that once considered themselves "suburban" are now, in fact, small cities with high-rises, traffic lights, noise, and parking meters. There are rush-hour traffic jams in Rye and Darien, and light industry has come to Greenwich. Suburban lakes, rivers, and beaches are polluted, and there is smog in both Hyde Park and

Indian Hill. Suburbs battle over big-city issues such as school bonds, zoning, and tax hikes.

There are, however, other reasons for the suburban exodus besides a search for better schools and more efficient police. Many families feel anonymous, socially, in big cities, where they find it difficult to meet people, make friends, and be "taken in." They hope vaguely that in a nice suburb, they will not only find a better way of life but will also make "a fresh start" in the social sense: meet and mingle with "a nicer class of people," and achieve, thereby, a boost in social status. But unfortunately, as once-small suburban towns have burgeoned, it is no longer quite that simple. Many suburban towns feel that they have grown quite enough, thank you, and they examine newcomers with unfriendly, even hostile, eyes. The first friendly face the new suburbanite may meet may belong to the Welcome Wagon lady, but after that, America's choicest suburbs can be extremely hard social nuts to crack. The fashionable country clubs, in the economically uncertain 1970s, have been experiencing financial difficulties. Memberships have declined, and there has also been a decline in clubs' use for large parties and weddings, due to the economic crunch. Golf has been losing favor over the last decade, particularly among younger people, though clubs must still maintain—and pay taxes on—vast golf course acreages. There has also been a decline of interest among young people in the whole idea of country clubs. Rye's Apawamis Club not long ago closed its beach and tennis facility, and sold off property, to make fiscal ends meet. The American Yacht Club, in order to appeal to a more diverse membership, has added such non-sailing enticements as a swimming pool and new tennis courts. The Manursing Island Club, which used to close for the winter, now keeps its doors open all year long.

Still, though the best clubs in the choicest suburbs may need money and often have yawning membership vacancies, they remain difficult to join. "We can't just take in every Tom, Dick, and Harry," says the manager of Darien's Wee Burn. If the club did, it would lose its precious reputation for "exclusivity"—its whole reason for being—and exclusivity means nothing more or less than keeping people out. To join clubs like the Wee Burn and the Apawamis, therefore, it is still necessary to have a sponsor, a second, and a third, plus letters of recommendation from as many as ten club members. New applicants are then subjected to interviews

173

and screening by membership committees. To newcomers, who know no one in the town, these conditions may present almost insurmountable obstacles. And in towns like Rye and Darien, where virtually the entire social life of the community—from dancing classes to teen-age parties and summer sports—revolves around one club or another, the newcomer may find himself feeling singularly left out of things. As the Planning and Zoning Commission chairman of Greenwich put it bluntly not long ago: "Intruders from any direction must be held at bay."

Still, though it is not easy, entry into suburban society is possible for the unknown newcomer. But to achieve social status in the suburbs requires special rules, and though many of the "rules" may seem like purest common sense, it is surprising how often they are ignored—with the result that the newcomer remains isolated, bored, unhappy, and frustrated. So for those determined to ignore Dr. Mead's warnings (after all, she has been known to be wrong in the past) and to abandon the city for a "nice" suburb where "nice" people live, there are a few tips and pointers to be borne in mind.

To begin with, it can be taken almost as a rule of thumb that the choicest suburb of any city will be the most inconvenient to get to—the farthest from the city, with no train or bus service, often inaccessible by any form of public transportation (like Cornwall, Connecticut), and reachable only by private automobile. There are a few exceptions to this, such as Grosse Pointe, Michigan, which is almost within walking distance of Detroit and which is still considered a very tough place, socially, to penetrate. (Bloomfield Hills, farther out, would argue this and point out that Grosse Pointe, which for years excluded Jews, now has not only Jews but also a few black families.) In general, the family wishing to move to an exclusive suburban enclave must forget about convenience. Inconvenience provides privacy, seclusion, and hence prestige.

It is important to remember that any newcomer to an established community is viewed with alarm and suspicion, and as a potential enemy—an enemy, that is, to real estate values. (Will the new family keep its lawn trimmed, its hedges clipped, its driveway weeded, its windows washed?) Whenever real estate changes hands in the suburbs, regardless of price, there is always fear among the immediate neighbors on the street that the new people "will let that beautiful place run down." So as quickly as possible, the newcomer should let it be known that he intends to spend money on maintenance and repairs. One can advertise this fact before one even meets

174

one's neighbors by giving the house a fresh coat of paint, a new roof, or a new driveway. These external details should be seen to first, for they will be the first things noticed, and they will be appreciated.

But it is important—even more important, in fact—that whatever exterior changes are performed on a new house not be extreme ones. If the house, when it was bought, was in reasonably good repair, it is likely that the immediate neighbors have been pleased with its appearance; at least they have grown used to it, and will react negatively to any dramatic alteration in color, façade, or architectural detail. In the wealthy suburbs, the rule to remember is that familiarity breeds contentment. A new couple in Darien bought a large Colonial house that had always been painted white. They immediately painted it blue, to the great distress of their neighbors and, indeed, the entire town. In Rye, a newcomer created a great local fuss—about which he, of course, was oblivious—when he erected a flagpole on his front lawn and flew the American flag from it. No one in the neighborhood, it seemed, had ever put flagpoles on their lawns, and the arrival could not understand why his neighbors appeared to be snubbing him. Similar unintended gaffes have been made by newcomers who placed garden furniture on front lawns in neighborhoods where such items were traditionally placed only in backyards, or by others who innocently failed to realize an unwritten rule of the community: garage doors that could be seen from the street should remain closed at all times. In certain towns it is permissible to give houses names (Twin Oaks, High View Farm); in others, even monogrammed doormats are taboo. Sometimes, a newcomer can be criticized for something that is not his fault at all. Shortly after a large place in Greenwich changed hands, a magnificent elm that had been the centerpiece of the front lawn fell prey to Dutch elm disease and had to be taken down. The new neighbor was blamed for having "neglected" the tree even though he had, in fact, spent several thousands of dollars trying to save it.

A worthwhile corollary to the above reminders would be this one: If a newcomer to a community is lucky enough to find, in run-down condition, a house on a street of otherwise well-tended residences, and will buy it and renovate it attractively, his new neighbors will clasp him to their collective bosoms, regardless of his race, religion, or color, for he will have improved, in theory, property values for one and all.

The new home buyer in the exclusive suburb should, after tending to such primary matters as exterior decoration, concentrate on interior window treatments. A new neighbor's windows are always the subject of scrutiny in the community, and needless to say, the windows that face the street are most important. The new arrival would do well to study the way windows of nearby houses are handled—whether draped, shuttered, or glass-curtained—and conform to the established community standard. Again, it is generally unwise to try to be too "different." If, in most suburban communities, people tend to mingle with people who are most like themselves, the windows will signal that identity of taste. Because this is the sort of problem that never affects the urban dweller, whose windows may be a dozen stories above the eyes of passers-by, it is one often overlooked by the neophyte suburbanite.

Next comes interior décor, which, in the suburbs, is generally given less emphasis than such exterior matters as the well-polished door knocker and the well-weeded pachysandra plot. Again, interiors should not be too showy; colors should be muted, soft. The new arrivals, hoping one day to entertain their neighbors, should plan on greeting them with interiors that are soothing, familiar, and unsurprising. A good grand piano will speak more of taste and breeding than a crystal chandelier. Good Orientals on the floor will say more than a heavy silver tea service. An original Andrew Wyeth will add more cachet to a room than half a dozen Andy Warhol prints, just as, in the suburbs, a well-cut raincoat and a good strand of pearls is more important than minks and diamonds, and a small Mercedes outranks the biggest Cadillac or Rolls, and a bowl of daisies on the coffee table makes a far greater impression that a Steuben urn filled with long-stemmed roses.

A further tip for the potential suburban hostess: Do not attempt to impress your new neighbors by serving so-called gourmet food. The rich are not accustomed to—and do not eat, nor do they serve—elaborate meals. Except at restaurants, where they can be adventuresome, the rich prefer not to be startled by what they see on their plates. Anything other than the familiar roast lamb or beef with parsleyed potatoes and buttered peas, or that smacks of a hostess who has taken lessons at Cordon Bleu, tends to make them feel awkward and embarrassed. Not long ago, when an aspiring young hostess, recently arrived in Bryn Mawr, attempted to dazzle her neighbors with an elegant French menu, one guest exclaimed: "Oh, you're such a fabulous cook! I wouldn't *dare* ask you to dinner at my house." The woman said it with a laugh, but the trouble was she meant it. Remember that what the establishment of any affluent suburb fears the most is change—which will inevitably be for the worse. To woo the members of the establishment, therefore, do not present them with anything that is new or bold or daunting. The most unwelcome person in the suburbs is the revolutionary.

Here are five other valuable pointers for serious suburban social climbers, or for those who at least would hope one day to penetrate suburban society's stern barricades:

1. It is helpful, when a family is moving to a new suburb, if they are parents of young children. Childless couples are often just as disadvantaged in the suburbs as unmarried women and divorcees. Children, on the other hand, make friends easily with other children, and through children, mothers inevitably meet other mothers and, eventually, fathers meet fathers. It is furthermore much easier to glide into suburban society—though here it is all a question of fate—if one's children are predominantly male. At all the junior dances and parties in the suburbs, boys are much more in demand than girls, right down to the preadolescent dancing classes. One young Westchester County mother, whose eight-year-old daughter was eager to join the Barclay Classes, was told flatly: "We can take in your daughter only if you enroll her two brothers as well." Other communities have a strict one-for-one quota: no girl accepted unless a matching boy, who is usually reluctant, can be offered up.

2. If there is a private day school in the community, enroll your children of both sexes in it. This is expensive and, of course, ironic, since many families move to the suburbs in quest of better *public* education. Still, though many communities deny it, it is usually quite apparent that the invitation lists to all the best children's dances and parties, at the best homes, are made up from the enrollment lists of the private schools.

3. It used to be that joining a church—particularly the Episcopalian church—was a good way to meet people and make friends in the suburbs. Alas, this is no longer true, and the churches have generally lost their social potency. Over coffee and cake in the church social room after the Sunday service, the newcomer today will meet only other newcomers looking just as out of place as he. Good works, on the other hand, still provide an avenue to social status for the ambitious. As a rule, the names of a community's social leaders will decorate the board of its local hospital or, if there is one, its art museum. Hospitals are more in demand than art museums, and so the new arrival who volunteers for, and toils dutifully at, the hospital thrift shop will find doors opening for her.

Any local charity that involves children is usually fashionable also. Obviously, if there is a local *children's* hospital, working for that can be the most socially rewarding of all.

4. If you get asked, by all means join the fashionable country club, but how you go about getting asked to join can be an arduous process. In fact, you really can't go about getting asked. You have to wait quietly in the wings and hope that it will happen. But there are a few subtle ways whereby you can let it be known that you will be a good club member. You can let it be inferred that, if invited, you will use the club frequently—for entertaining, for large parties, for tennis, and for golf. Clubs, after all, are not run as charities and have taxes and wages and other bills to pay. Nowadays, clubs have little interest in taking in the young couple, however attractive they might be, who will drop into the club once or twice a year, have a quick drink at the bar, and then go home. Let it be understood—without quite *saying* so, of course, which would give the game away—that you will be a big spender at the club. Sample hint (if you have a teen-age daughter): "I hear that the Smiths gave the most beautiful party the other night for their daughter at the club, and that everything was absolutely perfect—the food, the wine, the orchestra, everything . . . ."

5. The strain of living without acceptance is much more trying in the suburbs than in the city. An urban family can enjoy a full social life during years of struggling for recognition by the city's upper crust, and have friends on many levels who are completely unaware that any struggle is going on. In the suburbs, the striver is more easily recognized; it is easier for him to show his hand. Once spotted in the suburbs, he is doomed. Therefore, in the suburbs, the most important watchword is Patience. Be patient; don't try to storm suburbia's walls too quickly; be polite and willing, but never eager. As Molly Harrison of Cincinnati puts it: "We're not *against* new people, really. But we like to watch them at a distance for a little while, and kind of get used to having them here. Once we're used to them, we feel relaxed with them. If they turn out to be nice, and attractive, we'll take them in—eventually, if not right away. We don't like to be *pushed* into taking them in, that's the only thing. Once we take them in, they'll find us very friendly and they'll have a wonderful time. But the pushy party-giver turns us off."

The suburban social climber, in other words, should never show his climbing tools. And like any alpinist, he should study the terrain carefully before taking his next step.

19

Swinging

*I*t is odd that men and women should flock to the suburbs to escape loneliness, when the suburbs can be such lonely places. There are ways, of course, of slaking loneliness other than by needlepoint, television, and sitting by the pool. One can take up gardening or tennis or interior decorating, or do volunteer work. Or one can, if one has gained a bit of entrée, swing.

The phrase "the swinging suburbs" came into use perhaps twenty years ago, and through carefully guarded underground sources, the word got out: the suburbs do indeed swing, or at least there is an element there that does. There are many people who insist that because groups who swing are small, and consist of people who know and trust each other well—and because suburban houses and estates offer a gift of privacy not always attainable in city apartment buildings—the suburbs are actually sexier than cities. "You mean they have orgies in Scarsdale?" one woman asked. Well, yes, some people do, and orgies have actually achieved a certain degree of social acceptability. At least, it is no longer fashionable to frown on them.

In Shawnee Mission, the select suburb of Kansas City, the home of a wealthy young citizen and his wife is shielded from the street by an avenue of trees. Inside the house is an impressive collection of fine furniture and Oriental rugs. For parties, the lights are kept rather dim, and the stereo is played rather low. In the corner of the large living room, in a porcelain dish, sits what appears to be a bar of honey-colored bath soap. It is Turkish hashish, and it cost two

179

thousand dollars. Guests—perhaps ten couples—sit in a rough circle on the floor while, with some ceremony, the host chips small, thin, oily-looking flakes off the hashish bar, using a penknife, and carefully tamps them into a little pipe. He then lights the pipe, inhaling deeply, holding the smoke in his lungs for as long as he can. Then the pipe is passed to a guest, who also inhales deeply. The pipe continues slowly around the room.

The conversation is muted, there is some knowing laughter. The quality of the hashish is commented upon; it is considered very good. The rhythm of a rock group continues softly in the background. It is Saturday night, the best time, with the week's work and worries out of the way, and nothing but a lazy Sunday morning to look forward to. These are all such old and such good friends and neighbors, except for one couple, who are newcomers. They were warned, before being initiated into the group tonight, that this evening's entertainment would be somewhat special, for somewhat sophisticated, even worldly, tastes. The newcomers, for whom this is decidedly a new experience, are a bit apprehensive, but they have agreed to go along with whatever the evening turns out to be. They have been told that, should they not care for the experience in the end, this will not be held against them. But it is also understood that no mention is to be made of this particular evening to anyone outside the little circle. For the most part, the newcomers are happy to be here, because assembled in the room are some of the leaders of Kansas City society's younger set—couples who shop in New York, ski in Gstaad, have discovered the nude beaches in Sardinia and Acapulco, and are otherwise committed to dispelling the impression that Kansas City, Missouri, is a provincial, one-horse town. After all, didn't Kansas City give the world its very first suburban shopping center, Country Club Plaza, as long ago as 1920? The little pipe circles the room a second time, is refilled, and begins a third circle. The music—more protracted now, a song that never ends—lingers on from the twin speakers. "Isn't this nice?" someone asks.

Gradually, hands touch, hesitantly at first and then with more determination and enthusiasm. Gradually, too, the lights are lowered on rheostats until they are completely extinguished, except for a single candle. The table on which it sits is a kind of altar. In the flickering light of the candle, hands grope toward bodies, and bodies touch, then lips. In the darkness, only beards provide a clue as to whether the person one is kissing is male or female, but that is the point. It isn't supposed to matter. Shoes and neckties come off first, then stockings, jackets, blouses, dresses, bras, trousers, and underwear. At first there are whispers, a few giggles, and then, besides the music, there are only sighs and soft sucking sounds, which rise, very slowly, to moans and gasps and grunts and little cries. When it is all over, everyone lies still, cuddled and curled together, caressing cheeks and eyelashes and hair—lies there for what seems the longest time. The first word uttered is unprintable, and is followed by laughter, a signal that this part of the evening is over. It is time to sort out clothes and underthings from the untidy array of garments tossed over chairs and sofas, and to dress to go in to dinner, where the wine will be excellent.

While this particular evening did transpire in Kansas City, it would be wrong to suppose either that Shawnee Mission suburban-ites are a particularly depraved lot, or that this sort of thing does not go on, in certain groups, in Westport, River Oaks, and Sausalito. Of course, there are variations—not many, perhaps, but some. In Yorktown Heights, New York, a secluded enclave of large estates in northern Westchester, it is the custom for a certain hostess to depart, after dinner, for an upstairs bedroom, there to make herself available to any or all of her male guests. Her husband, meanwhile, has permission to repair to another bedroom with the lady guest of his choice. There are, of course, plenty of other bed-rooms in the house available for other random couplings. In Beverly Hills, where things might be expected to be carried off with a certain amount of flair, guests at the home of a well-known tax-payer are met at the front door by a uniformed maid. Each guest is handed a loose-fitting robe, and is ushered into a dressing room to change. Then, in their robes, the guests proceed into the party, where, among such traditional substances as alcohol and cannabis, a white powder is offered for sniffing.

"The important thing is to be discreet, not to get the whole town talking about it," says one suburban woman who, for obvious reasons, does not wish to be identified. "One rotten apple in the bunch can spoil the fun for everybody. It's not that we're ashamed of what we do. We're sophisticated, educated people who happen to take a liberal view of sex. We were practicing open marriage long before they wrote a book about it. What we enjoy doing doesn't hurt anybody, even though it might not meet what the hypocrites call 'community standards.' What we do at our parties doesn't involve the community. It just involves ourselves. But if someone blabbed, and the rest of the community found out about it, there

181

would be hell to pay. Our kids could be affected, our parents, our other friends who simply have no idea—even our husbands' businesses and professions. But as long as everything is kept within the group—there are four couples who get together fairly regularly, and a fifth who join us from time to time—there's no problem. It's like a little club, and it's very, very private."

It was apparently "one rotten apple" in Buffalo, New York, who let it be known that certain unorthodox carnal goings on were taking place involving two socially prominent couples in suburban East Aurora. Buffalo is a small, socially inbred city, and rumors spread rapidly. As they did, both sets of parents of the couples involved learned of the gossip and scandalized fathers confronted unrepentant sons and daughters. Soon, everyone in the Buffalo Tennis & Squash Club had heard the stories. Though the suburban "scandal" never reached the newspapers, it did billow sufficiently to persuade one couple to move out of town. The second couple were divorced.

Sex in the suburbs may have the advantage of increased privacy, but still a certain furtiveness is necessary, at least for some people. The men's room at the Greenwich railroad station, for example, is said to be a popular rendezvous for homosexuals during commuting hours. And, at the other end of the line, the men's room, public dressing rooms, and showers at New York's Grand Central Station were the scene of so many hasty trysts in the hours between 5 and 7 P.M. that the station closed much of the area off. Conservative Rye, on the other hand, pretends to be unaware that a bar operates on its main business street which offers a female impersonator for entertainment on weekend evenings.

Defenders of the suburbs point out, rightly, that according to the United States Census Bureau, the divorce rate per hundred is nearly twice as high in urban areas as it is in what the bureau calls the "urban fringe." From this the conclusion could be drawn that the suburbs exert a stabilizing influence on American marriages. But what statistics cannot measure is how many suburban marriages are enduring simply as the result of economic pressure. For the city apartment dweller, divorce can seem relatively simple. There is little property to divide other than books and furniture. But the couple who owns a suburban home has a considerable investment in it, which neither partner wants to lose. It could be argued, then, that the Census Bureau's figures suggest that the suburbs are holding together many marriages which, under other circumstances, would long ago have come apart.

Herbert Gans, a sociologist at Columbia University, has pointed out that "People who have problems in the city bring them with them to the suburbs," and this is no doubt true. Other researchers have found that suburban life itself has little effect on mental health. It has been noted, however, that certain groups of people tend to find the suburbs stressful. These include adolescent children, who find the lack of city activities boring; women of working-class backgrounds who have been thrust upward in society and find it difficult to deal with the social demands of a new environment; cosmopolitan individuals who simply miss big-city life; and educated women who want to work in interesting jobs.

In some cases, too, a move to the suburbs can put financial burdens on a family that it did not anticipate. In buying the new house, such matters as the extra cost of commuting, the need for a second car, the cost of keeping the grass cut and hiring baby-sitters had not been considered. This was the case of a Detroit couple who bought a new house several years ago in the "General Motors suburb" of Bloomfield Hills (as opposed to Grosse Pointe, which tends to attract Ford and Chrysler people.) Let us call them Mr. and Mrs. M. The M.'s had been married for eight years, and had two small children, when they made their big move. At the outset, the M.'s realized that they were paying more for the house than they had planned. But it was a lovely place, on two rolling acres, and was a temptation. Shortly after moving in, the M.'s discovered that the water supply was inadequate, and a new well had to be drilled. A new roof was also needed, and when that was completed, the assessment on their house was raised and their taxes went up. Additional furniture, rugs, and curtains were also indicated, but because of the unexpected expenses, these were temporarily ruled out. So was the second car Mrs. M. had planned to buy. Fortunately, the children's school was within easy walking distance, but shopping was not. Without a car, Mrs. M. was required to order groceries from a store that had a delivery service—at extra cost. In the beginning the M.'s had considered theirs a happy marriage. But soon their hours together were spent in bitter arguments over money matters.

Without an automobile, Mrs. M. began to feel isolated, abandoned, stranded in a half-furnished house. She believed that there was no way she could move out and join the community. She missed, all at once, the corner drugstore in the city where she and her neighbors had met for coffee and sandwiches. Because of his commuting, her husband was gone from the house for longer hours than before, and yet, without companionship during the day, she demanded more companionship from him in the evenings than he could supply. In the new position which had prompted him to buy his new house, Mr. M. was required to do a certain amount of traveling. While he was gone, in her loneliness, Mrs. M. convinced herself that he was being unfaithful. When he returned from his travels, she confronted him with suspicious questions. He confronted her with unpaid bills.

Mrs. M. did meet one neighbor who genuinely wanted to be her friend, though one friend is not a community, by any means. Also, the neighbor was an alcoholic, who helped feed Mrs. M.'s traitorous suspicions about her husband with cheerful assurances that "all men play around." The neighbor worked, but had Wednesdays off. "Every Wednesday she calls me and invites me over," says Mrs. M. "I don't really want to go because I know what she really wants is a drinking companion. But then, out of boredom, I go—she's just down the street. I can feel myself becoming an alcoholic right along with her, simply because I have nothing else to do. Now I find myself, around noon, going to the refrigerator to get myself something—a beer or a glass of wine. I think I'll just have one beer. But I usually have more. I drink now from noon until the kids come home from school, until there's somebody else in the house. I know this is not good. Every morning, I think: Well, maybe today I won't have anything to drink. And then my neighbor calls or comes over, and I have a beer with her, and before I know it I've had three or four. And then I think: Oh well, I won't tomorrow. And then tomorrow comes and I start drinking again, and before I know it, it's tomorrow and tomorrow and tomorrow." About a year ago, Mrs. M. tried to break off her friendship with her neighbor. There was an angry quarrel, followed by a reconciliation, followed by a second quarrel and more long, lonely hours, for which Mrs. M. consoled herself with beers from the refrigerator. The M.'s quarreled about Mrs. M.'s drinking, the rising bills for beer and wine, the state of the half-empty house, the lawn, which had grown too tall and rank for the power mower, and about the fact that Mrs. M. was gaining weight. Mrs. M. made a feeble, unsuccessful attempt at suicide—"Mostly to try to get him to pay some attention to me." Currently, the M.'s are seeing a psychologist and marriage counselor.

"Of course I've thought of divorce," says Mrs. M., "but where could I go, what could I do? We own the house together. He owns the car. My neighbor"—the two are once more friends—"says that the court would give me the house. But how could I make the mortgage payments?" The psychologist, meanwhile, who charges eighty dollars an hour, is adding to the couple's already overburdened budget and money worries.

Ulrich Franzen is a New York–based architect who has designed a number of expensive houses in Westchester County and on Long Island—houses which favor much use of glass and steel and stone, houses which have won prizes for their design and which have been photographed by all the leading house and architecture magazines. He takes a somewhat cynical view of the houses he builds and of the clients who hire him to build them. "I never pay any attention to what the client says he wants in a house," says Franzen. "I don't build the house for the client. I build it for the person who will buy it from the client. I design my houses for the *next* owners. I started doing this long ago, when I realized that my clients never lived in any of my houses very long. Most couples, when they hire an architect to build them an expensive modern house in the suburbs, think that building the new house will save their marriage. Of course, building a new house won't save a marriage. When the house is finished, the marriage breaks up anyway, and the house is sold to someone else, who will really appreciate it. Building the new house may *postpone* the breakup of the marriage for a while, but it will never save it. Building a new house is easy. It's so much easier to change your address than to change yourself."

20

The Vanishing Living Room and
Other Phenomena

Mr. and Mrs. Leonard Goodstein of Scottsdale confess
that they never use their living room—in fact, hardly ever go into
it. It exists, large as life, down a short flight of steps, and it is
prettily and expensively, if a little stiffly, decorated. Decoration,
indeed, has become the room's sole function. It has no other. It is a
room to be viewed and admired, but not entered. This, of course, is
not a new phenomenon in America, where, as early as Victorian
times, the formal "parlor" existed mainly for show. Though it was
dusted daily, and was often the largest room in the house, the parlor
was not for family use, but remained as forbiddingly untouchable as
the folded monogrammed linen guest towels in the bathroom.

In today's suburbs, however, in comfortable houses like the
Goodsteins' across the country, the role—or nonrole—of the living
room is a little different. The Victorian parlor was at least put to
occasional use—for weddings, funerals, or important entertaining.
But today's suburban living rooms offer only perpetually dead
space. The living room today has little more than symbolic value, as
an advertisement for a family's success. In it are placed the best
pieces of furniture, the most valuable paintings, the most expensive
rugs—all of which give it a roped-off look. In the rest of the house,
meanwhile, can be seen what suburbia is really all about, which is
essentially women and children.

It was women and children who invented the suburbs, who first
saw them as a necessity, and it is they who continue to rule them.

186

The cities, to which the men commute, are masculine; the suburbs feminine. For suburban women and children, contemporary architects of suburban houses have, to replace the living room, come up with that room called "the family room." The family room was a post–World War II invention, and today virtually no suburban house of consequence is built without one. Furthermore, it has come to serve a purpose that is perhaps unique in the history of human habitation. The family room is located hard by the kitchen, where the meals are prepared, and it inevitably contains a stereo, a radio, and a television. It is here—not in the dining room—that the family eats its meals, on trays in front of the set. Usually, the family room contains a bar too—one concession to male needs—and it is here that the cocktail hour is spent. The family room is for lounging and for napping, and for horsing around. It is also for entertaining, and it is here—not in the living room—that guests gather for parties when it is too chilly to be outside on the terrace by the pool. It is, in other words, an all-purpose living space where there are no real rules and where every domestic activity, including sleeping, can take place. The personality of the family room makes the living room, by contrast, all the more chilly and aloof, more ornamental and museum-like, a place one passes on one's way somewhere else. The family room is, as its name implies, a nest—a place where the woman of the house goes to relax and be comfortable, with her children and husband, her brood, nestled around her. Now that kitchens have become streamlined and impersonal, the family room is the heart of the house.

This nest is sometimes rather a messy one. If the living room is pristine and sterilized, the family room is cluttered and drink-stained. The rules of the family room permit that this be so. This makes a family room an easy room for a housewife to take care of, since it requires no care—nor does the living room, since how much care is required of a room that is never entered? Surveys have shown that women are, by nature, less tidy souls than men—or, rather, that most men *think* that women are untidy and disorganized. In a recent study, one hundred fifty recently divorced men were asked what they considered the primary reasons for the divorce. The responses followed a predictable pattern: "Our backgrounds were different"; "Our religions were different"; "Her mother was the domineering type"; "She was immature"; "We were incompatible"; "She and her psychiatrist ganged up against me." But 80 percent of those interviewed included, as at least *one* important reason: "She was a lousy housekeeper," or "The house was always a mess." The family room, perhaps, solves that problem. Also, since the Women's Movement has thrown terms such as "housewife" and "homemaker" into disrepute, the family room has conveniently provided a place where housekeeping and homemaking do not apply. The family room is for *family*, and family means kids, and kids mean kicked furniture and finger-spotted woodwork. As Jeanette Goodstein says proudly of her typically battered family room, "This is the room where we do our real *living*."

The family room is where the kids park their bicycles and skateboards, their surfboards and skis. It is okay, in the family room, to find a sneaker on the coffee table, a fielder's mitt on top of the television set, and a partly eaten apple wedged between the sofa cushions. All these details provide, after all, living proof of "living." And yet it is possible that the permissive ambience of the family room—a phenomenon that did not exist a generation ago—has prompted many families, and many men in particular, to sour on the suburbs, which have disappointed them in other ways that they would not have dreamed possible, such as rising crime rates and traffic problems, reminiscent of the city they left behind.

Perhaps, in the long run, the family room has been an unhealthy development. It has been popular, in recent years, to speak of urban communities as manifestations of a "sick society." And yet there is very recent evidence that this may not be the case at all. Dr. Leo Srole, a psychiatric sociologist at Columbia University and a director of the Midtown Manhattan Study, has come up with new findings which indicate that, if the cities are sick, the suburbs and rural areas of America are even sicker. In a 1977 meeting of the American Psychiatric Association in Toronto, Dr. Srole reported that his researches indicated that, in general, mental health was better in the cities than in the suburbs. "At minimum," he said, "the data stand in total refutation of the prejudgment continually pressed since the eighteenth century that urban mental health is on a one-way slide downward."

Dr. Srole referred to the anti-urban bias of many social commentators, politicians, and writers such as Erich Fromm as part of an "undocumented indictment"—or conspiracy—against the big cities, adding that cities may offer a far healthier accommodation to the human condition and spirit than small towns do. "We've got to realize that urban life does an awful lot of good through the cultural and other resources that it provides and that many people thrive on," says Dr. Srole.

To support his thesis, Dr. Srole produced a number of pieces of evidence, including an unpublished study conducted by the National Center for Health Statistics, a federal agency. The survey, involving 6,700 subjects across the country, was designed to uncover signs of stress and other difficulties—such as trouble sleeping, feelings that "everyone is against me," that a nervous breakdown was imminent, and that "worries get me down physically." It was found that people who lived in rural areas and in towns of under 50,000 population had "symptom scores" nearly 20 percent higher than those who lived in cities of 50,000 or more. Another bit of interesting evidence came from a comparison of people living in midtown Manhattan with those in remote Stirling County, Nova Scotia, where the population density per square mile is twenty persons, compared with mid-Manhattan's 75,000. After drawing subsamples from each group that matched demographically, Dr. Srole compared the mental health scores and found that the mid-Manhattanites were far better off. The scores, says Dr. Srole, "offer no support whatsoever to the antique presupposition of the superiority of rural mental health. On the contrary, Stirling County's mental-morbidity rate is higher than midtown Manhattan's by a wide and highly significant statistical margin."

Furthermore, Dr. Srole concludes that mental health in the cities has improved markedly over the years. Going back to a research project that was conducted in Manhattan in 1954, Srole reinterviewed as many of the original sample of 1,660 New Yorkers as he could find twenty years later—695 of the original group. Of these, 44 percent still lived in Manhattan, 17 percent had migrated to one of New York's four other boroughs, and another 26 percent resided within the New York–New Jersey metropolitan area, figures that indicate a certain loyalty among New Yorkers to their city and to city living. Comparing the mental-health ratings of people who are in their forties today with those who were in their forties twenty years ago, Dr. Srole found that the proportion of those in need of psychiatric help had dropped by 50 percent. A similar decline was measured when people in their fifties today were compared with those in their fifties twenty years ago.

Of course, other factors than "quality of life" in New York City must be taken into account when examining these rosy figures—

189

such as a general improvement in social and economic conditions, parental influences, and the social forces that shaped the parents themselves in the era in which they grew up. Still, Dr. Srole's findings are encouraging. It is currently quite the fashion among New Yorkers to deplore their city and the life it provides, and at Manhattan cocktail parties there is always a certain amount of agonized talk about rapes, muggings, and burglaries, from people who, it usually turns out, have never actually experienced any of these discomfitures. It may be that New Yorkers, like everyone else, enjoy acting out dramatic fantasies and are helping to feed a myth of New York as a dark and dangerous place—while in reality New York's crime rate is lower than that of Cleveland, Houston, or Washington, D.C. New Yorkers, figuratively speaking, may be complaining happily all the way to the bank.*

True, United States Census figures do show that urban areas have a higher divorce rate than suburban or rural areas. But since one out of five American marriages now ends in divorce, sociologists like Dr. Srole would probably not claim any connection between divorce and mental illness. In fact, he might conclude that divorce was a sign of mental health—our ability to make difficult decisions and to move away from unpleasant situations. What the lower suburban divorce rate may indicate, as we have noted, is that many unhappy suburban marriages are being held together merely by the weight of children, jointly owned property, and co-signed mortgages.

At least one Scarsdale man, recently divorced, says that it was the physical fact of the big suburban house which kept his marriage

*It is curious, in New York, how stories circulate and how, if the story is good enough, it is repeated again and again, with each person who tells it prepared to swear that it happened to her or to him. There is the Bloomingdale's ladies' room handbag story, for example. It goes like this. The person telling the story went into the ladies' room at Bloomingdale's and, inside a booth, hung her handbag on a hook that projected from inside the door. After seating herself, she suddenly saw a hand reach over the door, remove her bag, and depart with it. She reported the incident to the store's security department. A day or so later, she received a telephone call from a person who identified himself as a Bloomingdale's detective. Her bag had been found. She must collect it at the store at a certain hour. When she arrived at the store, however, the security staff had no information on her bag and no idea who might have called her. Returning to her apartment after this fruitless trip, she found it had been burglarized. This author, being male, has never visited the ladies' room at Bloomingdale's to see whether the doors on the booths have inside hooks or apertures at the top through which a bag could be snatched. But having heard the tale from so many New York women who insisted that they had been victimized in this identical fashion, he did check with the security department of Bloomingdale's. The store has no record of any such incident.

together longer than was good for either his former wife or himself—the house, the lawn, the garden, the swimming pool. "Owning a house means endless expenditures of time and money," he says. "For years, while the marriage was going sourer and sourer, we could occupy ourselves—and keep our minds off the situation—with the house, with things that had to be done. The new roof, getting the place painted, keeping the hedges clipped, and getting rid of the crab grass." Finally, he decided to divest himself of all this, and as usually happens, his former wife got the house. Also, as usually happens, he plans to move back to the city, where he feels life for a bachelor will be more congenial. "There's an elegance to New York City social life that was always missing in the suburbs," he says. "There's a European quality, a 'salon' feeling that you get in cities like Paris and Rome and London and Madrid, when people uncertain. A salon in the suburbs is ridiculous on the face of it. But in a city, it is possible."

It is interesting that he should talk fondly of a "salon." A salon is perhaps the direct antithesis to a family room—a room that city apartment dwellers are happy to live without.

21

Back to the City?

*P*erhaps the reasons are psychological. Perhaps they are topographical. Perhaps topography influences psychology (the way ontogeny is alleged to recapitulate philogeny), but it is certainly true that some cities attract in-city dwelling—and a fiercely loyal band of "downtown" lovers—more than others. No one who could afford not to would want, say, to live in downtown Atlanta, Dallas, Detroit, Los Angeles, Washington, or Salt Lake City. Metropolitan apartment living is, on the other hand, quite acceptable in New York, Boston, San Francisco, Chicago, New Orleans, and Philadelphia. When a city provides views of water, in-city living tends to become more attractive. Four of New York's five boroughs are on islands, and the fifth, the Bronx, which is not, is probably the least fashionable of the five in which to live—with the exception of the western strip, called Riverdale, which provides views of the Hudson River and the New Jersey Palisades. "River view" is an asset that is always stressed in advertisements for New York apartments that can boast one, which, as a rule, command higher rents.

Our feelings about water are basic and complex. Our primordial origins were watery, and our bodies are largely composed of water. Water sustains our lives as importantly as air, along with the crops we eat, and has sustained trade since the beginning of human commerce. The great port cities of the world remind us of the success of that commerce. At the same time, in an almost paranoid way, we cast our wastes into the water, leaving it to carry away all unpleasant

192

things. There is a perverse urge to toss the empty beer can over the side of the boat or to hurl the worn-out tire into the river. At the same time, when we look out over water we are somehow reassured.

Chicago has its shimmering lakefront, and San Francisco's hills overlook bay, ocean, and bridges. Because of San Francisco's hills, city dwellers there can achieve their water views from hilltop town houses. In relatively flat New York and Chicago, the views of water are attained from tall apartment buildings, and city ordinances prevent new buildings from interfering with existing water views. Both San Francisco and Boston are peninsular cities, and where San Francisco has the bay, Boston's Back Bay and Beacon Hill have the Charles River. Also peninsular, in a sense, is New Orleans, with the Mississippi River on one side and Lake Pontchartrain on the other, and so is Charleston, South Carolina, where downtown living near the water is even more fashionable than living in the suburbs. It could be theorized that cities which must be approached by bridges carry a special aura of mystery and romance—the excitement of getting there across a ribbon of pavement in the sky, a symbol of man's conquest of water—that makes urban living in these cities more appealing. The recent renaissance of New York City's Roosevelt Island, approachable via a thrilling aerial tramway, would fit this theory: it was created in the heart of the metropolis, and yet it is separate, apart, remote from it.

Cincinnati is another hilly city that relishes its river views, which it likes to compare with the water views of San Francisco. Though the setting of Cincinnati's Hyde Park section, where the best views are, is suburban, residents proudly point out that Hyde Park is technically a part of Cincinnati proper and is therefore "city." Recently, "artistic" Cincinnatians have discovered the pretty hilltop of Mount Adams, which really *is* a part of downtown Cincinnati, and have been attractively renovating and restoring turn-of-the-century brick and frame town houses with river views. (A passer-by recently asked a pedestrian: "Is this the Mount Adams section where everybody's fixing everything up?") The great romantic cities of the world—London, Paris, Florence, Venice, Rome—have all been cities of bridges, and cities where urban living is treasured.

Philadelphia, meanwhile, defies the water-view theory. Though Philadelphia has a river, downtown Philadelphia takes little advantage of it, and the parts of downtown where it is fashionable to live—Rittenhouse Square, for example—have no views of water.

Los Angeles also turns its back on the water. In fact, Los Angeles is possibly the only port city in the world where if one lives near the beach, one lives in a slum.

Mountain views seem, for some reason, to repel in-city dwellers, and urban living is unpopular in Salt Lake City, Denver, and Phoenix—cities which are, incidentally, virtually bridgeless. In cities like these, where the affluent have fled to the suburbs, to go "downtown" at night is to visit empty, and often dangerous, streets and sidewalks. These are the cities where the flight to the suburbs has left an inner city that falls to disuse and decay. Inner-city businesses fail, and shops are boarded up. Doctors, lawyers, and other professional people move their offices to the suburbs. Even the policemen in cities like these dislike the downtown beat at night; they would rather be in the suburbs.

The problem of dealing with inner-city decay has been faced by a number of American cities over the last decade, and expensive attempts have been made to lure people back from the suburbs. Most of these, however, have been unsuccessful. Salt Lake City has lined its main shopping streets with tubs of trees, flowers, park benches, and reflecting pools, without noticeably increasing the number of downtown shoppers. Atlanta several years ago created "Underground Atlanta," which flourished for a while as a tourist attraction and then, as expensive shops and restaurants failed to do the amount of business expected of them, gave way to cheap gift and novelty stores, poster shops, and "head" shops selling hash pipes of futuristic design. In downtown Salt Lake City, Trolley Square has been developed out of what was the city's trolley car barn. Appealing though the idea might sound, Trolley Square has not been successful and is deserted after 5 P.M. In Houston, the same sort of thing was tried in Market Square. It, too, has fizzled, as the owners of buildings grew greedy and charged inflated rents, forcing shopkeepers to overprice ordinary "gifte shoppe" wares. In romantic San Francisco, on the other hand, where in-city living has always had charm and popularity, the renovation of Ghirardelli Square—originally the site of a chocolate factory—has won favor among residents and visitors alike, and is an economic success.

Cleveland is another city with a lakefront but, unlike Chicago, Cleveland has turned its back upon the water and abandoned the shore to a sports arena, a gaggle of factories, and an airfield. The reason generally given for the two cities' opposite feelings about

194

their respective lakes is that Chicago is on the west shore of Lake Michigan, whereas Cleveland is on the south shore of Lake Erie. Great Lakes tides, it seems, move generally in a north-south direction, causing erosion on the southern and northern shores. Cleveland's lakeshore keeps slipping into the lake, and near the water, billboards advertise for landfill. The situation could, of course, be corrected by levees, but these would be expensive, and Cleveland's city fathers have addressed themselves to other matters rather than consider ways in which the lakefront could be improved. Cleveland's lake is little used for boating or other water sports; though Lake Erie is now cleaner than it has been for years, no man-made beaches have been developed as they have been in Chicago; and though the big lake continues to provide a dramatic view, new buildings face the other way. From the new Holiday Inn, only the multilevel parking garage has a view of the lake. Cleveland blames political corruption for the fact that funds have not been made available to beautify and shore up the sagging lakefront but are now being proposed for a project, much more commercially alluring, to extend a giant jet runway into the water. This would surely destroy the lakefront forever. Still, the possibilities for graft in such an enterprise are mind-boggling.

It is probably too early to assess Detroit's recent attempt to "breathe new life" into its downtown area with the Renaissance Center, but if it follows the pattern of Cleveland's Park Centre, the outlook is not cheerful. Park Centre was designed as an immense downtown apartment and shopping complex, with expensive shops and luxury housing. Again, it was hoped that so many attractive substitutes to suburban living would be offered that the flight to the suburbs would turn around, or at least be stemmed. Today, after a series of receiverships, most of Park Centre's large apartments are untenanted. They have become popular, it is said, with Cleveland's black gangsters, and a recent visitor was told: "Every numbers runner in town lives there." From the street, one sees tattered curtains flap from broken windows in the apartment tower, and the building's general appearance of poor maintenance and ill repair have done little to attract affluent suburbanites back to the inner city. In Cleveland, with its murder rate higher than either Washington's or Houston's, the local joke is that "Even the muggers and the hot-watch peddlers leave the city at night for lack of business—and head for Shaker Heights." And even in Shaker Heights, that once famous pocket of suburban wealth, there is trouble as suburbanites move farther and farther out. The Shaker Square shopping center today looks almost as woebegone as Park Centre.

Park Centre's shopping mall is, meanwhile, in even worse shape than the apartment tower that rises above it. More than two thirds of the available shopping space is still unrented and uncompleted, and the wide indoor plazas, corridors, escalators, and courtyards are almost spookily deserted. More shops seem to close than open, and an air of fiscal failure is pervasive. As one wanders through these empty vistas, amid abandoned construction, one wonders what sort of folly could have prompted men and women of supposedly sound business sense to presume that such endeavors could possibly have succeeded. On the lower level, an area that has been given the name Eat Street boasts the largest seating capacity of any dining area in the state of Ohio, and in the unpatronized vastness of Eat Street's many fast-food operations—offering everything from pizza to burgers to fried chicken and back again—one can easily believe this extravagant claim.

One wonders whether the cause of Park Centre's economic woes may be not the venality and greed of the local merchants but the curious view held by chambers of commerce across the country that what the public wants is something cute. Is it for being cute that the suburbs appeal to so many millions of people nowadays? If so, the chambers of commerce in cities like Cleveland are fighting cute with supercute. It is the brand of cuteness that seems to think it is cuter, or fancier, to spell "Centre" Britishly, rather than the way most Americans—and certainly most Middle Westeners—spell it, and that feels dining will be enhanced when it takes place in something called "Eat Street." Cuteness abounds in Park Centre shop-naming. An emporium called Incredible Edibles, for example, is a delicatessen. A clothing shop is called Clothes Circuit. One of Eat Street's fast-food outlets is named Tummy Acres. And so it goes.

Because all the cuteness smacks of Madison Avenue hucksterism, or at least an imitation of it, and because the merchandise offered at the cute-named establishments is of an assembly-line quality that can be found in an airline in-flight gift catalogue, cuteness not only becomes quickly cloying but begins to smack of the second-rate and of retailing desperation. Cute becomes synonymous with cheap—with sandal shops and candle shops and shops that sell macramé and inexpensive jewelry. (Along Scottsdale's much-touted Fifth Avenue, the "exclusive" shops now confine themselves almost exclusively to extravagant examples of the sandalmaker's and the candlemaker's arts, along with a number of stores that sell nothing but imitation Indian squash-blossom necklaces and artificial turquoise rings.)

What the real estate developers of these costly complexes have failed to realize, along with the chambers of commerce with whom the developers work in happy collusion, is that all the archness and coyness add up, in most Americans' minds, to silliness and vulgarity. They underestimate Americans' present sophistication and, in terms of taste, are at least twenty years behind the times. Even the man who delivers your milk has, in all likelihood, been to Europe at least once, and having seen the real thing, he will not be impressed by—in fact, he will be repelled by—a fake trattoria in the basement of a Midwest high-rise.

Cuteness is certainly one of the forces that is doing in Park Centre. In Boston, on the other hand, the restoration of the Quincy Market area—where, among other things, the nineteenth-century architecture around Faneuil Hall was treated with respect—real charm has been substituted for cuteness, and the venture has been a great popular and commercial success. But then inner-city Boston has always been an appealing place to live and visit.

One thing that has happened in the affluent suburbs over the years is that their affluent residents are growing older. The young couples who flocked to suburbia in the years immediately after World War II and who, in a deflated postwar real estate market and with GI loans, bought properties and built houses—to which have been added swimming pools, saunas, tennis courts, and burglar-alarm systems—are now past middle age. Their children are grown and in many cases have children of their own. In Rye, for example, the average resident in 1955 was thirty-six years old. Today, he is forty-seven. With age has come a conservative stance—an opposition, for instance, to increased school taxes, from which suburban school systems have suffered. If the cities have become predominantly Democratic, the wealthy suburbs have become predominantly Republican. In the so-called Five Towns area of southeastern Long Island, everyone talks of how things have changed. The Five Towns—Hewlett, Woodmere, Cedarhurst, Lawrence, and Inwood (the first four were considered fashionable, while the fifth, Inwood, was "where the help lived")—were originally settled by prosperous Jews who had emigrated from Eastern Europe around the turn of the

197

century. They had made money in such endeavors as New York's garment industry, but they still had decidedly socialist and trade-unionist views that they had carried with them from the pogroms of czarist Russia and Poland. For years—particularly during the 1920s, '30s, and '40s—the Five Towns comprised a truly golden ghetto, and life revolved around the Lawrence Beach Club and Woodmere Academy, a private school. Five Towns boys and girls married each other and moved away and so, in time, did their parents—back to the convenience of Manhattan or to the roomier reaches of Westchester County. Into their pleasant houses moved conservative Orthodox Hasidic and Yemenite Jews. Today, according to novelist Beverley Gasner, who, along with her husband, grew up in Lawrence and now lives outside Washington, "It's all different. It used to be lovely—cozy and homey, like a little club, like an extension of your family. Today, the streets are deserted on Saturday because of the Sabbath. The rest of the week, it's a sea of beards, side curls, and yarmulkes."

Blacks have begun moving to the suburbs too—in small numbers, to be sure, but still at a rate that has not particularly delighted the predominantly white suburban establishment. Economic factors—particularly the high price of land and houses—remain the primary barrier to suburban integration. But equal-opportunity programs over the past decade have placed more and more black families at an income level where they can afford the open space and green lawns that first attracted whites. Still, black leaders say that there is a strong psychological reason why blacks remain reluctant to buy homes in white suburbs, where they have been conditioned to expect snubs and discrimination. As one black woman declares: "It's easy enough to get kicked around where we are. Why spend a hundred thousand dollars to get kicked around somewhere else?"

Economically successful blacks have therefore tended either to stay in their old neighborhoods or to move to affluent black communities—such as Collier Heights outside Atlanta, or Baldwin Hills, Ladera Heights, and Leimert Park, south of Los Angeles. In the sprawling San Fernando Valley northeast of Los Angeles, only 2.4 percent of the population was black as recently as 1975, as opposed to a 19 percent black population in Los Angeles as a whole. Recently, a campaign sponsored by the Fair Housing Council and the Ford Foundation has been urging middle-class blacks to move into the Valley. A commercial jingle that chants: "Move on in, move on in, move on in to L.A.'s Valley," has been promoted on

198

local black radio stations, while billboards depicting black and white families sipping cocktails together and enjoying other convivial suburban social situations have sprouted along local highways. Mr. Ken Kelly, a black real estate man and chairman of the campaign, conducts guided tours of San Fernando Valley towns for prospective black buyers, and says: "What we're trying to do is communicate that times have changed, that the mainstream is open to blacks—use it if you want to. I won't say that all discrimination is gone, but we are trying to tell them that it's a lot different than it used to be." It is too early to say how successful this particular promotion will be, and Mr. Kelly admits that many blacks are unwilling to leave black communities because of generations of fear of what happens when a black tries to rock the white man's boat. The campaign came at a time when the Los Angeles Board of Education faced a court order to bus in order to integrate schools, and emotions were running high among both blacks and whites on the busing issue. But Mr. Kelly takes the attitude: "If somebody had done something like this ten years ago, maybe you wouldn't have needed busing. The schools would already be integrated."

The suburban population growing older, more stodgy, more set in its ways ... neighborhoods changing, either for the worse or becoming prohibitively expensive ... integration, or the lack of it ... school systems that are threatened ... taxes ... battles for (and against) zoning changes ... widening streets to accommodate heavier suburban traffic ... the noise from the thruways ... the air-pollution level. These are the topics that dominate the suburban Friday- and Saturday-night cocktail parties in the late 1970s, that are discussed around the pool and outdoor barbecue, within the indoor sauna, at the beauty parlor, in the supermarket, and at the garage sale. These issues, and others like them, have turned a younger generation sour on the suburbs, and sent them fleeing to farms in rural Vermont, or back to the cities their parents fled, in order to see whether, perhaps, the answer isn't city living after all. "We worked so hard to get away from Houston Street!" wails a New York Jewish mother whose daughter has moved into a SoHo loft.

The back-to-the-city movement has already had disruptive side effects, because as the middle-class young move back into the urban core, the poor—who were originally forced in—are now being forced out. Not long ago, the *New York Times* reported the cases of two Washington, D.C., neighbors who had never met and yet whose fates were closely linked. One was a twenty-eight-year-old white architect named Robert Corcoran, and the other was a poor black woman named Beatrice Poindexter, who lived just down the street. Mr. Corcoran, repelled by what he called the "sterility" of suburban living, had bought a run-down house on a mostly black street in Washington's Adams-Morgan section, not far from downtown. He had paid very little for his house, but had the wherewithal to undertake an elaborate plan for its renovation and restoration. All at once, the street became "hot" real estate property, and Miss Poindexter was being evicted from her $84.50 a month apartment because a real estate developer wanted to convert the whole row of houses on her street into "town houses" to sell for $70,000 and up. Miss Poindexter had no idea where she was going to go.

This "resettlement of urban America," as the sociologists call it, is of course an ironic reversal of the blockbusting that turned many cities black in recent years. In Washington, for example, the 1970 census showed the city to be 71 percent black. In mid-1977, however, the Washington Center for Metropolitan Studies reported that the city had begun to gain white population again, and that most of these newcomers were young, and college-educated, and from the middle and upper middle class. Suddenly, this is a process that is being repeated in many cities—in the South End of Boston, the Park Slope section of Brooklyn, and Queens Village in Philadelphia.

On the one hand, the well-to-do young newcomers are a blessing to the old cities. By rehabilitating once-fine houses, they are reviving decayed neighborhoods. Run-down tenements are being sand-blasted and gutted, fitted with skylights, new plumbing, and air conditioning. Run-down areas become both prettier and safer, and they attract new businesses—all of which help a city's often sagging tax base. But then there is the inexorable consequence. Like displaced war refugees, thousands of the poor are pushed elsewhere, often deeper into the poorer black or Puerto Rican ghettos. Already a torrent of eviction notices is falling on the residents of Adams-Morgan, and the area is now nearly one-third white. It is getting whiter by the day.

Though Beatrice Poindexter does not know Robert Corcoran, she bitterly resents what is happening to her old neighborhood. She refers to the man who gave her a two-week eviction notice as a greedy "speculator," and it does not help that the particular developer who bought her building happens to be Jewish. Blacks have long distrusted Jews, and regarded them as their natural enemies.

200

The developer, Jeffrey N. Cohen, sees things somewhat differently and says: "We are not speculators—we are investors and developers." He insists that he does not buy and then sell houses to run up their prices, a tactic known in real estate circles as "flipping." Instead, he renovates houses in order to deliver a "quality product," and gain a good but not excessive profit for himself. Like many developers, he blames the woes of people like Miss Poindexter on the city government, which encourages the middle class to come to—and stay in—town, without making any provision for the poor who are supplanted. "I say the developer has the moral responsibility to pay for an evicted tenant's moving," says Mr. Cohen, "but he should not have to subsidize them to stay in the area—which is what most of them seem to expect us to do."

It is, meanwhile, another irony that one of the aspects of the street which Mr. Corcoran particular likes is its "racial diversity"—though he admits that this pleasant diversity will soon disappear as more people like him move into Adams-Morgan. And as more people like Mr. Corcoran move in, it will not only be poor rental tenants who will be displaced. A number of black property owners in the Adams-Morgan area are nervous—but for economic, not racial, reasons. One of these is Robert Corcoran's next-door neighbor, Ernest Gordon, a fifty-four-year-old black man who is a clerk at the Pentagon. Mr. Gordon gets along well with Mr. Corcoran—in fact, the two men are quite friendly—but Mr. Gordon is unhappy with what's happening to his block. The reason is that his property taxes have nearly doubled in the last two years, since Adams-Morgan all at once became chic. The fact that his house has also soared in value does not impress Mr. Gordon, for the simple reason that he has no wish to sell and move. "Where would I go at age fifty-four?" he asks. Still, he may be forced to go—somewhere—if the day comes when he can no longer afford to pay his taxes.

A number of community advocates have been searching for means to allow at least some city residents to buy their houses—cooperatively, perhaps—before prices climb out of reach in neighborhoods like Adams-Morgan. Margarita Suarez, head of Adelante, a Hispanic group in Washington, said before a hearing of the Civil Rights Commission not long ago: "The only way to stay in a community is if you own some of the land, because then you can control what happens on it." Thus far, however, no way has been found to accomplish this "only way." Others are more cynical about

201

the situation. Paul Tauber, a businessman who recently opened—and then sold at a considerable profit—a tavern that caters to the well-heeled newcomers to Adams-Morgan, says that the displacement of the poor by the better off is just "part of city life." When it happens, it happens. When change occurs, he says, "Someone has to suffer, someone has to lose," adding that the city, in not making adequate provision for the displaced, "was not reacting to the reality of what is required." What the reality of what is required *is*, Mr. Tauber does not say.

One requirement that seems obvious is that the cities cannot survive if they are abandoned to the poor. One reality is that city, state, and federal governments have failed so abysmally and systematically in helping the poor that both the middle class and the poor have despaired of this sort of salvation's ever coming from any government at all. Another reality is that government cannot afford to intrude itself into the redevelopment of inner-city life, nor can it afford to leave matters to the realtors and developers with whom government politicians have worked so profitably hand-under-the-table-in-hand.

Neighborhoods, throughout history, have always had an uncanny ability to care for themselves. Even the most egregious-looking block in Harlem has its sense of neighborhood. But when, under the guise of slum clearance or better housing, these old neighborhoods have been razed and replaced with government housing projects, the results have been, without exception, disastrous. On the other hand, old neighborhoods have been, and can be, revived by individuals in the neighborhoods themselves. Salvation of the cities can be accomplished through personal involvement—people in neighborhoods being encouraged to work *for* their neighborhoods. City politicians must realize that only the middle and upper classes—not the poor—can rebuild cities, but they can do so only if the terms are made attractive to them, if they are not penalized for upgrading neighborhoods through increased taxes, and if they are convinced that the money they spend will allow them to live a life free of terror. Encouraging the rich to come back to the city, and not penalizing poorer property owners like Mr. Gordon by doubling his taxes in two years' time because he happens to live on a street that is taking on an air of swank, should not result in the displacement of the poor. Instead, such neighborhood renewal should create more jobs for the poor, which would give them more money to live wherever they chose—in the suburbs, for example.

Though there are doubtless some who would say that this approach to urban renewal would never work, it must be conceded that it has never been tried on any sort of consistent basis. And meanwhile, in neighborhoods like Adams-Morgan, the rich and the poor, the white and the black, circle each other like suspicious dogs, sniffing and snarling at one another.

Elsewhere, this sort of thing happens: In the Mount Adams section of Cincinnati, a number of people have bought old houses and expensively renovated them. The neighborhood has not "gone rich" in any sense, but less affluent neighbors have caught the newcomers' spirit and have added decorative touches, such as window boxes, to their houses, and all at once, a formerly dowdy neighborhood has taken on an air of turn-of-the-century graciousness. One Mount Adams man, who is not rich, owns an empty lot next to his house which he operates as a small parking lot, and from which he derives a small income. Recently the city raised his taxes on the lot, offering as an explanation: "A nice house could be built there." Now the owner of the lot is forced to raise his parking rates, and this neither helps the garage-less, less well off neighbors who use his lot, nor does much to build good feeling in the neighborhood. "If cities would leave neighborhoods alone," he says, "neighborhoods would get along just fine." Which makes more than a little sense.

One wonders what the next generation—Mr. Corcoran's children, say, if he has children—of the affluent in-city people will do. Will city life lose its luster for them, will rising taxes push them outward to some unnamed suburb of the future? Will neighborhoods like Adams-Morgan and Mount Adams in time become slums again—the rich and the poor shifting backward and forward against each other as inexorably as the tides of Lake Erie? After all, once upon a time Adams-Morgan was a good address. Then it deteriorated. Now it has become fashionable again. Are American life and American living always to be engaged in this seesaw interaction? Some city planners believe so. "The traditional approach in America is that we use up places, and then move on," says Harvey S. Perloff, dean of architecture and urban planning at the University of California at Los Angeles. When Adams-Morgan is "used up," the likes of Robert Corcoran will find another address.

Of course, if the direst predictions about future shortages of fuel and energy come true, the suburbs will be in even deeper trouble. There will be no gasoline for the automobiles that propelled the rush to the suburbs in the first place, and are still the suburbs' lifeline. There will be no gas for the power mowers that manicure suburban lawns, to say nothing of fuel for heating swimming pools. But meanwhile the suburbs continue to expand and proliferate. At latest count there were more than twenty thousand suburban communities in the United States, and the number grows daily. It has been estimated that the suburban population in the last fifteen years has accounted for 75 percent of the nation's growth. The suburbs are emerging as our newest majority. As Samuel Kaplan, director of the New York City Educational Construction Fund says: "The quintessence of America is now suburbia. It is in suburbia that most of the nation's growth is occurring—in population, in jobs, and in power. After growing from a nation of farms to a nation of cities, it is clear from all signs that America has become a nation of suburbs."

To be able to "move on" is a luxury that is still not affordable by everyone. It is a truism to say that the rich have always had it better than the poor, and that the haves—at every level of society and at every stage of history—have had more mobility than the have-nots, whether the move is by camel caravan or air-conditioned limousine. It is also true that the American rich are often bored, often restless. It seems certain that the restless privileged of America will never be content to be settled in one place for very long, and will always be pushing outward or inward—into the bustling cities one moment, out to the wooded hills the next, searching for something of the past with one hand and something of the future with another, in pursuit of some suburbia of the mind, chasing the dream of the good life, the *perfect* life, that must exist, or be made to exist, on some patch of real estate or another. Hooked into the dream of the "upwardly mobile"—a term we Americans invented—is the certainty that whatever inconveniences life may present us at the moment, wherever we may be, this, too, shall pass. To help it pass, we move on. To a new house in, we hope, a better neighborhood.

Index

ASPCA (American Society for the Prevention of Cruelty to Animals), 96, 97
Adams, John Quincy, 45
Adams-Morgan section of Washington, D.C., 200–203
Adelante, 201
age of suburbanites, average, 197
Ailey, Alvin, 143
alcohol, availibility of:
  in Hudson, Ohio, 34
  in Salt Lake City, Utah, 22–23
Ali, Muhammad, 5
Allen, Ivan, 81
Allen O'Neill Drive, Darien, Conn., 103–104
Alta Club, Salt Lake City, Utah, 27
Amberley Village, Ohio, 51
American Bar Association, 76
American Psychiatric Association, 188
American Yacht Club, 80–81, 117, 120, 173
Anderson, James Bonbright, 35
Anderson, William P., 149
Annenberg, Walter H., 134, 139
Anti-Defamation League, Southern Council, 72, 76
anti-Semitism, 78–82
  in Atlanta clubs, 68–73
  See also Jews, acceptance of
Apawamis Golf Club, 78, 120, 173
Archbold, John, 127
Ardmore, Pa., 134
Ardsley Club, 129
Arizona Ballet, 15
Arizona Republic, 15
Arizona State University, 13, 15

art museums, as means of social entry, 177
Ashland, Linda, 160
Atherton, Calif., 153
Atlanta, Ga.:
  old families, 75–76
  private clubs, 68–77
  urban life in, 192, 194
Atlanta Constitution, 75, 76
Atlanta Journal, 75, 76
Autry, Gene, 7

Baker, James A., site of house, 7
Baker, John, 50
Bala-Cynwyd, Pa., 134, 135
Baldwin Hills, Calif., 198
Barclay Classes, 78, 177
Barlow, Haven, 28
Bell, Griffin, 68, 75, 79
Belvedere, 124
Benjamin, Allan, 158–159
Berwyn, Pa., 134, 135
Best, Mrs. Hugh, 136
Beverly Hills, Calif., 166, 172
  sex practices in, 181
Bing, Rudolf, 71
Birmingham, Mich., 64
Birnam Wood Club, Santa Barbara, 164
Black, Mrs. Jennie Prince, 127
blacks, acceptance of, 174, 198–199
  in Atlanta clubs, 71, 77
  in Grosse Pointe, Mich., 174
  in Philadelphia suburbs, 67, 139
  in Rye, N.Y., 119
Blood and Money, Thompson, 6

Bloomfield Hills, Mich., 64, 174
    financial burdens of life in, 183–185
Bloomingdale's ladies' room handbag story,
        190 n.
Boston, Mass., 131, 141
    Quincy Market, 197
    urban life in, 192
    water views, 193
Boulders, The, Ariz., 16
Brace, Dr. Charles, 125–126
Brando, Marlon, 60
Brigham Young University, 25
Bronfman, Edgar, 106
Bronfman, Samuel, 124
Brown, Franklin Q., 126–127
Brown, Walston H., 126–127
Bryce, Mrs. Angelica Schuyler, 165
Bryce, Peter Cooper, 165
Bryn Mawr, Pa., 133, 134, 176
Buffalo, N.Y., sex practices in, 182
Buffalo Tennis & Squash Club, 182
Burlingame, Calif., 153
Bush, George, 5
Butes, James, site of house, 8
Butler, Michael, 161

Camargo Country Club, 48, 51
Candidate, The, 154
Candler, Asa W., 76
Candler, John S., II, 76
Capital City Club, 68–69, 73
Carefree, Ariz., 16–18
Carnegie, Nancy (Mrs. Percy Rockefeller), 94
Carroll, Gen. Howard, 123
Carrollcliff, 123–124
Carter, Frank, 69, 82
Carter, Jimmy, 68
Carter, Victor, II, 8
Carter, Victor, III, 8
Castellane, Count Paul Ernest Boniface de, 125
Castro, Raul, 13
Cedarhurst, N.Y., 197
Center for the Study of Democratic Institutions,
        165
Chambers, Ann Cox, 75–76
change in suburbs, causes of, 197–200
Chapin, Roy, 64
charity, local, as means of social entry, 178
Charleston, S.C., 131, 193
Chase, Harold, 165
Chase, Pearl, 162, 165
Cherokee Club, 72
Chicago, Ill., 192, 194–195
    water views, 193
children, advantage of, in suburbs, 177
Churchill, Winston, 127
church membership, 177
Cincinnati, Ohio, 39–46, 131, 141
    Blue Book, 54

Cincinnati, Ohio (cont'd)
    cultural life, 52
    Fountain Square, 41–42
    Mount Adams, 193, 203
    old families, 44, 49–55
    Procter & Gamble, 43–47
    skyline, 41
    Spring Grove Cemetery, 39–40
    suburbs:
        Amberley Village, 51
        Clifton, 48
        Glendale, 43, 44, 46, 47
        Grandin Road, 48–49, 55–56
        Hyde Park, 42, 43, 48–49, 50, 51, 55–56
        Indian Hill, 39, 40, 43, 47–48, 51, 53
        Madison Road, 48
        Mariemont, 43, 50
        Terrace Park, 43, 53
    urban center, 41–42
    urban problems, 171
    water views, 193
    Wesley Chapel, 45, 172
Cincinnati, 45
Cincinnati Country Club, 48, 51
Cincinnati Enquirer, 45, 53
Cincinnati Post, 45
city life, 188–191
    problems of, 171–173
    mental health in, 188–189
    return to, 191, 192–197
Cleveland, Ohio, 33–38
    crime rate, 190
    old families, 33
    suburbs, 33, 122
        Hudson, 34–38
        Peninsula, 37
    urban life, 37–38, 194–197
Clifton, Ohio, 48, 171
club cars on commuter lines, 110–113
clubs, private, see private clubs
Coca-Cola families, 76
Cohen, Dolly, 53
Cohen, Jeffrey N., 201
Cohen, John, 71
Collier Heights, Ga., 198
Commerce Club, 72
commute, definition of, 106–107
commuting, art of, 107–114
Connecticut Turnpike, 86–87, 99
Conrad, Barnaby, 161
Coral Casino, 166
Coronado High School, Scottsdale, Ariz., 12
Corbett, Patricia (Mrs. Ralph), 49, 55
Corbett, Ralph, 49
Corbett Foundation, 49
Corcoran, Robert, 200, 201
Cornwall, Conn., 174
Country Club of Detroit, 60
Country Club Plaza, shopping center, 180

country clubs, *see* private clubs
Courtlandt Place, Houston, Texas, 8–9
Cox, Lori, 11–13
Crest Hills Country Club, 51
crime:
  comparative rates, 190
  in Darien, Conn., 100–102
Custance, James D., 69, 79

D. B. Cooper's, 23
Dallas, Texas, urban life in, 192
Darien, Conn., 87, 99–105, 172, 174, 175
Darien Review, 104
Darlington, Thomas, 17
Dartmouth College, 93
Daylesford, Pa., 134
Daylight Time, 16
decor, interior, 176
Denver, Colo., urban living in, 194
Depew, Chauncey, 130
Detroit, Mich., 57–64
  old families, 57–58, 61, 62
  Renaissance Plaza, 59, 195
  suburbs:
    Birmingham, 64
    Bloomfield Hills, 64
    Grosse Pointe, 57–64, 122, 135, 174, 183
    relationship to city, 59
  urban life in, 192
Detroit Symphony, 59
Devereaux, Marion, 53–54
Devon, Pa., 134
Dillman, Bradford, 161
Disabled American Veterans, 13
discrimination:
  against blacks, 61, 69, 78–82
  against Jews, 68–73, 78–82
  against single women, 156–158
divorce, incidence of, 190
  in Hudson, Ohio, 35
  reasons for, 187–188
  in suburbs, 182
Dodge, Marcellus Huntley, 90–91
Douthit, Claude, Jr., 146
Dow, Earl, 4
Downs, Hugh, 17
dress:
  Main Line, 136
  Santa Barbara, 161
  Scottsdale, Ariz., 14
  Watch Hill, R.I., 148
Drulie, Sylvia, 143
Drury, Samuel S., 147
Duchin, Peter, 148
Dykema, Mrs. Raymond, 63

Eagle's Nest, 14
earthquake at Santa Barbara, Calif., 163
East Aurora, N.Y., 182

East Ridge Shopping Center, 154
Eccles, George, 26
Einstein, Albert, 145
Elite Directory, 128
Elson, Edward, 72, 76
Emeny, Brooks, 92
Emery, John, 49–50
Emery, Mary M., 43, 50
Emery Auditorium, 50

Fadiman, Clifton, 161
Fairfield County, Conn., 87–105, 122
family room, 187–188
Federal Heights, Utah, 21
financial burdens of suburban life, 183–185
Finneran, Jane, 54–55
Fish, Mrs. Stuyvesant, 147
Five Towns area of Long Island, N.Y., 197–198
Flagler, Henry Morrison, 133
Florestal, 165
food, in suburbs, 176
  eaten by rich people, 74
Ford, Eleanor (Mrs. Edsel), 62
Ford, Emory, 62
Ford, Frederick Clifford, 62
Ford, Henry, Sr., 61, 63
Ford, Henry, II, 61–62, 64
Ford, John B., 62
Ford, Walter Buhl, 62
Franklin, DeJongh, 71, 72
Franzen, Ulrich, 185
Frisch, Mrs. Robert, 81
Fromm, Erich, 188

Gable, Clark, 75
Galleria Shopping Center, 6
Gans, Herbert, 183
Gasner, Beverley, 198
Geier, Inga, 51
General Motors families, 165–166, 183
Geraldine Rockefeller Dodge Foundation, 97–98
Ghirardelli Square, 194
Gilligan, John, 55
Giralda, 90–91, 98
Gladstone Car, 111–113
Gladwyne, Pa., 133
Glendale, Ohio, 43, 44, 46, 47, 171
Godfather, The, 60
Goldwater, Barry, 11, 12
Gone with the Wind, 75
Goodsell, Almira Geraldine (Mrs. William
    Rockefeller), 89
Goodstein, Jeanette (Mrs. Leonard), 186–188
Goodstein, Leonard, 15, 186–188
Gordon, Ernest, 201, 202
Gordon, The Rev. Ernest, 146
Gould, Anna (Duchesse de Talleyrand), 125
Gould, Jay, 124

Gracemere, 129
Grand Central Station, N.Y., homosexual rendezvous in, 182
Grapple St., Rye, N.Y., 119
Grasso, Ella, 111
Gratz, Helen (Mrs. Godfrey Rockefeller), 93
Gratz, Rebecca, 93
Great Salt Lake, 27–29
Green, Adelaide Browning (Mrs. H. Stuart), 129
Greenwich, Conn., 87–98, 99, 117, 167, 172, 174, 175
  railroad station, homosexuals in, 182
Grey, Mrs. Horace, 165
Griffin, Merv, 167
Grosse Pointe, Mich., 57–64, 122, 135, 174, 183
  automobile people in, 183
  development of, 63
  Ford families in, 61–62
  Lake Shore Road, 64
  relationship to Detroit, 59
Grosse Pointe City, Mich., 59
Grosse Pointe Farms, Mich., 59, 60
Grosse Pointe Park, Mich., 59, 60
Grosse Pointe Shores, Mich., 58, 59
Grosse Pointe Woods, Mich., 59, 60
growth of suburbs, vii–viii, 122–130
Gulph Mills Golf Club, 67

Hall, Seymour, 111, 113
Hamilton, Alexander, II, 127
Handy, Helen Parmalee, 58
Hanna, Mark, 34
Harvard University, 93
Harkness, Rebekah (Mrs. William Hale), 143
Harkness, William Hale, 143
Harlow, Harry, 79–80
Harness, Edward G., 43
Harrison, Benjamin, 51
Harrison, Charles Learner, III, 51–53
Harrison, Edmond, 52
Harrison, Learner Blackman, 52
Harrison, Molly (Mrs. Charles L., III), 51–53, 178
Harrison, Pegram, 69
Harrison, William Henry, 45, 51
Haverford, Pa., 133
Heirloom Cities, 131
Heminway, Mrs. John, 148
Herring, Joanne (Mrs. Robert), 4–5
Herring, Robert, 4–5
Hewlett, N.Y., 197
Hill, Jesse, 77
Hill, Joan Robinson (Mrs. John), 6
Hill, John, 6
Hillsborough, Calif., 153, 154
Hitchings, Nancy, 102
Hite, Kathleen, 17

Hodge, Shelby, 5
Holliday, Benjamin, 124
homosexual rendezvous points, 182
hospital work as means of social entry, 177–178
Houston, Texas, 3–10
  Courtlandt Place, 8–9
  crime rate, 190
  Heights, 7
  old families, 7–8
  River Oaks, 3–7, 9–10
  urban life in, 7–9, 194
Hovas, Alessandra (Sandra) (Baroness di Portanova), 5
Hovhaness, Alan, 154
Hudson, David, 34
Hudson, Ohio, 34–38, 141
  social distinctions in, 35–36
Hudson Country Club, 35
Hughes, Howard, 25
Hurley, Mrs. Collier, 4
Hussein, King of Jordan, 4–5
Hutchins, Robert, 165
Hyde Park, Ohio, 42, 43, 48–49, 50, 51, 55–56, 171, 172, 193

Indian Hill, Ohio, 39, 40, 43, 47–48, 51, 53, 171, 173
Indian Village, Rye, N.Y., 117
Ingersoll, Anna, 131
inner city life, see urban life
interior decor, 176
Inwood, N.Y., 197
Ireland, Harry, 108

Jackson, Mr. and Mrs. Keith, 3–4
Jackson, Maynard, 71
Jagger, Mick, 161
Jamail's, 6–7
Jews, acceptance of:
  in Atlanta clubs, 68–73, 76
  in California suburbs, 166
  in Cincinnati, 51
  in country clubs, 67–82
  in Darien, Conn., 103
  in Five Towns, Long Island, N.Y., 197–198
  in Grosse Pointe, Mich., 61, 174
  in Hudson, Ohio, 37
  in Los Angeles Country Club, 37
  in Philadelphia suburbs, 67, 133, 134, 139
  at Procter & Gamble, 47
  in Twigs, 117–118
  in Watch Hill, R.I., 145
Joy, Helen Newberry (Mrs. Henry B.), 57–59, 64

Kansas City, Mo., suburbs of, 179–181
Kanzler, Mrs. Robert, 62
Kaplan, Samuel, 204
Kelly, Ken, 199

Kimball, Spencer W., 27
King & Spalding, law firm, 73, 79
Kinsolving, Arthur Lee, 146
Kirbo, Charles, 75
Korda, Michael, 159–160
Krumm, John M., 146

Ladera Heights, Calif., 198
La Grange, Gerald, 120
Lake St. Clair, Mich., 58, 63
Lance, Bert, 68, 79
Lawrence, N.Y., 197, 198
Lazarus, Irma (Mrs. Fred, III), 42, 49, 55
Lazarus, Ralph, 49
Lehr, Harry, 147
Leigh, Vivien, 75
Leimert Park, Calif., 198
Levittown, N.Y., 37
Lewisohn, Adolph, 89
Light, Goddard, 119
Lighthouse Book Store, 119
Lincoln, Florence, 92
Lincoln, Frederic, 92
Lindsay, Samuel, 146
Lipschutz, Bob, 73
liquor laws:
    Hudson, Ohio, 34
    Salt Lake City, Utah, 23
Little Town Club, 162, 164
living rooms, use of, 186–187
Longworth, Alice Roosevelt, 48
Los Altos, Calif., 153, 154, 156–158
Los Angeles, Calif., 159
    urban life in, 192
    water views, 194
Los Angeles Country Club, 67
Losantiville Country Club, 51
Loudon Woods, Rye, N.Y., 117
Lyndhurst, 124–125

McAllister, Ward, 147
McDaniel, Hattie, 75
McDonald, Duncan, 21
McIlvain, Alan, Jr., 140
Mack, Mrs. Edgar, 48
McMillan, James, 58
MacMullan, Mrs. Katherine, 139
McQueen, Butterfly, 75
Mad River, Vt., 94
Maddox, Lester, 71
Mafia:
    in Arizona suburbs, 14
    in Detroit suburbs, 60
Main Line suburbs of Philadelphia, 131–140, 141
    dress, 136
    manners, 137–138
    old families, 135
    speech peculiarities, 135–136

Manhattan, mental health in, 189–190
Manny, Elizabeth (Mrs. Ralph), 117
Manursing Island Club, 120, 173
Mariemont, Ohio, 43, 50
Markel, Mrs. Babette, 155
Martineau, Harriet, Society in America, 57–58
Massell, Sam, 71
Mazzola, John W., 143
Mead, Margaret, 171–172, 174
Mendenhall, Mrs. Joseph, 20, 24
Menlo Park, Calif., 153–154
mental health, 183, 188–191
Merion, Pa., 134
Merion Cricket Club, 67
Merion Golf Club, 67
Merritt Parkway, 85–86
Metropolitan Opera, 71, 96, 97
Midtown Manhattan Study, 188
Milton Point, Rye, N.Y., 117
Misquamicut Club, 143, 145, 148, 149
Miss Doherty's College Preparatory School, 52
Mitchell, Margaret, 75
Mixter, Mr. and Mrs. James, 50
Mizner, Addison, 164
Model, Jean, 91
monkeys, experiment in discrimination, 79–80
Montecito, Calif., 167
Montecito Club, 164
Montessori School, Hudson, Ohio, 36, 37
Montgomery, Jim, 75
Moore, James, 112
Morgan, J. Pierpont, 129
Mormons, life style of, 22–27
    notable families, 27
Mosbacher, Emil, Jr. (Bus), 80
Mount Adams, Cincinnati, 193, 203
Mountain View, Calif., 153, 154
mountain views, 194
Mount Desert Island, Maine, 147–148
Myers, Paul and Suzie, 141–142, 146, 149–150

Narberth, Pa., 134, 135
National Center for Health Statistics, 189
National Patriotism Week, 13
neighborhood relations in Calif. suburbs, 159
neighborhoods, city, 202–203
Neiman-Marcus, 6
New Canaan, Conn., 87, 99
New Haven Railroad, 87
New Orleans, La., urban life in, 192
    water views, 193
New Rochelle, N.Y., 172
New York, N.Y.:
    crime rate, 190
    suburbs of:
        Fairfield County, Conn., 87–105
        Westchester County, N.Y., 115–130
    urban life in, 192
    water views, 192–193

New York City Educational Construction Fund, 204
New York Journal-American, 92
New York Yacht Club, 80, 117
Newark, N.J., 172
Newberry, John Stoughton, 58
Newberry, Oliver, 58
Newberry, Truman, 64
Newberry, Walter, 58
Newberry & McMillan, Capitalists, 58
Newport, R.I., 147
Noroton Yacht Club, 103
Northeast Harbor, Maine, 147–148

Ocean House Hotel, 144
old families:
  Atlanta, 75–76
  Cincinnati, 44, 49–55
  Cleveland, 33
  Detroit, 57–58, 61, 62
  Houston, 7–8
  Philadelphia, 135
  Salt Lake City, 27
  Santa Barbara, 164
  Watch Hill, R.I., 142
  Westchester County, 127–129
Oliver, John L., 58
Olympia Tea Room, 144
Olympus Cove, Utah, 21
Ophir Farm, Purchase, N.Y., 124
Operation Mailbag, 13
Oquirrh Mountains, Utah, 21
Overbrook, Pa., 134
Owen, Annie, 4–5

Palmer, K. T., 17
Palo Alto, Calif., 153, 154
Paoli, Pa., 134
Pappenheimer, Eloise, 71
Paradise Valley, Ariz., 16
Park Centre, Cleveland, Ohio, 195–197
Parker, Suzy, 161
Pasadena, Calif., 166
patriotism in Arizona, 11–13
Peabody, Endicott, 147
Peachtree Plaza, 73
Peninsula, Ohio, 37
Pennock, Liddon, 139
Penn Valley, Pa., 134
Pepper, George Wharton, 147
Perloff, Harvey S., 203
Piedmont Ball, 74, 75, 76
Piedmont Driving Club, 68–77, 79–80, 81–82
Pinnacle Peak, 14
Philadelphia, Pa., 133
  food in, 131
  old families, 135
  suburbs of, 67, 131–140
  urban life in, 192, 193

Philadelphia Country Club, 67
Philadelphian, The, 132
Phoenix, Ariz., 11–18
  cultural life, 15
  life style, 15–16
  patriotism in, 11–13
  political orientation, 13, 15–16
  real estate speculation in, 14–15
  restaurants, 14
  schools, 12–13, 18
  sports, 15
  suburbs:
    Boulders, The, 16–17
    Carefree, 16–18
    Scottsdale, 11–16
  urban living, 13–14, 194
Phoenix Symphony, 15
Pocantico Hills, 88, 89, 94, 124
Poindexter, Beatrice, 200
political orientation of suburbs, 197
  Darien, Conn., 104
  Five Towns, Long Island, N.Y., 198
  Hudson, Ohio, 35
  Philadelphia, Main Line, 138
  Salt Lake City, Utah, 21
  San Francisco, Calif., 153
  Scottsdale, Ariz., 13, 15–16
polygamy in Salt Lake City, 24
Portanova, Baron Enrico di, 5
Port Huron, Mich., 167
Price, Leontyne, 71
Princeton University, 93
private clubs:
  Alta Club, Salt Lake City, 27
  American Yacht Club, 80–81, 117, 120, 173
  Apawamis Golf Club, Rye, N.Y., 78, 120, 173
  in Atlanta, Ga., 68–77
  Birnam Wood Club, Santa Barbara, 164
  Camargo, Cincinnati, 48, 51
  Capital City Club, Atlanta, 68–69, 73
  Cherokee Club, Atlanta, 72
  Cincinnati Country Club, 48, 51
  Commerce Club, Atlanta, 72
  Coral Casino, Santa Barbara, 166
  Country Club of Detroit, 60
  Crest Hills, Cincinnati, 51
  in Darien, Conn., 103
  discrimination in, 78–82
  Gulph Mills Golf Club, Philadelphia, 67
  Hudson Country Club, 35
  Jews in, 68–82
  Little Town Club, Santa Barbara, 162, 164
  Los Angeles Country Club, 67
  Losantiville, Cincinnati, 51
  Manursing Island Club, Rye, 120, 173
  membership in, 173–174, 178
  Merion Cricket Club, 67
  Merion Golf Club, 67

private clubs (cont'd)
  Misquamicut Club, Watch Hill, R.I., 143, 145, 148, 149
  Montecito Club, Santa Barbara, 164
  New York Yacht Club, 80, 117
  Noroton Yacht Club, 103
  Piedmont Driving Club, Atlanta, 68–77, 78–79, 81–82
  Progressive Club, Atlanta, 72
  Radnor Hunt Club, 67
  in Rye, N.Y., 118, 120
  Shenerock Shore Club, Rye, N.Y., 118
  Standard Club, Atlanta, 72
  Valley Club, Santa Barbara, 164
  Wee Burn Country Club, Darien, 103, 104, 173
  Woodway Club, Darien, 103
Procter, William Cooper, 43, 47
Procter & Gamble, influence in Cincinnati, 43–47
Progressive Club, 72

Quincy Market, Boston, 197

race discrimination, 78–82
  in Atlanta clubs, 69
  in Cincinnati, 55–56
  in Darien, Conn., 103
  in Detroit, 61
  in Philadelphia suburbs, 67
Radnor, Pa., 133, 135
Radnor Hunt Club, 67
real estate speculation, 14–15
Redford, Robert, *The Candidate,* 154
Redwood City, Calif., 153, 154
Reid, Whitelaw, 124
religious discrimination:
  in Cincinnati, 51
  in Salt Lake City, 21–22, 25
  See also Jews, acceptance of
Renaissance Plaza, 59, 195
renovation of slum areas, 200
Reserve Inn, 35
resorts, summer, 141–150
restaurants and bars:
  D. B. Cooper's, Salt Lake City, 23
  Eagle's Nest, Phoenix, 14
  Olympia Tea Room, Watch Hill, R.I., 144
  Pinnacle Peak, Phoenix, 14
  Reserve Inn, Hudson, Ohio, 35
Rice, H. B., site of house, 7
Rich, Michael Peter, 69–70, 76
Rich, Morris, 69, 70
Rich, Richard, 69, 70
Riverdale, N.Y., 192
River Oaks, Texas, 3–7, 9–10
river views, Cincinnati, 42
Robinson, Ash, 6
Robinson, Oscar, 55–56

Rockefeller, Andrew, 95
Rockefeller, David, 88
Rockefeller, Emma, 89
Rockefeller, Geraldine (Ethel) (Mrs. Marcellus H. Dodge), 89, 90–91
Rockefeller, Godfrey, 91, 93
Rockefeller, Mrs. Godfrey, 94
Rockefeller, Godfrey Stillman, 88
Rockefeller, James Stillman, 94–95
Rockefeller, John D., Sr., 88, 89, 124, 129
Rockefeller, John D., Jr., 88, 89
Rockefeller, John D., III, 88, 106
Rockefeller, Laurance, 88
Rockefeller, Molly (Mrs. William), 95, 96
Rockefeller, Nelson, 88, 93
Rockefeller, Percy, 89, 91, 92, 93
  children of, 91–92
Rockefeller, William, Sr., 88–90, 95–96
  estate of, 92
Rockefeller, William, 94, 95–96, 97–98, 120
Rockefeller, William G., 89, 90, 91
  children of, 91–92
Rockefeller, Winthrop, 88
Rockefellers, Greenwich branch, 87–98
  life style, 94
  summer camp, 95–96
  wealth of, 92, 97
Rockefellers, Tarrytown branch, 88–98
  life style of, 94
  wealth of, 96–97
Rogers, Henry H., 89
Rojas, Mr. and Mrs. Manuel, 161, 166
Romney, Melbourne, 23
Roosevelt Island, N.Y., 193
Rosemont, Pa., 134
Ross, Mr. and Mrs. Lee, 72
Rothblatt, Donald, 156
Rothschild, Baron Philippe de, 166
Rowan, C. W., 155
Rye, N.Y., 95, 96, 115–121, 172, 174, 175
  average age of residents, 197
  Grapple Street, 119
  schools, 119, 120–121
  sex practices, 182
Rye Country Day School, 78, 96, 119–120
Rye Town Hilton, 118

St. David's, Pa., 134
Saltair, 28
Salt Lake City, Utah, 19–29
  availability of alcohol in, 22–23
  founded by Brigham Young, 19–20
  Great Salt Lake, 28
  life style, 22–27
  notable families, 22, 27
  polygamy in, 24
  religious conflicts in, 21–22, 25
  schools, 25
  suburbs:

Salt Lake City: suburbs (cont'd)
    Federal Heights, 21
    Olympus Cove, 21
  urban life in, 192, 194
San Antonio, Texas, 167
San Fernando Valley, Calif., blacks in, 198–199
San Francisco, Calif., 166–167
  suburbs, 153–160
  urban life in, 192, 194
  water views, 193
San Jose, Calif., 154
San Jose Symphony Orchestra, 154
Santa Barbara, Calif., 122, 160–167
  architectural style, 163
  earthquake in, 163
  old families, 164
Santa Clara Valley, Calif., 154–156
Savannah, Ga., 131
Schlotman, Mrs. Joseph, 64
Schnitzer, Kenneth and Joan, 4
schools:
  in Carefree, Ariz., 18
  Coronado High School, Scottsdale, Ariz., 12
  in Darien, Conn., 103
  economics of, 172
  in Hudson, Ohio, 36
  integration of, in Los Angeles, 199
  private, 177
  in Rye, N.Y., 119, 120–121
  Rye Country Day School, 78, 96, 119–120
  in Salt Lake City, 25
Scott, Mrs. Harold, 125–126
Scott, Sir Walter, Ivanhoe, 93
Scottsdale, Ariz., 11–16, 186
  Coronado High School, 12
  dress, 14
  Fifth Ave., 196–197
  life style, 13–14, 15, 16
  Mafia in, 14
  patriotism in, 11–13
  Pinnacle Peak, 14
Seal Harbor, Maine, 95, 147
service organizations as social entry, 177–178
sex practices in suburbs, 179–182
Seymour, Mrs. Mary, 119
Seymour Electric Co., 119
Shaker Heights, Ohio, 122, 172
Shaker Square, shopping center, 196
Shawnee Mission, Mo., 179–181
Shenerock Shore Club, 118
Shepard, Helen Gould (Mrs. Finlay), 124
Sherman, Roger, 121
shopping centers:
  Carefree Shopping Center, Phoenix, Ariz., 17
  Galleria, Houston, Texas, 6–7
  in Phoenix, Ariz., suburbs, 14, 17
  in Santa Clara Valley, Calif., 154–156
  ZCMI, Salt Lake City, Utah, 24
Sloan-Kettering Cancer Center, 96, 97

Smith, George Washington, 164–165
Smith, Joseph, 27
social entry, means of, 176–178
Social Register:
  Atlanta, 74
  Cincinnati, 52–53, 54
  New York, 117, 128, 146
  Santa Barbara, 166
Sondheim, Stephen, 143
Sound of Music, The, 115, 119, 121
Southport, Conn., 99
Spalding, Hughes, Jr., 75
Spalding, Jack, 75
Springer, Gerald, 55
Spring Grove Cemetery, 39–40
Srole, Leo, 188–190
Stamford, Conn., 87, 172
Standard Club, 72
Steinburger, Mrs. Harvey, 7
Stettinius & Hollister, law firm, 50
Steuben Glass staircase, 4
Stillman, Elsie (Mrs. William G. Rockefeller), 91
Stillman, Isabel (Mrs. Percy Rockefeller), 91
Stillman, James, 89, 91
Stirling County, Nova Scotia, mental health in, 189
Stolp, John and Kathleen, 154
Strafford, Pa., 134
Strauss, Mrs. Carl, 49
Suarez, Margarita, 201
suburban life, vii–viii, 122–130, 174–176, 186–188
  changes in, 197–199
  financial burdens of, 183–185
  mental health in, 183, 188–191
  migration to, 171–172
  sex practices, 179–182
  social entries, 174–178
summer homes, 43, 141–150
Summer Social Register, 43
Summit County, Ohio, 33–34
Sundial Realty Company, Phoenix, Ariz., 17
Sunnyvale, Calif., 154

Taft, Charles P., 51
Taft, Elizabeth (Mrs. Walbridge), 149
Taft, Martha Bowers, 50
Taft, Robert, Jr., 50
Taft, William Howard, 50
Taft Art Museum, 50
Talleyrand-Perigord, Duc de, 125
Tanner, Obert J., 26
Tarrytown, N.Y., 89, 123, 129–130
  Afternoon Drive, 127
Tarver, Jack, 75
Tauber, Paul, 202
Taubman Company, 155
Taylor, Mrs. J. Madison, 148

212

Terrace Park, Ohio, 43, 53
Thaw, Harry K., 165
Thompson, Becky, 102–105
Thompson, Thomas, *Blood and Money*, 6
Tokeneke Road, Darien, Conn., 103–104
Tolstoi, Countess Cyril, 63
Town & Country, 160
Tutko, Thomas, 155
Twigs, 117–118
Twinsburg, Ohio, 35, 37
Tyler Davidson Memorial Fountain, 41

Union Terminal, Cincinnati, 40
United States Census, divorce rates, 182, 190
University of California, Santa Barbara, 165
University of Cincinnati, 48
urban life, 171–173, 188–191
    mental health in, 188–189
    return to, 191, 192–197

Valentine, Michael, 102
Valley Club, 164
Vandenberg Air Force Base, 165
Vanderbilt, Cornelius, 129
Vanderlip, Frank A., 126–127
Van Dyke, Dick, 17
views:
    of mountains, 21, 194
    of water, 42, 193–194
Villa, Mrs. Anthony, 4
Villanova, Pa., 133, 134
volunteer service as means of social entry, 177–178

Wainwright, Stuyvesant, Jr., 121
Warren & Wetmore, architectural firm, 8
Wasatch Mountains, Utah, 21
Washington, D.C., 199–203
    crime rate, 190
    urban life, 192
Washington Center for Metropolitan Studies, 200
Watch Hill, R.I., 58, 141–150
    dress, 148

Watch Hill (cont'd)
    old families, 142
water:
    feelings about, 192–193
    views of, 42, 192–194
Wayne, Pa., 134, 135
Wee Burn Country Club, 103, 104, 173
Weil, Sydney, 45
Wendel, Ella, 127–129
Wendel, J. G., 127–129
Wendel, Rebecca, 127–129
Wesley Chapel, Cincinnati, 45
Westchester County, 122–130
    old families, 127–130
Western Reserve Academy, 34, 36
Western Reserve of Conn., 34
Western Reserve University, 34
Weston, Conn., 87, 99
Weston, Phyllis (Mrs. Leo), 55
Westport, Conn., 87, 99
Wheelwright, Mrs. Michael, 166
White, Stanford, 164, 165
Whitehead, Robert, 143
Whitney, Mrs. Cornelius Vanderbilt, 101
William Howard Taft School, 50
Wilson, Mrs. Russell, 48
Windmill Pointe, 60
windows, treatment of, 176
Wintersteen, Mrs. John, 140
Wittenstein, Charles, 72
women, single, discrimination against, 156–158
Women's Wear Daily, 55
Woodmere, N.Y., 197, 198
Woods, William S., 70
Woodway Club, 103
Wynnewood, Pa., 134, 135, 138

Yale University, 93, 94, 95
Yorktown Heights, N.Y., 181
Young, Andrew, 70, 77
Young, Brigham, 19–20
Young, Harry, 111, 112

ZCMI Center, Salt Lake City, 24